MY RED BUTTERFLY

Avinash Pushkarna

NIYOGI
BOOKS

Published by
NIYOGI BOOKS
D-78, Okhla Industrial Area, Phase-I
New Delhi-110 020, INDIA
Tel: 91-11-26816301, 49327000
Fax: 91-11-26810483, 26813830
email: niyogibooks@gmail.com
website: www.niyogibooksindia.com

Editor: Gita Rajan
Layout: Shashi Bhushan Prasad

ISBN: 978-81-926939-1-0

Publication: 2017

Printed at: Niyogi Offset Pvt. Ltd., New Delhi, India

Dedicated to my late father and my mother who brought me into this world;

To my wife **Susmita** and my children **Ankita** and **Kunaal** who have given meaning to my life

How do I love thee? Let me count the ways.
I love thee to the depth and breadth and height
My soul can reach, when feeling out of sight
For the ends of being and ideal Grace.
I love thee to the level of every day's
Most quiet need, by sun and candle-light.
I love thee freely, as men strive for Right.
I love thee purely, as they turn from Praise.
I love thee with the passion put to use
In my old griefs, and with my childhood's faith.
I love thee with a love I seemed to lose
With my lost saints, - I love thee with the breath,
Smiles, tears, of all my life! - and, if God choose,
I shall but love thee better after death.

Elizabeth Barrett Browning

Contents

Love is in the Air

Love! A beautiful feeling!

Love is enigmatic. Erupting anywhere, anytime, between perfect strangers; tying them together in a bond: mystic, pious.

No one knows when one may get struck by Cupid. I had no idea either, about its profoundness, till I too was smitten.

How can I forget that sunny noon, that Sunday of November 1975?

Science is fun. I had crafted a pinhole camera using a cardboard shoebox. Abundant sunshine prompted me to put my contraption to test. Winter had not fully set in. The days were balmy. The skyline was teeming with piles of cumulus clouds; like heaps of fluffy cotton floating on a blue screen; the bright sun according them a distinct glow. The brilliant golden sunshine had lit up everything: tall green trees, dwellings, blooms of colourful perwinkle, chrysanthemum, petunia, roses and marigold. The air was salubrious: sparrows, bulbuls, mynas, pigeons and hoopoes animatedly chirping and trilling, flitting around; kites soaring high. A serene, mirthful setting! I came to the rear balcony of my house.

My house was on the first floor in a square block with rows of eight double-storey houses along each side of the square. Every house had two independent floors. Their rear balconies faced a common courtyard: square and open. Right in the centre there was a municipal tap which served well in times of water scarcity, ever common to Delhi. The courtyard would be used by children for playing local games and by adults for spending summer evenings and nights. Delhi was safe in those times—not plagued by terrorism, loot or extortion, and people would sleep in that open courtyard, without fear or inhibitions. At night, in summer, around a hundred charpoys could be seen; lined side by side, with residents chatting lazily or feverishly, depending on their individual mood or temperament. During winter again the yard would be put to optimum use. Adults and children soaked up the sun, getting their daily dose of Vitamin D. Clothes would be spread out on clotheslines strung across poles. The more enterprising ones would put out spices to dry, even expose woollens, quilts or mattresses to the sun to kill moths. It was a great community setting, a flavour of village life in an otherwise truly urban locale.

Coming back to my story; with that contraption in my hand and filled with excitement, I moved my camera with its pinhole facing the courtyard, peeking through the one-inch upper hole. O my God! I was thrilled to see the distinct inverted images: big bushy trees, a street dog, clothes hung on steel wires; some scattered cots, two small children running around and a fat elderly lady looking askance; interesting vignettes of city life. I was jubilant, and my heart craved for more. Just then …

I was stupefied! I got riveted to an image. Had I captured it or had I been captured? I was captivated by the image of a lovely young girl, attired in red kameez and black salwar; her lustrous black tresses, well-oiled and tied in two plaits; her resplendent face lit with a lovely smile and her nose stud gleaming. She was looking towards me: partly bemused, partly inquisitive and a little apprehensive. I remained transfixed, appreciating the sheer beauty of the female figure and the pretty face for a while. I lifted my head and beheld the real thing. Exquisite she was! How could an inverted image on an oiled paper, in a ragtag contrivance match the real beauty! Smitten by the gorgeous face, its glow accentuated by the effulgence of the radiant sun, I stood still for a moment, but that moment was a wee bit longer. The girl too didn't move. Then, reality dawned upon us, interrupting the dreamy spell we had been under. The girl blushed, I felt embarrassed. She collected herself and rushed inside her house. It was on the ground floor, at right angles to my home, separated by just five houses. I was left stranded. That was the encounter—the first encounter. It left lingering memories in my mind and stirred me deeply. I just couldn't come to terms with it. Just then I remembered I had to practise a few numerical problems of optics as a class test was scheduled for the next day.

I didn't see the girl for a few days nor did I have the means to ascertain the identity of that lovely, mysterious face. However, destiny has its own ways. One afternoon while returning from school, I found a big tent pitched in the rear courtyard, near *that house*; about thirty people, squatting on the rugs spread inside the tent, with grim faces; a few ladies weeping softly. There was a pall of gloom. On reaching home I heard my sister Nalini's voice, 'Mummy, what has happened in that house? Why are the ladies crying?'

'Someone told me an old man has died there. That family has shifted to our locality only a month back as tenants. They were earlier staying in Loha Mandi. Because of the demolition drive, their area was bulldozed. Poor old soul was here for just a month.'

'Mummy, my classmate Shobhana has also shifted here in the adjoining house. I think they are related,' Nalini said.

'Kanta Auntie told me that they have been allotted plots in Janakpuri, and their houses are under construction; at the most they are here for another six months,' Mummy said.

Those were the days of the Emergency. The government had decided to demolish certain areas; trade and markets were being relocated. The big iron and scrap market (Loha Mandi) and wood market (Lakkad Mandi) were shifted from the Motia Khan area of Delhi to Narayana and Mayapuri. Many of the old houses beside the market had been demolished, and the displaced people were offered houses in upcoming localities like Janakpuri.

After changing and washing my hands and face, I stood in the rear balcony, expectant, watching the tent, the people, and their actions. The wait yielded dividends. The mystery-girl came out of her house, and started tending to friends and relatives assembled outside, offering them tea on that winter afternoon. While serving, she casually looked towards my balcony, and was stunned to see me. Our eyes met—again a trifle more than normal, and then she blushed. I was stupefied; caught in a time-warp. A strange sensation ran all over my body: from my eyes to my head, to my spine, to my arms, to my legs; as if I had touched a live electric wire. My heart was beating faster and my breathing accelerated. My throat and lips became dry. I tried to move, but found my body frozen; I felt a thud in my heart. On that slightly cold winter afternoon, my hands were full of sweat. What had gone wrong? I couldn't comprehend. And how could I? It was the onset of the game which God, the ever-playful, plays with the lives of ordinary mortals. The girl shifted her attention back to the guests, casting furtive glances towards me. But I couldn't grasp their import. I stayed there for a while; my mind commanding me to move, to attend to the loads of school assignments; but my heart was adamant; it desired more glimpses of that mystic face.

I was studying in the tenth standard, harbouring dreams of becoming a doctor, imagining myself in a white coat with a stethoscope dangling from my neck, running around in a hospital, helping patients in distress.

Our house was compact; a simple middle-class home with just two rooms: a large drawing-cum-bed room and a smaller bedroom. There was a small kitchen, a bathroom, and a toilet. The front balcony was actually a continuous common corridor for all the houses on the first floor. Only the small rear balcony was our private one. In the 15'x 10' drawing room, we had a sofa set and a divan. There was a round table in the corner and a rectangular table along the sofa.

Papa was a junior level government officer. To augment the family's income, Mummy ran a coaching centre at home, tutoring students of primary and middle classes. Papa too, after returning from office, would teach students of higher classes. Whole day long those two rooms would be full of students of all ages; and the incidental din and bustle. I too was involved in the process, teaching mathematics and science to students of middle school. I had a few select like-minded friends. Overall it was very enjoyable; life was on a smooth roll. The students would be sitting on a durrie on the floor, while my mother would occupy the divan or the chair.

I had very loving parents. They tried to give us the best they could afford. Both were good-looking. Mummy was of medium built, fair complexioned, round-faced with large beautiful eyes. Papa was of medium height, well-built, with wheatish complexion, a long face and square jaw. And, even in those times when awareness had not spread much, they had planned their family, just two children: Nalini, younger to me by four years, and me.

When I was small, around five, we were at Chandigarh. One day Mummy came to fetch me from school. On the way there was a sudden downpour. We didn't have an umbrella handy. Mummy lifted me in her lap, and covered me with the pallu of her saree. All the way long while I was comfortably ensconced in the cocoon of her love, she withstood the torrential rain. We reached home: she completely drenched, but I mostly dry.

Papa would become a child with me. Chandigarh is a beautiful city, green, clean and full of butterflies and motley insects. I was very fond of butterflies; enthralled by their lovely colours, elegant flight and tantalising glide. Nalini was just eight months then. It was a bright and scorching day of June, when I pleaded, 'I want to catch butterflies.' Papa tried to reason, it was too hot to venture out. Mummy too dissuaded me. But I was adamant.

Ultimately Papa gave in and indulged me; he took me to a nearby garden, with our caps on to ward off the sun and an empty glass bottle for the catch. Amongst green grass, tall trees and blossoming sunflowers, periwinkles and roses, were flying myriad butterflies—the swift cabbage whites; the twinkling and small yellow ones with dark dots; and very small grey ones. My fickle mind was besotted with a big tiger butterfly flitting from flower to flower; black body with white striations, its lovely red wings were a mosaic of black bands and white and black dots.' I want that,' I pleaded. After fifteen minutes of hot pursuit in the searing sun, while it flew and dodged, Papa could trap it in the glass bottle, and hollered, 'Got it.' He put a small sunflower and some periwinkles, and covered the bottle's mouth with a thin cloth. We returned home triumphant. 'Look,' I revealed our trophy to Mummy and to Nalini leaning on a cushion, 'See, how beautiful it is! Look at the way it is dancing!' Nalini attempted to hold the bottle; but I moved away, lest my prize escape.

Nalini and I shared a great bond since childhood; with periodic incidents of altercations–the hallmark of affinity and fraternity. We would laugh over trivial occurrences. The magnitude of laughter, at times, would leave the people around bemused.

Together we used to move around in circles with steel tumblers against our ears ... listening to the churning of sound. We would sing ... a chorus of cacophony and the occasional melody; we used to watch sunbeams entering the dark rooms through slits of the doors, creating a riot of colours and weaving sheets of light with dust particles twinkling like stars. We would catch insects and get scared by lizards and cockroaches.

Nalini and I were standing and chatting in the rear balcony after finishing our lunch. Suddenly a cow appeared from nowhere, and started nibbling a petticoat hung out to dry. The owner of the petticoat, a fat lady, ran after the cow. But the bovine was agile; it escaped with the prize, leaving her distraught.

'Oh, my God, what will that cow do with the petticoat? I don't think she wears a saree,' Nalini quipped.

'May be there is a bovine party. She has the petticoat and will soon find a saree to match,' I rejoined. Nalini burst into laughter but she had to hide her face, lest that lady took offence.

Hardly this spectacle was over when we were presented with another funny sight. Three small children—Bobby, Golu and Chintu—were playing cricket with a bright yellow rubber ball in the courtyard. Chintu bowled and Bobby swung his bat and hit. The ball was in the air for a long time and landed about twenty feet away, near a stray dog of our locality. The canine mistook it for a bird, grabbed it in its jaws and sprinted. Golu followed it. The dog was faster and dodged him; but later realising that it was not edible, dropped it almost twenty steps ahead.

'Today all animals seem to be in a party mood,' Nalini observed, 'the dog was having a ball with the ball.'

'Why not? One feels hungrier in winter. The ball must have been appetising,' I remarked. Golu was crying. The ball had lost its shape. The dog was standing with a befuddled expression. We giggled. Suddenly, that mysterious girl emerged from her house, looked at us, and then smiled on spotting Nalini. 'Is she your friend Shobhana?' I asked nonchalantly.

'No, Shobhana lives in the adjoining house; this is her cousin, Shama. She is elder to Shobhana by four years. She studies in the ninth standard in Hari Mandir School. Shobhana is in my school.'

Shama was dressed in a coffee brown salwar, a matching kameez and a light brown cardigan. Her black hair, in two braids, had cream-coloured ribbons at the end. She was picking up the clothes from the clothesline. My heart got entangled in those lovely cream-coloured ribbons!

Nalini and I chatted a little longer. But my mind was turbulent. Unknown to myself, I had lost my heart!

Shama had woven her magic. Her radiant and innocent face, her doe shaped eyes, her shimmering tresses parted in the front and tapering into two plaits, her lissom torso draped in salwar suit and her smart gait had bowled me over. Her impressions were etched on my subconscious mind … I wished to see her at least once in a day. Whenever I felt exhausted after studies, the rear balcony was my recourse. Pulled by a strange magnetic attraction; always in the hope that she would be there, I would go there for a glimpse of her. Off and on, I would succeed. That ritual would rejuvenate my tired body and jaded mind. For me she was a novelty—a child's new possession, a fountainhead of exhilaration. I was just fifteen; my physicality knocking at the doors of the teenage kingdom; but my mind and heart had the purity and innocence of a child.

Time moved on.

Dreams of Future

In December, 1975, my maternal grandfather expired, after a prolonged illness. Loved and adored by all, *Bauji*, as he was fondly addressed, was born in 1900. He had special affection for my cousin Neelima, (the elder daughter of Om Mamaji, almost my age) and I. Bauji was always pleased with our academic inclinations. I shared a special bond with Bauji. He was a wellspring of unalloyed love. All through our visits to his place during the summer vacations, we would avidly follow his daily chores. Despite his age, Bauji was an embodiment of fitness. An early riser, he would begin his day with a glassful of lime water; exercise for forty-five minutes, doing yoga *asanas* and *pranayam*. After daily regimen and bath, he would get dressed classily: white shirt and dhoti, neat and well ironed; followed by a white turban—well starched, tied elegantly. He was the cynosure of all eyes as he would go cycling to a temple almost two kilometres, and later for home tuitions. He had an aura of simplicity, tidiness, wisdom, warmth, and affection.

I had eighteen cousins from my maternal side. Mummy was the youngest of six surviving siblings: two brothers and four sisters. The family had migrated as refugees from Sialkot province of undivided Punjab during the Partition. It was a cohesive family which had faced the trauma of Partition; witnessed the communal frenzy with attendant sufferings. We children were always curious about their past. Only when I grew up and was wise enough to understand worldly matters, could I appreciate what they had undergone.

During summer vacations, it would be a great reunion with endless exchange of anecdotes, jokes and stories and of course a never-ending array of simple inexpensive games, often self-invented, both indoors and outdoors. Bauji would bring sweets for children and gave us pocket money in the evening to buy crisp bread toast or kulfi or some other delicacy. At night Bauji would mesmerise us with fairy tales: of palaces, queens, kings, princesses, princes, fairies, and magnificent animals; fabulous lands, thieves, robbers; and mythology in his unique style. We would relive them in our dreams.

Pabiji, our maternal grandmother too loved us very much, but we were scared of her. She was lean, with tremendous stamina, firm voice and short temper. A devout early riser; everyday she would collect fresh flowers, to offer puja. Consecrated in a small room of the house was a temple, where she would religiously do bhajan-kirtan for at least an hour in the morning and evening. And, we all would join the chorus. We learnt domestic chores by working as per her command. Pabiji would cook and serve us with love. There was a large, dense *jamun* tree in the veranda of their house providing shade. In summers it would be laden with plenty of *jamuns* which we would feast on. It attracted lot of houseflies as well. I developed an uncanny expertise in catching or killing them! One fine morning, Neelima said, 'Can you capture two live houseflies for me?'

I was ready. Armed with a small glass bottle with a rubber lid, I could spot four houseflies resting on a leaf. Very calmly, with my hand under the leaf, I put the open end of the glass bottle on the flies. Three got captured. 'Come on, put that lid on the leaf,' I prompted. Neelima obeyed. Overjoyed she said, 'Thanks a lot dear bro.'

I earned the nickname, 'The fly catcher' from Bauji!

I was naughty. One night all of us were sitting in the drawing room when suddenly a coca cola bottle cap started moving, its serrated edges rasping on the floor. Neelima jumped and Naresh, my cousin hopped, shrieking. 'What's happening? Is it some ghost?' Everyone shouted or screamed. I alone laughed. When asked for the reason, I replied, 'Almost an hour back, I had seen a wood insect sitting there. I covered it with that bottle cap. I had forgotten about it.' The wood insect remained immobile for a long time and then tried to free itself; but it was difficult for it to come out. Everyone burst into loud laughter. 'Rohit is very naughty. He has great fondness for insects.'

Childhood was full of innocence and curiosity. We would keenly watch: the cobbler cobbling shoes; the fellow sitting on a stationary cycle, sharpening knives and scissors on his rotating grinding wheel, set in motion by his pedalling, while sparks would fly all around; the carpenter cutting wood, levelling it, creating frames and structures; tinning of utensils on a makeshift hearth; painting and whitewashing of houses and so on and so forth.

Bauji died of abdominal cancer. Naresh, his eyes red with crying, came to inform us on a chilly December morning. The scene at our grandparents' house was gloomy. There was a huge gathering. Bauji's body covered in a white sheet; motionless and serene. The sight made me cry. I accompanied the procession with my elder cousins to the crematorium, and saw Bauji's mortal remains being consigned to flames amidst the chanting of sacred mantras. I had, till then, seen people crying over serious issues and even trivialities; but seeing death so closely with concomitant grief and lamentation was a unique experience. I returned with a sense of deep desolation. Sweet memories of Bauji haunted me for a few days.

In April 1976, I got promoted to the eleventh standard. It was going to be year of trial–of my attitude, my tenacity and my perseverance. My performance in the eleventh would decide if I would enter my desired stream in pursuit of my dream of becoming a doctor.

Summer vacations commenced mid-May onwards. I was geared up to utilise them to the fullest possible. I didn't have an idea that it would add another dimension to my life. I would rise early at five, and after getting ready, would spend long, arduous hours for my studies in the rear balcony till ten in the morning, when it would not be too warm. Later, inside the house, my gruelling schedule would continue.

One day, a distant cousin Amit, a young boy of twenty, visited us. His disposition was endearing and friendly. 'Auntie, the meal was so tasty that I ate like a glutton. And, I am now feeling heavy. If you don't mind, can we go out for a stroll,' Amit proposed after dinner. 'Oh yes!' my parents agreed.

We moved out. The sky was a vast expanse illumined by balmy moonshine and dotted with twinkling stars. The soothing fragrance of *raatrani*, wafted across with the cool breeze. The park was lovely, dim lights all around, and a cascading fountain in the centre. Water was flowing into a small pool below, its sound dulcet and sonorous. We took two rounds of the park, and then sat on the soft, silky cool grass.

'Amit, what do you plan to do after your graduation?' Papa asked.

'Uncle, you know Daddy wishes me to join his motor parts business which is flourishing. Earlier we were merely dealers. Now Daddy has a factory at Sonepat. We manufacture piston rings, brake pads and some accessories,' Amit responded and asked, 'What are Rohit's plans?'

'Well, he aspires to be a doctor.'

I was enjoying the conversation which moved on to anecdotes of the fond times Amit's father and Papa had during their childhood. Mummy too was remembering Amit's mother. An ice-cream vendor found us ready customers and the conversation continued over ice-cream.

All of a sudden, I found my mind wandering; I was no longer involved in the chat. No matter how I tried to sustain my attention, it was of no avail. Shama's thoughts started haunting me; I could see her lovely face wherever my eyes moved. Once I felt, she was descending on a moonbeam from the luminescent moon, and in no time was near me; her face beaming, her nose stud gleaming.

My mind was in a spin. I picked up a stray straw, and started scribbling on the wet soil of the grassless space: Shama, Shama, Shama … I was perplexed by my action. And, to avoid getting noticed, I camouflaged it, pretending to be revising some chemical formulas. Little did I know that I was smitten by the love bug! My senses had been overtaken by a powerful sensation! Shama had entered my life through that small aperture of the pinhole camera and transformed the plain and insouciant canvas of my life with a rainbow of novel sensations and emotions!

Shama had entered my mind, my stream of thoughts. While doing my normal jobs, while interacting with people, while being seriously engrossed in studies, I would, time and again, be inundated by the lovely, innocent image of Shama smiling at me, watching me intently. I would get disconcerted: on the one hand I would be disturbed by her uninvited intrusions into my smooth and regular routine, on the other hand I would be submerged in very enjoyable currents tingling my nerves and sinews. It was love! And, my young mind was unable to understand. But one thing I was becoming conscious of—I wanted to be in Shama's vicinity forever.

Luck seemed to be on my side. Shama's four siblings—two young brothers studying in sixth and seventh and two young sisters studying in second and third—took admission in our coaching centre. In a short span, they became very friendly with me. I would teach them, the mere fact of their being Shama's siblings stirred a strange chord within me! I learnt that they were in total six siblings with a sister even elder to Shama. Her father was having a saree shop in Chandni Chowk: Arora Saree Emporium.

Since we stayed on the first floor, there was an apprehension regarding the safety of our scooter. With the approval of Shama's immediate neighbours, it was decided to park it in the backyard near that house, close to a peepal tree. I thus got an opportunity of having a close glimpse of Shama daily.

Every night at around nine-thirty or ten, I would start the scooter, and go racing to the coveted spot. Being a novice, I would drive in first gear, with the headlight on, announcing my arrival with screeching brakes. Then I would rotate the accelerator for one last time, creating another loud sound with the secret purpose of attracting Shama's attention. She would generally be there, sitting on a cot, under the peepal tree, conversing with her mother and siblings. My ploy would invariably succeed; there would be a cursory meeting of eyes, apparently a casual look. That casual look would send my spirit soaring, satiating the deep recesses of my heart, initiating a chain of happy stirrings within.

Sometime during mid-June, my cousin Yogesh visited us. He was older than me by three years, a bit of an extrovert and very fond of roaming around the city. He had great interest in new consumer electronic goods and appliances entering the markets. At home, he would try to understand the anatomy, circuitry and functioning of the electrical or electronic products. Studies didn't appeal to him. He was pursuing graduation from a private college, and believed fate alone would translate his dream castles into reality.

'Why don't we both go out and have some fun Rohit?' Yogesh proposed one day, while I was deeply engrossed in my chemistry book.

'I have to finish this,' I replied.

'What man? Whole day long you are studying. A few hours' outing won't hurt you,' he argued. 'Come on. Let's go to Red Fort.'

'Oh, I have been there twice.'

'I am not planning to go to the monument. Let us go to that interesting market area near Red Fort. '

'Okay. But let's keep it for the evening; around five. It will be too hot now,' I said.

In the evening, we went there by bus. The population of Delhi has really exploded in present times, but in the late seventies there was not so much of crush or rush. It was intriguing to go into the narrow, crowded roads and lanes of Lajpat Rai market and Bhagirath Place, in front of the majestic Red Fort. It's predominantly a market for electronic goods, electrical items and medicines. Yogesh would stop at some shop, enquire about an electrical part, then move on to another.

I was exposed to new items displayed in the showcases of the shops. The most appealing item was a transparent glass cylinder containing a blue or red viscous liquid in which golden or silver coloured shining particles moved up and down when plugged in and electric current passed through it.

There were many other interesting electric and electronic articles: portable fans, irons, shavers, massagers, colourful radios and transistors and battery-operated toys.

'What are you looking for?'I asked Yogesh.

'Nothing specific,' he replied.

But he would stop at various stops, enquiring about the mechanisms and prices, and even entering into discussions and arguments. I was getting apprehensive as Yogesh didn't seem to be interested in buying anything. I prayed that he would not come across an irate shopkeeper who might insist on our buying something, and turn nasty noticing that we were only amusing ourselves.

'Are you not scared of the possibility of any shopkeeper losing his temper on discovering that we are here to just loaf around,' I asked.

'Why should we worry about that? We are enquiring, and maybe we may take time to make up our minds. Shopkeepers have to sell their wares. Anyone can be a prospective customer; and even if one doesn't buy, one can be a source of advertisement. Shopkeepers are used to all types of customers. And, they would not turn down people as they wouldn't like to lose a potential customer. So when we go out shopping, we can afford to be a little shameless,' Yogesh explained.

Yogesh's philosophy didn't appeal to me. But, perhaps that *was* or *is* the reality.

Chandni Chowk, our next destination, appeared like a vast river of humanity, bounded by rows of shops throbbing with activity. There were shops of jewellery, electrical goods, grocery, garments; goods of almost all kinds. Far away, in the backdrop, could be seen the 'Town Hall,' the municipal office, built during British period. Lot of pigeons were hovering in the sky and resting on the sills and roofs. And, on the ground, we were moving around like aimless wanderers. Suddenly, I saw one saree shop with the board 'Arora Saree Emporium'. Immediately it struck me. Oh it's Shama's shop, I whispered under my breath. In the window, a few mannequins had been displayed nicely draped in colourful sarees. I stood there for a moment, glued to one mannequin. To me she seemed to be Shama, tall, beautiful and elegant. Her face smiling and her nose stud gleaming. It appeared she was looking at me through her doe shaped eyes which had a very captivating magnetic twinkle.

'What has happened Rohit?' Yogesh asked and then started laughing on discovering me appraising the saree clad mannequin. 'Do you wish to buy a saree?'

'Oh no, I was just watching the colours and prints. Mummy has a similar one.' I lied to cover my embarrassment. But that figure in the shop and that sign board had disturbed me.

We moved and after walking almost a hundred steps, Yogesh stopped in front of a sweets shop. There was a huge rush there. The fellow was selling jalebis—thick, tortuous and tantalisingly red, made from *maida*. With the adroit twisting and circular movement of his hands, the *halwai* was allowing *maida* paste fall through the small hole of a cotton pouch into a pan of boiling ghee. The twisted mass would swell into intricate jalebis; and would be transferred to a pan of concentrated sugar syrup. People were madly devouring jalebis, which nutritionists would term unhealthy.

'One plate,' Yogesh ordered. And, we too devoured it to our hearts' content.

Later I entreated, 'Yogesh. I think it's time to go home.'

Yogesh found it difficult to stay at home. He was always restless. The next day, he made another proposition, 'Come on, you bookworm. Let us go for the matinee show of *Dus Numbri.*'

I had to give in and got ready.

Before we could proceed, Mummy said, 'Rohit, get me half a kilo of curd from the market.' Attired in smart black denim bell-bottoms and a pale printed polyester shirt with small red and black coloured apple-like motifs, I must have appraised myself ten times in the mirror, and felt good about the fact that I was looking smart. And, this was confirmed by Shama's brother Babloo too when he remarked, 'Bhaiyya! You are looking great.' With enthusiasm and verve, I went out. And, coincidentally while returning, I bumped into Shama, standing in the backyard, holding a hanging steel rope. She was in a red kameez and black salwar. I was reminded of my favourite red butterfly which I had caught in Chandigarh. And like that butterfly her movements were vibrant and elegant. I saw her and blushed. Then I lifted my eyes. Our eyes met. I could discern red striations in hers. I had heard red strings in someone's eyes were a manifestation of intoxication or a high level of excitement. Her eyes had a twinkle. 'Was it because of me?' I wondered. But I had no means of finding out. Eager at the prospect of watching an entertaining movie and having been blessed with such a spectacle, my heart leapt with joy. I was basically a shy person, especially in the matter of girls. I wished to remain in the midst of that trance a little more. But my introvert nature and the awareness of being in full public view made me lower my eyes and flee from the scene.

The movie was real fun: a simple love story interspersed with lilting songs, some hilarious fighting sequences, and a very happy ending. I enjoyed every bit of it. But, I don't know how in those scenes involving the hero and the heroine, I had the illusion of me being there with Shama; and Hema Malini exuding Shama's vivacity. Shama was ubiquitous: dancing and singing; emoting and evoking. I was drenched in exultation—incomprehensible and unparalleled.

Yogesh left the next day.

Flame of Love Glows

Two days later, I had just gone to bed after my gruelling routine. Shama's thoughts started pervading my subconscious, her images dancing like coloured glass pieces in a kaleidoscope: one after another in various postures and moods; sometimes coming from the horizon with colourful haloes. I tossed and turned in bed. Then benevolent sleep enveloped me. And, in my dreams she was sitting beside me while I was opening my heart out to her:

'Shama, why do you play this hide and seek? You know whenever I happen to meet you, my lips get sealed, and I am unable to see you properly. What to do? I am so shy and timid. I don't want anyone to get a whiff of my liking for you. You don't know what you mean to me. I wish you could come to my house.'

And, I saw Shama's angelic face smiling affectionately as if appreciating my feelings. Her beautiful black and lively eyes had a magnetic twinkle.

'Why don't you come to my house?' I asked.

She didn't reply, but her eyes moved mischievously, her smile became enigmatic.

You know, in that combination of red kameez and black salwar, you look marvellous; please come in that very dress; you don't know how much I pine for your glimpse and wish to talk to you, but I am not that bold; the moment I see you I become limp and speechless; something goes wrong; and against my own wishes, my heart loses to my timid self, and I am unable to face you for long; I hide, I run away; my heart longs for you, my eyes search for you every moment; they want to capture your image, drink your beauty, seek your presence, but they are never satisfied; but I don't know why I consciously deprive them of that elixir; I am undergoing queer feelings, they are indescribable; for me one glimpse of you is the most important thing—the most revered. Please do come, do come. Oh my Shama! Please do come.'

I drifted into deep slumber, with sweet feelings; and woke up fresh and alert the next morning.

Three days later at around ten thirty in the morning, I was seated on a sofa in our drawing room, engrossed in studying the respiratory system of *Rana tigrina*–the Indian frog. Mummy was on the divan, teaching students. Suddenly, the curtain of the front door parted, and in a flash entered a girl, in red kameez and black salwar, I was stunned. Shama—the face that had hypnotised me for the last few months. I looked at her but was spellbound and speechless at the sheer splendour of her visage; the enchanting loveliness and innocence was beside me; it was unbelievable. My *dream had materialised into reality*! I glanced sideways, and then tried to refocus on the respiratory system of *Rana tigrina*; but the magic of a female *Homo sapiens* was more powerful; it unsettled my own respiratory system; I became breathless while my heart was racing!

I lifted my eyes again; I saw Shama, seated beside my mother, discussing about the progress of her siblings' studies. When my eyes met Shama's, I saw a queer and powerful gaze—not suggestive but inquisitive; I was benumbed; in turmoil. My heart was pounding and goading me to keep looking at her. But my mind was rationalising, 'Is it appropriate?' I tried to shift my focus back to *Rana tigrina*, but my concentration vanished. I kept casting furtive glances at her till my sense of guilt and timidity overtook me. Surrounded by so many students, and in the presence of my mother, I didn't want my special feelings to be exposed. I got up and moved over to the adjoining room. However, my heart and mind remained hooked on to my beloved soul.

Since the door was open, I overheard their conversation, concentrating on her sweet and melodious voice which I had the privilege to hear for the first time.

'Auntie, Babloo and others would be having their interview in the first week of July for admission to schools in Janakpuri; there would be written tests also. Can you prepare them for that?'

'Don't worry. I have been giving those mock tests almost every second day so that they are well prepared. But make sure they are regular. By the way, when are you people shifting?'

'Around the last week of June,' she replied.

The words poured into my ears like molten lead and singed my heart. I didn't hear the rest of the conversation; my ears were only appreciating the pitch and timbre of her voice.

Well, their relocation to Janakpuri was inevitable, I agonised.

Now, I was swallowing a bitter-sweet pill. I could sense the powerful vibrations of someone, to whom I had unknowingly lost my heart; I was enjoying every bit of her presence, although not before my eyes. Simultaneously, the stark reality of the family's imminent departure was staring at me; my heart ached; tears welled up in my eyes, trickling down. A teenager was sobbing—an act not becoming of a man as it is generally considered a sign of weakness. I couldn't help it; it was my nature!

What a tragedy! Till Shama's arrival that day I had never seen her so closely or heard her voice. That day, my surreptitious glances, captured and transported her image to my heart: that perfectly chiselled, small, oval, lovely and innocent face; two large black, sparkling and doe-shaped eyes; nicely arched eyebrows; long aquiline nose with a shining nose stud, lustrous black hair, parted sideways and in two braids, some vagrant wisps partly covering her brow and eyes; fair, silky complexion; medium height and slim figure; graceful and elegant demeanour; and her musical voice. I was flabbergasted, absolutely! The image was deeply engraved on my heart; forever! A name was etched on my sixteen-year-old innocent heart: Shama! Shama! Shama! Her name would always be resonating in my ears and echoing in my surroundings. She was the red butterfly I had caught in Chandigarh!

What an irony! While she was there, I didn't return to the room, to have a final glimpse. I had to steel my heart so that I could bid farewell to my beloved!

My visits to the rear balcony continued. Off and on I would find Shama: sometimes chatting with her sisters or wringing and drying clothes on a clothesline; *perhaps symbolising the bond of our love that was like a tenuous steel wire between two poles; far apart*!

One day her siblings did not turn up for tuition. Mummy was a bit concerned, 'Babloo and the rest have not come. Their interview date is fast approaching. They should not miss a single class. Rohit beta, go to the balcony and if you see someone from their family in the courtyard tell them to send the children across.'

'Of course, Mummy, no problem.' I was ecstatic. It was my lucky day. I sprinted to the balcony and was amazed to find Shama in an onion pink salwar suit, along with her cousin Shobhana, wringing and hanging clothes. Despite my increased heartbeat, I steadied myself, and without betraying any nervousness, hollered, 'Why have your brothers and sisters not come for tuition? Mummy has asked them to come immediately. It's getting late.' I was surprised at my authoritative tone. Shama too seemed momentarily disconcerted, the washing slipped out of her hands; but then her eyes evinced concern and amusement. I felt embarrassed at my behaviour. Shama simply nodded and went inside. In no time her siblings came for tuition!

Shortly before Shama's departure for Janakpuri, my restlessness grew. My mind started racing and heart suffered pangs; there was an urgency to convey my emotions and feelings. I didn't know when I would ever meet her in my life; at which juncture and in what circumstances? I merely wanted to express my love. I thought of meeting her somewhere. But where and how? I was lost in thinking, designing and planning. I was too naïve, simple and shy. I couldn't gather enough courage to translate my wishes into action. I thought harder with my heart with its emotional baggage on the verge of exploding. Finally, there was a flicker of hope. I poured down my feelings, facts and reasons for harbouring those feelings, on a paper thus:

'Dear Shama,

Hi; I know you are surprised to receive this letter.

First of all I have a humble request. Please don't let this letter be known to anyone. I know I have taken a huge risk while writing to you. Please understand that since the day I have learnt about your leaving this locality, I have been restless. And, I thought before you leave, you must know what I feel for you.

Shama, I have fallen in love with you. Your face is so sweet and magical. Since the day, I saw you last winter, something strange started happening to me. I felt like seeing you time and again. Your glimpses gave me life, and the day I didn't see you, I felt empty. Slowly, I realised that I am in love with you. I had heard tales of people falling in love and seen many such stories in movies. I never knew what love was till your magic enveloped me. I am so timid and shy. I always wanted to speak to you; but whenever I faced you, I couldn't gather courage. That day when you came to our home, I wanted to be near you and talk to you. But my shy nature made me run away to the other room. Shama you are always in my thoughts, in my dreams and around me.

And, now you will be leaving. This mere thought is giving me a lot of pain. Shama, I don't know when I shall be able to meet you. But, if this letter reaches you, it will give me relief that at least I could convey my feelings. I can only say that my love for you is true.

Very lovingly yours
Rohit'

Very reverently I put the letter before the idol of Goddess Durga, consecrated in a small niche in our home, invoking her blessings to impart me the wisdom to decide whether to deliver that; if so, how? I prayed that it may not cause any commotion or damage to both of us and our families' reputation. I applied some sindoor on the letter, caressed it, and packaged it lovingly in a small transparent polythene packet. I delved on the timing, mode, and messenger for its delivery. 'Whether I should do it myself or give it to my sister?' I mulled over. But the mere thought of giving it personally sent shivers down my spine, with that letter slipping from my perspiring fingers. How could I face Shama? I considered Nalini to be my messenger. But I had not confided in her. Time was slipping by, and only two days remained before Shama was to leave. After persistent thinking, with my waking hours in turmoil and my nights tearful, I got a wild idea: Why not through her younger brothers, who respected and loved me. But how would they take it? How would they react? My mind wavered; my hands itched to convey the outpourings of my bottled up emotions. I invoked mother Goddess, incessantly seeking her permission to deliver that precious letter of my life. The Goddess didn't approve; I backtracked with a heavy heart!

On the day of the family's departure I stood in the balcony, watching the proceedings. I saw Shama roaming around, participating actively. To accentuate my pain and perhaps, for a lasting impression, she, coincidentally, was wearing *red kameez and black salwar*. My red butterfly was flitting and gliding, fluttering her wings; her eyes glowing and probing, occasionally in my direction. What did they encapsulate? Was there love for me? Did she wish to talk to me? I was searching for reflection of my thoughts and emotions in those two lovely, innocent, doe-shaped eyes; but the distance was far too much to capture and comprehend what they contained. It appeared that something remained unsaid—something was amiss. But I was too young; only a student, with my prospective career and ambition. I was not courageous like Sir Walter Scott's hero Lord Lochinvar, who being daring in love and dauntless in war, could elope with his beloved on a galloping horse nor was I like Prithviraj Chauhan to come riding atop his horse to the *swayamvara* of his beloved Samyukta, lift her, and flee. I was to merely witness and bear the separation. Was it really the separation?

The cavalcade left with *my* Shama. I was left musing, crying and clinging to that neatly wrapped letter, the embodiment and expression of my love and emotions, my prized possession!

That was a deep, depressing day. I wept, crestfallen, alone, no one to offer me a shoulder of sympathy, a shoulder to lean against or cry on, a shoulder of comfort or a touch imbued with care—to understand and alleviate my pain, to mitigate my grief. My lips were quiet, but my heart was singing the title track of the movie *Chalte Chalte* exhorting Shama to never say goodbye:

Chalte Chalte mere ye geet yaad rakhna,
Kabhi alvida na kehna, kabhi alvida na kehna…

That day was a milestone in my life. Earlier in my life too I had faced separation, either temporary or permanent; and had felt the pain. But this was unique; much stronger and much deeper. It was a mortal wound—ever festering, but wrapped in queer joy, that would transmute me into a different soul. It was something out of the world; a strange mixture of pleasure and pain that only God's chosen few are visited upon!

Summer vacations were still on…
My studies became more focused and strenuous.

Shama's absence devastated me deep inside. I needed divine support to sustain me in my agony. I started accompanying my mother to the famous Jhandewalan temple; around twenty minutes walk from our home. The temple was primarily devoted to Vaishno Devi: the mother goddess, astride a tiger, her eight hands carrying an assortment of weapons: trident, scimitar, mace, etc. The goddess symbolises power and righteousness. I became her ardent devotee. I would religiously kneel down in obeisance to idols of Vaishno Devi and other gods and goddesses; and pray for bestowing me with will power and tenacity to work hard to achieve my goal. Besides, there would be special prayers for the well-being of Shama, my love. In a small cavernous subterranean sanctum in the temple, with one way entry, was housed the idol of Lord Hanuman, the son of Vayu covered with greasy vermillion.

Love engenders peculiar idiosyncrasies. I too couldn't remain untouched. Every day, after bath, I would write Shama with a ball pen on my chest, on the spot beneath my heart, taking all pains to conceal it from all. In that cavernous sanctum sanctorum—like all devotees—I would apply God's pious vermillion on my forehead. Then after ensuring that no one was watching, I would apply it on my chest, on Shama's name. I would feel Shama and her love.

Praying in a temple, religiously and from the heart, brings peace and solace. And, if one is also imbued with the feelings of love for someone, the impact is heavenly.

And while in the bed, before going to sleep every night, I would observe another ritual. With a pillow over my left arm, I would fantasise Shama lying beside me, with her beautiful innocent visage, her dark shining and wavy hair. I would sweetly tell her that I loved her; that she was everything for me. I would kiss her lovingly, passionately and innocently as a two-year-old child fondling his doll. It would soothe my mind and body, and transport me to a tranquil world of dreams; my subconscious mind wading through the ethereal world. Waking up fresh to the chirping of sparrows at dawn, I would be ready to jostle with another day.

In our sleep we become part of one common universe, where flows continuous energy of one source, where realism is eclipsed by surrealism.

I also started identifying myself and Shama with the heroes and heroines of romantic Hindi movies whether with a happy ending or a tragic one; empathising with the characters, living the circumstances and emotions in the romantic songs and songs of separation. Besides, I got obsessed with the name Shama. Hindi and Urdu cinema and its songs are replete with the word Shama, and I got tethered to the same. That one word would resonate and reverberate in my ears, in my mind, and in my heart, bringing sweet memories of my beloved's innocent and lovely face; of her dark luminescent eyes; vagrant wisps of her black shimmering hair; her restrained and captivating smile. I would be lost—away from the rigours of reality; I would be rejuvenated, forgetting all the pain of the day's toil. For me that name was the only life-sustaining support—like a rope for a person caught in deep morass, like a stray wooden plank coming to the rescue of someone lost in the deep sea. Her thoughts would resuscitate me; lifting my sagging spirits, whenever the going became tough and dreary.

I would be fascinated by the soulful and beautiful songs from the Hindi movies that echoed my sentiments. I would memorise them by heart and sing them alone or many a times in my class or even in certain gatherings. I would sing the duet from *Chitchor*, which literally meant 'The stealer of heart' like its hero Amol Palekar singing with the heroine Zarina Wahab, craving for a rendezvous when the lamps are lit with the arrival of evening:

Jab deep jale aana, jab shaam dhale aana,
Sanket milan ka bhool na jana,
Mera pyar na bisrana…

or I would imagine Shama as an innocent, delicate and beautiful girl of the movie *Shankar Hussein*, and sing the Muhammd Rafi song:

Kahin ek masoom nazuk si ladki,
Bahut khoobsoorat, magar sanwli si …

I would sing and immerse myself in many such songs in my lonely times, with my aching heart. I would cease with tearful eyes and choked throat. But, in public I would be in control. With Shama's love running like fire in my arteries, veins and nerves, and her angelic face deeply embedded in the recesses of my mind, I would impart life to my singing, pouring all my emotions into it. People would appreciate that I sang from the core of my heart; emoting the pathos etched in the lyrics. A song from the movie *Anand* was closest to my heart:

Kahin door jab din dhal jaye,
Saanjh ki dulhan, badan churaaye,
Chupke se aaye …
Mere khayalo ke aangan me, koi sapno ke,
Deep jalaye, nazar na aaye … nazar na aaye …

Time moved on.

One day while I was having lunch on my return from school, my sister announced, 'Shama, has come to our locality with her elder sister; perhaps to pick up some left over articles.'

'Oh that girl! She is so sweet and well-mannered, always elegantly dressed,' Mummy said.

'Her cousin Shobhana used to praise her. I wish she had stayed here a little longer. I wanted to be friends with her,' Nalini said.

I felt like flying out for a precious glimpse of my Shama! But I restrained myself; lest anyone may have a clue of my feelings, my yearning and my craving for her. I denied myself that opportunity with immense pain in my heart. I was training myself in self-abnegation as what cannot be achieved should be avoided. Moreover, I was not sure whether Shama too loved me.

'*Pursuit of love at an inopportune moment only aggravates the agony; whereas, if the image of the beloved is consecrated in one's heart and worshipped, it gives heavenly bliss*,' I, philosophised, at the tender age of sixteen.

If you love someone and your love is reciprocated, you at least know that you are loved in equal measure. But here, it was purely a one-sided story; I didn't have any inkling of what was brewing in her mind. I lacked courage to elicit her response. In coming times I would be steeling my nerves and heart even further. But Shama was forever with me apropos a song from the movie *Mera Saya:*

Tu jahan jahan chalega, mera saya sath hoga,
Mera saya, mera saya...

A few days later ...

I was returning from school, in my school uniform: white trousers, white shirt, white canvas shoes and white socks; my hair ruffled, my school bag dangling from my shoulders, undulating with the rhythm of my motion and my mind lost in Shama's thoughts. I was at the end of the backyard from where the path would narrow down to the staircase. I was thoroughly confused as suddenly who should I see but Shama! Coming from the opposite side at a leisurely pace! I, for a few seconds was immobilised; it was totally unexpected, but a living proof of telepathy. I was gripped by mixed feelings of euphoria, discomfort and bewilderment. I didn't know what to do. I was not mature enough to handle such situations. I kept walking nervously, caressing the strap of my schoolbag, from top to bottom. Those twenty seconds seemed like aeons; causing elations and commotions; as if I was on a boat eddying around in a whirlpool. My head was spinning and my heart thudding. I did not know whether I was in motion or at rest. I raised and lowered my head a few times, fighting a number of wars inside, contemplating whether to stand and talk to her or run away from the scene. I could not decide. Yet, despite the shyness and the persistent fear, I, perhaps for the first time and in the shortest span available, appraised her contours, dress and visage: the slim lithe figure;, the printed pink salwar -kameez with a pink dupatta partly resting on her bosom and the rest dangling down to her knees; her face, innocence writ large on it and the glow of her fair complexion accentuated by her sartorial pink and bright sunshine. I gathered courage and looked directly into her eyes. It appeared that Shama was a bit discomfited though she too maintained eye contact. That moment, it seemed would never end, holding us in a trance. Then my inner turbulence took over: I wanted to remain standing there and imbibe her image till eternity, but didn't have the gumption. I felt like pouring my heart out to her to convey the intensity of my feelings and emotions to tell that I loved her from the core of my heart. But I was equally apprehensive of her reaction to such outpourings; wary of the possible public outcry on my confabulations in such lonely circumstances with a young and beautiful girl. Whether she too had similar feelings for me? Or her temporary petrifaction and reciprocation of eye contact were merely curiosity and equal discomfort. After all she too could have felt awkward being caught alone in the presence of a young boy in a public place. What if on taking a step even towards initiating a conversation could result in a slap from Shama, thereby compromising my dignity and reputation? I just could not say anything and trudged along with so many unsaid feelings and emotions; my silence, my eyes, my face betraying all that my lips could not utter.

One has to be little bold in the matters of the heart. Boys are generally expected to take the initiative and risk in such affairs as girls are shrouded in the veil of dignity, decorum, upbringing and their innate shyness.

But poor me; I was neither an extrovert nor had I divulged my entanglement to anyone else. Who could have come to my aid?

That episode compounded my anguish. On reaching home, I rushed to a solitary corner, thrust my face into a pillow, and burst into sobs. I cried because of my helplessness, because of my inability to covey my emotions and feelings which would remain bottled up, because of a sense of tremendous loss. Still I hoped, '*Perhaps, Shama would still be there; perhaps, she too might be waiting for one courageous move from my side!*' I felt like rushing out to Shama and shouting at the top of my voice, proclaiming before her and before everybody in the world:

'*O Shamaaaaaa, I am madly in love with you; I will wait for you forever; please, wait for me too.*'

But the shackles and manacles of social conduct, my parents' dignity, Shama's honour and my future—my aspirations and goals—nipped such outrageous adventure in the bud.

The renunciation of that idea would change the course of my life and also my character was something I did not know then.

Days passed …

I slowly learnt to live without Shama. My studies became intense. I was quite attentive in class: learning chemical processes; understanding laws of physics; solving tedious mathematical problems; and then my favourite biology. I listened carefully to my English teacher's renditions of poetry and prose, visualising Shama in stanzas and paragraphs imbued with romance and emotions.

An episode of 'A *Tale of Two Cities* by Charles Dickens, involving Sydney Carton and Lucy deeply moved me:

Sydney Carton expresses his unconditional love for Lucy, but on learning about Lucy's love for Charles Darney, makes a graceful exit, promising to render all help to her in case of any need during his life.

I was amazed by Sydney Carton's sacrifice in the end when he embraces the guillotine in place of Darney and facilitates Lucy's union with him. I genuinely wanted my love for Shama to rise to such heights—purely unconditional, not causing any harm to her honour or reputation; no emotional blackmail. I wanted to first achieve my goal, and then, at the opportune moment, pursue and propose to her. I was clear in my mind that I would take further steps only if she would reciprocate my feelings; else I would accept her verdict, and always remember her and worship her as my first and most sacred love.

I knew her address: B-56, Janakpuri; but wanted to use it only five to six years later!

Oh to Be Young!

No matter how much, I tried to console myself; my smouldering emotions seared me deep inside. My heart would writhe with pain. Such feelings don't remain hidden for long. They find expression sooner or later; one feels like confiding in one's close friend or sibling. Sometimes I thought of sharing it with Neelima or Nalini but was apprehensive. One day in class, I sang the song from *Chitchor* in a singing session at the insistence of my class teacher:

Jab deep jale aana, jab sham dhale aana,
Sanket milan ka bhool na jana,
Mera pyar na bisrana...

There was huge applause. Much later, I was having lunch in the garden with Inder Arora, my close friend.

'Rohit, since your return from vacation, you seem to be lost,' Inder commented, 'You have become very quiet, and your singing expresses a lot of pain. Any problems?'

Almost all my friends were in the same age group—about sixteen years old, the time when teenage sensations lurk in the body and mind. People start understanding your emotions.

'No, nothing,' I denied, hotly.

'Come on, Rohit. Something seems to be bothering you,' Inder put an avuncular arm on my shoulder. That was enough to prompt an eruption of the volcano of my emotions. I felt a strange sensation in my body, and the pent up feelings that had been tormenting me gushed out. Tears flowed from my eyes.

'Hey, what happened? Why the tears?' Inder caressed my shoulder and back, 'What will other students say? Come on, control yourself.' Inder was very affectionate. We used to play games together and would also discuss academic issues. But that day the issue was different. I couldn't keep myself in check. We stood up and started walking towards a lonely corner of the playground.

'I am in love,' I blurted out, 'No one can understand what I have undergone in the last few months. I can't tell my parents or sister or cousins. They will either take me to task or make fun of me. I just can't explain how deep my feelings are and what place that one person holds in my heart.'

'Who is she? Do you meet her often? Does she also love you?'

'Her name is Shama. No, I have never spoken to her. I don't even know if she loves me. And, to add to my misery, she has shifted to Janakpuri.'

Inder laughed. 'You're impossible? Never talked to her! Don't even know if she loves you! And, now she has moved away from your vicinity. This is incredible.' He laughed even more.

His reaction annoyed me. 'That is why I didn't want to disclose it. Nobody will realise my sentiments.'

'Oh, come on pal. I do appreciate your feelings. But this is unbelievable. What do you intend to do now? Do you think it is the right time to pursue love? You have to think of your career, your future. Do you want to become another Romeo or Ranjhah or Majnu, losing your all in love?'

'Oh, no yaar. You haven't understood; in fact no one can. I know my career is important. I appreciate my parents' concern; I shall strive hard to become a doctor. I have made a pact with myself.' And, then I revealed my decision of pursuing Shama only when I would have achieved something in my life.

'Rohit, dear buddy, I am proud of you. I never knew that love could transform someone like this. May God shower his benevolence on you and your love,' Inder squeezed my shoulder.

But that day, I felt as if a load had lifted off my heart. Inder and I would be sharing a great bond; much more than friendship—a bond of affection and trust!

With the passage of time, I learnt to endure Shama's absence. But I also felt that Shama was always somewhere nearby. One day on my return from school, Nalini confronted me, mischievously holding something in her fist. With her eyes twinkling and a naughty smile, she said, 'I know; howsoever hard you may try to hide.'

'Know, what?' I countered.

'That you love Shama.'

'Shama? What are you talking about?' I protested. But I felt weak in the knees.

'I know and now don't try to cover up,' Nalini opened her fist, and out tumbled the neatly packaged paper from the polythene bag—the manifestation of my love and outpourings of my emotions—which I had wanted to smuggle to Shama, a day before her departure. *I had been caught! My well concealed secret was out.* I had no choice but to accept my indiscretion.

'Please don't tell anyone,' I pleaded. Nalini laughed, and assured that she would oblige.

But things were not that simple. A month later, I was stunned when Mummy asked with an amused expression, 'So, you liked that girl Shama.' *So, Nalini could not keep the secret to herself.* I adopted the best course available in such situations—denial; yes, absolute and outright denial.

'Who told you? Nalini! She is always in the habit of telling lies. Don't believe her.' My defence was of no avail. Mummy was too smart. But she had a lot of faith in me. Mummy used to proclaim that my shyness and purity were equivalent to that of a dozen girls. She firmly believed my moral strength and ethical resolve and that I would never go astray.

She just smiled, 'Okay, so what if you like someone. But one must maintain some restraint.'

'O Mummy you know me well! How can I do such a thing? I am serious about my studies,' I replied.

'Why are you so upset? I was just curious, teasing. I have ample faith in you, my child. Forget it.'

'Yes Mummy,' I heaved a sigh of relief but vowed to myself to take Nalini to task later.

You have to be cruel to yourself to prove your goodness. You have to suppress your emotions, kill your sentiments, and steel your nerves, never to flinch or waver. A boy certified as bearing a good moral character has to pose like a tamed horse, wearing blinkers, not looking sideways; following a virtuous though torturous path. Such was my fate too!

As time went on, the desire to excel in the exams grew stronger. My burning desire to earn a meritorious position drove me on. December, with the usual chill, was upon us. I would study late at night with all the necessary accessories to ward off cold—kurta pyjama, a thick sweater, a muffler, a cap, and an old overcoat. I would sit in the same rear balcony, which at night would be covered with tarpaulin. The lull of harsh winter nights and the fresh air sneaking through the uncovered gaps of tarpaulin would provide a congenial setting for late-night studies. Even otherwise the rear balcony had the sweet and vivid memories of Shama!

One night, at around ten thirty, I was deeply engrossed in my organic chemistry book, trying to understand the chemical structures of ketones and aldehydes. All of a sudden, a melodious song emanated from the radio of a distant neighbour; it was Lata Mangeshkar at her best for the movie *Woh Kaun Thee*:

Naina Barse…Rimjhim Rimjhim,
Piyaa torey aawan ki aas…

The lyrics, the melody and the pathos of the song caused irrepressible catharsis. Far away from Shama, in the solitude of night, I was shaken, and like the wordings of the song, tears were raining from my eyes. Emotions of love could be so powerful!

I had an urge to look far away at the peepal tree where I used to park our scooter. I was under a spell. In the calm of that chilly night, eerie darkness, there stood the magnificent and resplendent figure of Shama in all its glory: her face aglow; her eyes gleaming and her nose stud sparkling. Her eyes were fixed on me; her serene face adorned with a pleasing smile. Her eyes and facial expressions beckoned me. I felt like running to her, and then somewhere a dog barked. Reality dawned. There was nothing but the cloak of darkness there. And … of course … no trace of Shama. Her apparition was merely a figment of my imagination conjured up by my psyche and my senses that had been deeply influenced by my feelings for her.

How could I be so attached to someone! To whom I had never even spoken! I couldn't understand. I could only see the image of Shama merging into the equations and structures of organic chemistry, then vanishing and reappearing. 'Oh God! Help me, let me concentrate,' I prayed, 'let Shama's love burn inside me forever and guide me in locating her and expressing it at the opportune moment—when I become a doctor with enough financial and social status.'

The enormity of the syllabus and paucity of time prompted me to become oblivious to everything. January and February flew past and the real test came in March. Board exams continued throughout the month. I did well but bungled in some crucial problems of maths and physics, committing silly errors. Finally the ordeal was over.

The results were announced about a month later. I had scored 535 out of 750, and was joint fourth in my class with one Jaideep Aggarwal. Inder Arora was third with 541 and Rajeev Dewan fifth with 526. Four of us got admission in Khalsa College at the University Campus: Jaideep, Inder and I in Zoology (Honours) and Rajeev in Botany (Honours). Neelima, my cousin scored 585, and got into Kirori Mal College. Unlike famous colleges like Hindu and Hansraj, Khalsa was not much heard of. However, Khalsa College's precincts belied all notions of ordinariness: sprawling complex with modern construction, a huge playground for cricket, basketball, football, and hockey. It had beautiful gardens ornate with lovely lawns, pruned trees and colourful flower-bearing herbs. The lecture rooms, laboratories, and library were all majestic, neat and well-equipped.

Although students of our class were meritorious, there was a conspicuous hiatus between those with convent or public school background and those from modest schools. We, from modest schools, shared constraints and inhibitions in speaking English, and secretly admired their fluency and palpable advantage of attracting the opposite gender.

In India a person speaking English is considered more cultured, and earns the tag of being naturally good while the Hindi speakers have to really prove that they too are people of substance.

I had to first think in Hindi, and then translate my thoughts into English before speaking. I remembered a few lines that I had picked up from a few Hindi movies. Before Inder came to the college, I met one Ajay Goel, a simple boy like us.

'Hullo, Good morning, I am Rohit, Rohit Sharma. May I know your name please?' I asked.

'I am Ajay; Ajay Goel. You are from which school? What was your percentage?'

'I am from Ramjas School, No. 4, Pahar Ganj. I got 71.32%. What about you?'

'I got 67%. I stay at Kamla Nagar, which is just nearby.'

Then I spotted Inder Arora, and introduced him to Ajay,

'Inder, he is Ajay Goel, our classmate. He stays at Kamla Nagar, and he scored 67%.'

'Okay,' Inder responded, 'I am from Adarsh Nagar. I got 72.13%.'

Our conversation was restricted to just these lines. Beyond that we neither had the material nor the skill to converse. On the first day, there were hardly twelve students in the class. Anita Paul, with protruding eyeballs and clad in salwar-kameez was in the first row. I was so shy that I would hardly look at or converse with girls; harbouring apprehension that any first move would be misconstrued. My nature to a large extent had also been shaped by not having been to a coeducational school. When I look back, I laugh at my own preconceived notions and trepidations.

'Hullo everyone,' said Preeti on entering the class when she saw our group of five boys. I blushed and replied nervously, 'Oh, hullo.' Preeti was a fair-complexioned girl with nice features, black hair, good height and elegant gait. She was mostly attired in tight jeans and short tops. Her movements did send electric waves in my body making me realise that I had come of age. But that feeling was different from the feeling I had for Shama.

Manjeet Kaur was of medium height, fair and with a cherubic innocent face. Though she did have a good figure and was clad in body-hugging jeans and T-shirts, her appearance would engender gentle feelings: of sweetness, innocence and serenity. I felt comfortable with her. On discovering my lack of fluency in English, she would speak in Hindi. She was very good-natured and simple and behaved in the same friendly way ... with everyone.

College life was in sharp contrast to school; replete with colour and glamour. No school uniform, lot of liberty! I had never seen such a large number of girls, all smartly dressed in T-shirts, trousers, tops, and jeans.

Strange are the creations of God. If reduced to its basics, what is a human body? A contrivance composed of seventy per cent water and mega-structure of molecules of carbon, hydrogen, oxygen, nitrogen, etc. But, what an impact it has on the fellow souls, especially the opposite gender! Only God knows why he created and wove the whole gamut of human drama; we mortals despite knowing it is ephemeral, an illusion, get trapped, get sucked into the quagmire.

I too was drawn into it, having just entered my youth. Occasionally, I found it difficult to take my eyes off those lovely creatures. But, it would be only momentary. Because I firmly believed that bodies bereft of emotional attachment are merely objects. One wishes to possess them, but their illusion vanishes in no time and the desire grows to have another object; just like a child's plaything. One may get bodies but souls are not revealed easily; souls are discovered only by the 'soul mates'. And, you don't get your soul mate with any planning. God has his designs, his timing, and he endows you with the sagacity to recognise your soul mate. Without his will you cannot find one, let alone choose. It is beyond the ken of human comprehension.

I was thus a spectator in the whole drama, rooted to Shama. I was in the college to pursue my dream, my cherished ambition, and not to get swayed by such mirages. But still a battle between the spirit and senses had started.

I always had a complex whether I looked good. Continuous studies had turned my wheatish complexion dark. I had a tall, wiry figure, thin, longish face with an aquiline nose which had always been an object of jest. I had doubts if girls could ever like me in college as there were so many tall, well-built, fair and handsome boys. Many of them were from public schools, fluent in English, having natural style and trendy mannerisms; hailing from rich families.

But since my childhood, I had heard that I had a very winning smile—the hallmark of a Libra male; that innocence was writ large on my face; and that I lacked any complexity. My family members used to say that I had large, beautiful and expressive eyes, which exuded liveliness and simplicity. I used to laugh heartily, like a child. But whether these traits compensated for the deficiencies in my features and complexion, I didn't have any idea.

Whenever someone would tease me about my complexion, I would tell Mummy. Lovingly she would console me, 'Things like complexion are temporary. You know your Papa was also dark. Don't worry; you will develop into a handsome individual. You never know who is waiting for you and where.'

'Have you taken down all the notes?' Preeti asked me the moment the Histology class got over. I was packing my bag. 'Yeah, I … I thinkkkkkksooo,' I replied, totally flustered on finding her standing near my desk. During the lecture she was just behind me in the second row. 'I saw you were sincerely taking down notes. You know, by chance my pen ran dry. Couldn't borrow from anyone as it would have disturbed the class. You know Sir doesn't like any noise or diversion,' Preeti clarified. I had meticulously jotted down notes on epithelial tissue although the professor had been dictating at a furious speed.

'Can I borrow your notes? I'll return it by tomorrow,' her tone was confident. She was in a yellow salwar suit. I lifted my eyes to respond. But my God! I was daunted by her dark, big shapely eyes. Her lips were pink and glistening. I tried to ward off her gaze; but when I put my head down, my eyes found that her yellow diaphanous dupatta had slipped from her bosom. Rattled by the sight I stammered, 'Okay, youuuumayyyytttttaketttthem.'

'What happened? Are you okay Rohit?'

'No, nothing, just some allergy,' and I screwed up my nose and deliberately sneezed.

I took out the notes.

She smiled while taking it; amused at my discomfiture.

College Blues

Shama's love helped me develop a strong character and enhance my goodness. When presented with an opportunity to sit close to a female, I would recoil from even a slight physical contact. While standing in a bus, I would try to shield any lady in my proximity from licentious males. I would create a secure space by using my body as a shield in between to block their manoeuvres. I would strain and shrink and remain balanced even while holding the handle-bar; defying the fast and wayward movement of the bus. I would also avoid any inadvertent physical touch from my side lest I may be mistaken for possessing a similar propensity. I knew by doing so I would be denying myself the pleasure of even looking at the girls; but I was prepared to forego such bliss. In the process I was evolving; weaving a strong web of self-restraint. After all, I loved and worshipped Shama—my companion forever. But little did I know that in the bargain I would be breaking many hearts.

I would look at any girl only when she would not be looking at me. If she happened to notice, I would avert my glance, and thereafter would not look back for a long time; thus dispelling any doubts. I didn't want to create any wrong notions. I was always guarded in my interaction with girls. I had begun treating them as if they were not human species; though in my heart and mind I would be fighting many wars, suppressing my urge, my intense desires. Perhaps, for girls too I had become an object of curiosity as my behaviour was not normal. They might have construed it as my inferiority complex or my bloated ego or something wrong with my physical and biochemical setup.

'Thanks. Here is your notebook. You really take down notes fast. And, I don't know why my pen runs dry so often,' Preeti said.

I was sitting in the corridor reading 'Life cycle of Malarial Parasite' when Preeti appeared out of nowhere dressed in tight blue denims and white cotton top.

I looked up, almost blushing, and said, 'I do, but I find it difficult to read my own handwriting. How are you able to read it?'

'Oh no! Your handwriting is bold and clear, as clear as your heart. Isn't it Manjeet?' Preeti asked Manjeet standing close by. Manjeet reminded me of Shama. But there was one big difference. Though I liked Manjeet, I could never love her, she could not replace Shama in my affections. Manjeet was a good friend but my heart did not recognise her as my soul mate. She too did not seem to harbour such feelings for me.

'Nooooo, nooo, my handwriting is not that, it's just about okay,' I said timidly, my tone betraying nervousness. 'Rohit, are you okay? Your face has turned red,' Preeti remarked. I could feel my rising pulse, sweat on my forehead and my wet hands. 'IIII ammmfffffine,' I stammered. Preeti laughed and was joined by Manjeet.

Yes, Preeti's presence disturbed me, and I had to win that battle against my biological cravings, which, thankfully for me, were only momentary. My heart spoke a different language. And, the heart never lies. "*I must listen to my heart*," I chided myself.

'Okay bye, Rohit, see you later,' they said and went their way.

Howsoever hard I tried but my voice failed me when I talked to girls. It took a long time for me to overcome this failing.

College studies were much tougher than school. The curriculum was vast and complex. There was additional pressure of studying for the MBBS entrance exam. Practical classes were now more elaborate. The whole day I would scamper from one floor to another in the Science block, attending lectures and practicals. Free time was utilised for gossiping, collecting books from the library and preparing notes. I would, on occasions look enviously at the group of students of Humanities enjoying in the gardens, in the cafeteria or basking in the sun. But that was not a life I had chosen for myself!

Inder and I also took admission in a coaching institute for MBBS entrance exams. It became exacting as I would commute from my place in Central Delhi to the university campus for college, and on Saturdays, Sundays and holidays, to coaching classes. Time progressed. In the late hours at night while studying, images of Shama would pervade my senses and mind, and a song from the movie *Kinara* in the voice of my favourite singer Bhupinder Singh, would resonate in my ears:

Naam gum jaayega, chehra ye badal jayega,
Meri aawaz hee pehchaan hai gar yaad rahe…

Whenever that song would be played on radio, my eyes would well up, and that lovely, resplendent face of Shama would dance before me; there would be pangs of harsh reality of separation; and a craving to see her would consume me.

Shama too would be in some college now. I would wonder. Whether she got admission in north campus or somewhere else in Delhi? Whether someday I would see her in some DTC bus? Perhaps yes? When? How? Where?

Such questions would crop up in my mind. I became a fatalist. If Shama was my destiny, I would find her and get her one day—yes, the day ordained by the Omniscient and the Omnipotent.

While lost in the studies I would wonder, at the exponential progress of time. How those 86,400 seconds of a day would vanish! The course content was interesting but vast and the competition tough. In times of exhaustion, Shama would always surface in my thoughts.

Autumn gave in to winter. Winter, though a guest only for three months, seemed to be in top gear, and in no time spring arrived. Gardens of Khalsa College teemed with ornate blooms of daisies, dahlia, carnation, asters, zinnia, roses, marigold, etc. in various hues, jutting out of green niches. The lawns were lush green with nicely mowed grass. Trees had acquired fresh appearance; small plants and shrubs became livelier. Nature was at its glorious best, exhilarating hearts and elating the spirits.

Mid June 1978…

Results started tumbling out. First the college exams: I missed first class by ten marks. I was disappointed but thought they were secondary; the entrance exam result was what really mattered.

Almost a week later, in the afternoon when I visited Om Mamaji's house, I learnt that results of the Delhi Pre-Medical Exam were out. I enquired about Neelima's result but their morose mood conveyed it all. I could hear Neelima sobbing in the other room.

Still I asked, 'What happened?'

'Rohit! She couldn't qualify. What about you? Why don't you go and find out.'

I was dejected to see Neelima's condition. I couldn't even console her. I had to find out what fate had in store for me. I hurried to the Science Faculty—totally nervous, my mind occupied by a single question: 'Would I succeed or would my fate be like Neelima's?' As I neared the Science Faculty my feet felt leaden and my heartbeats increased. On the way I met Jaideep along with another student of my coaching college.

'Hey! How was your result?' they asked.

'I am yet to find out.'

They had been selected, I learnt. On seeing my nervousness they tried to boost my morale, 'You have to give us a treat as you are going to be in Maulana Azad Medical College.'

'Let us see.'

I rushed to the hall where the results had been pasted on a board. A number of students were going through the long list. With bated breath, I gingerly went through it. 'O my God!' I sighed with disappointment! I couldn't make it. Inder and Jaideep had made it. Rajeev Dewan too had missed narrowly. I felt as if I would faint. Exercising extreme self-control, I came out of the Science Faculty enveloped in depression.

Suddenly, I saw Inder. He was ebullient, but my result saddened him. He consoled me, and we walked together. I put up a brave front, and said, 'All is not over; I will work hard next year, and shall get through.' While conversing animatedly we reached the bus stand near Patel Chest Institute. Inder had to now catch a bus for Adarsh Nagar and I had to walk down to Vijay Nagar where we had shifted to a few months earlier. 'Okay Inder goodbye,' I said with a choked throat and tearful eyes. I couldn't speak further. Inder was perturbed. He put his hand on my shoulder. That avuncular touch aggravated the storm raging within. I started sobbing. A few passers-by noticed me. I was feeling the loss I had suffered: my failure and the loss of a very good friend, whom I would now see rarely, whose regular company had been severed by fate's cruel hands.

The bus arrived and Inder boarded it. I stood there in tears, waving emptily, disillusioned, sorrow writ large on my face. *That was the beginning of a new life*. I somehow collected myself, and trudged along homewards—absolutely devastated. Mummy and Nalini did not need many words—they understood. 'Why do you cry? Look, even Neelima, who is more diligent than you are, couldn't make it. What can you do? There are so many good candidates to choose from, and the number of seats is limited. The whole system is full of uncertainty and probability,' Mummy consoled. 'Don't lose heart, try harder next year.'

Unfortunately nothing succeeds like success; success alone is the yardstick by which the world measures you. We judge ourselves by our capabilities, while others judge us by our achievements.

All night in bed, I was tormented by thoughts of failure; sleep eluded me. I kept on pondering; but there were no answers. When the restlessness continued till very late into the night, I implored God to shower His mercy and give me refuge in sleep. I thought of Shama and entreated, 'Despite this failure, please don't desert me, don't ever desert me.'

The Dream Crashes ... But Life Goes On

Mourning over, I got on with my second year. Instead of dissecting human bodies in a medical college, I was to now study the life history, anatomy and body systems of invertebrates like cockroaches, prawns, snails, houseflies, mosquitoes, etc.

Compared to the first year I could take a little more freedom as I had the confidence of having studied most of the course. The composition of my class was now more colourful than the first year. There were many new students, and girls were in majority. They would come colourfully attired in attractive dresses, many of them were very beautiful and smart; their mere sight would unnerve the passers-by. And, I discovered that I too had become an object of interest for a few. *Maybe, my looks had improved.* I started appraising myself in the mirror.

I was under the influence of two competing factors: my biological self—governed by androgens, natural for my age; and my emotional self—governed by my basic nature. But my ability to strike a balance between the two was being put to test in that vivacious environment replete with tempting sights and infinite possibilities.

New admissions through migrations were still on.

'Hi, is this B.Sc (Hons.), Second Year?' A beautiful fair complexioned girl dressed in an orange salwar suit asked me while I was browsing through my notes, seated on the first bench. Two other students were sitting on different benches. We had come in early. Her shining black hair was plaited in a nice braid. Her eyes had a twinkle, and her round face was lit up with a natural smile; in short, she was petite and pretty and had a nice figure, not a voluptuous one.

I looked up and replied casually, 'Yes.' And, to my surprise, she sat next to me, and introduced herself, 'Komal, Komal Bajaj. I have migrated from Daulat Ram.'

'Rohit Sharma. I have been here since First Year.' Then she made small talk of a general nature. She was like Manjeet, without any airs. By the time the others came in and the lecture started, we had established a good rapport.

Just after the lecture Komal shrieked when an elegantly dressed girl in a peach salwar suit and dupatta approached her, 'Hi Sonam, why so late? You were to join earlier.'

'Got delayed; payment of fees and other formalities. Good, we'll be together now.'

I gave them a cursory glance. Sonam was smiling. I smiled in return. She was a slim and pleasing girl of fair complexion, average height, normal features, an oval face and brown boy-cut hair. Her light brown eyes had gentleness and innocence.

Days passed.

'Rohit, your shirt is looking really good,' one day Komal just remarked off hand, 'and it goes very well with your light brown trousers.' I just smiled. 'And, I always find that your clothes are well-matched. How do you manage?'

I blushed. Such a comment from a girl was totally unexpected.

'I … I … don't do anything special. It is entirely Mummy's choice. She selects my clothes.'

'Oooo, so you are mama's boy. Don't you like wearing good clothes and others praising you, especially girls?' she winked.

'I … don't know. I just wear whatever Mummy brings,' I said innocently. I just didn't know why she said that. But during our conversation, Sonam, standing nearby, gave a naughty smile.

I found Komal very affectionate. Exchange of smiles between us was spontaneous and we were ready to render mutual help in the laboratories whenever necessary. The level of comfort was so good that I sometimes felt like sharing the 'Shama Chapter' of my life with her. But I always wondered what she would think.

But then, I was oblivious to something else brewing. I, from day one, had observed that Sonam's way of looking at me was a little different. One day I had to go to the Administrative Block for collecting refund of last year's laboratory security. Clad in black trousers and a striped pink shirt, I strode exuberantly. That day I had the affirmation of my good looks from my reflection in the mirror.

There was a long queue. Suddenly I saw Sonam standing there among others, calmly looking at me. I hesitated for a moment, but then, without much premeditation, approached her, 'Will you please get me a security form?'

She flushed. Something palpable in her eyes: appreciation! In five minutes her turn came and she got me the required forms.

'Thank you,' I said formally, and left with utter nonchalance.

There were many occasions when I happened to be near Komal and Sonam, but I liked talking to Komal. It was always a very neat interaction. Slowly I became comfortable with other girls too. But on many instances I discovered Sonam gazing at me, her eyes conveying fondness. Gradually, she would even intervene in my conversations with others.

'Rohit, will you explain the Circulatory System of the leech. I find it a bit complicated,' Vandana asked me one day.

'Yeah, best person to ask; Rohit must have read that at least twice. I saw him lost in his book for two hours in the library,' Sonam replied. She was standing nearby.

I was surprised. *When did she see me? Was she keeping tabs on me even in the library?*

Once I was sitting on the cemented space in the corridor adjoining the lawn, copying notes from Rakesh's notebook. All of a sudden, my pen popped out of my hand and fell on the grass. I had to close my notebooks and put them aside to reach for it. The moment I got up, from nowhere came a fair and soft hand offering me my pen. When I lifted my eyes, I found Sonam's smiling face. 'Oh, thank you so much,' I said with gratitude and a restrained smile. 'Welcome,' she said softly.

While conducting a dissection of a cockroach, one day in the lab, my forceps dropped on the floor. I moved my dissection tray aside to get up. But before I turned, Sonam, who was just two seats away, picked that up and gave me. There were so many signs. But, despite her being decent and beautiful, my heart was not stirred.

Our chemistry lecturer was in a lighter mood one day. He was generally of serious disposition. But his moustache was funny, it twirled like the Greek letter omega. Few of us had nicknamed him 'Omega Sir'.

That day, Omega Sir gave us a shock, 'Students we have had enough of chemistry. I am a bit drained out. Let us hear some songs. Any volunteers? I have heard you guys singing in your free time.' We all started passing the buck on and most of us were hesitant. Rajiv Malik, a naughty friend of mine suggested, 'Sir, Anant Basant,' knowing fully well that Anant was tone deaf. Anant growled, 'Oye, I don't sing.' And, then Savita Dheer, a good-natured plump girl volunteered. She sang a lovely song from the movie *Gharonda* which had actually been sung by Bhupinder Singh:

Ek akela iss shehar mey,
raat me aur dopahar mey,
aabodana dhoondta hai,
aashiyana dhoondta hai...

The song was my favourite. It did not suit Savita's soft female voice. The ice having been broken, I was itching to sing; but wanted some goading and prompting. And, to my amazement, I found both Komal and Sonam proposing, 'Sir, Rohit sings well.' I refused only once, out of formality, and when coaxed by Omega Sir relented, 'Okay, I will sing the same song which Savita just sang.' I put my heart and soul into the song and the effect was superb: my voice resembling and reverberating like Bhupinder; and the resemblance was accentuated by the common cold that I had; the lyrics of the song conveyed my loneliness in the crowd without my dearest Shama. Shama alone was the succour and shelter for me in this world!

I, in those five minutes of singing, had transcended into a different world—a world illuminated by the luminescence of Shama, the world submerged in the thoughts of Shama. When the spell was broken, I heard loud clapping in the classroom, and saw Sonam's eyes riveted on me. When our eyes met, I looked elsewhere. Once again I looked in that direction but didn't have the courage to look straight; instead I dropped my gaze to the floor. I didn't want to give any false signals!

With the passage of time I noticed Sonam staring at me almost every moment and everywhere: in practical classes, in theory classes, in the corridors, in the library and in the canteen. To be truthful, I did enjoy such attention. Who doesn't like getting such appreciative approval from the opposite gender? *After all, such visual appreciation within the confines of decorum engenders feelings of completeness and well-being.*

Sonam's behaviour and her feelings were now crystal clear. But for me she was merely a classmate. She did not evoke any special feelings. In fact my heart didn't have any special feelings for any of the girls: whether in my class or my college or in my neighbourhood. Although, I was disturbed biologically by the presence of a few girls, none could invade my emotional domain.

Strange is this world. Strange is the web of human emotions. You love someone madly, obsessed; but that prized one may like you only as a good human being. Love is not cultivated, it just happens! Lucky are the ones whose love is requited. Paulo Coelho says that 'soul mates' identify each other by a 'special light' they emit. Only the soul mates are able to discern that 'light' as God has blessed them with that sagacity. And, one may have more than one soul mate in a single incarnation!

I had seen my soul mate in Shama. And, with a heavy heart, I started ignoring Sonam. Whenever I found her looking at me, I would return blank stares. Despite her overtures, I posed as a dunce. Sonam was very fond of cricket and especially Sunil Gavaskar. She used to carry a pocket radio-transistor which she would hear at low volume.

The world outside was changing fast. Jimmy Carter became the President of America. In India the Janata Party experiment—which had overthrown the Congress regime of Mrs Indira Gandhi after the 'Emergency'—was turning out to be tentative and shaky. Too much of infighting ultimately led to the removal of Morarji Desai and brought Choudhary Charan Singh, a leader of farmers, as the Prime minister of India.

In Hockey, India was losing, but in Cricket, a sparkling Indian star Kapil Dev emerged. He captured the imagination of Indians with his fast-scoring and swashbuckling approach. He was bold in his fast bowling too. He set cricket stadia on fire in Pakistan and India with his buccaneer hitting, unfazed by bowlers' reputations. Whenever I found Sonam's conversations veering in a different direction, I would divert her with a query. 'What is the latest score?'

I cannot forget the commotion that occurred one day in the zoology lab. We were to dissect cockroaches. A few students had already entered the lab while the rest including me were about to reach. All of a sudden, a few students started rushing out of the lab, screaming. While we hurried to the lab to find the cause, I, in the melee, collided with Sonam. She came running with her eyes closed wailing, 'Oh, save me, save me, I just can't put up with those animals.' She, little realising it was me, held me with both her arms with her head resting on my shoulder, and squealed, 'My God, they are so awful, irritating and dirty; filthy creatures.' Her body was quivering and her act was purely spontaneous, like a scared child rushing to safe sanctuary. My hand too reached her head, and I started caressing it gently. Her hair was smooth, well-shampooed. She felt a little assured, her body no longer shivering. 'Hey Sonam, come on, calm down. What happened?'

Sonam, opened her eyes, and felt embarrassed at the situation we were in.

'Oh, I am so sorry,' she moved away embarrassedly and looked around.

Good, no one had paid us too much attention. We felt relieved.

I left her and proceeded to the lab, and was welcomed by flying cockroaches, criss-crossing in the air and falling on the ground.

Anant Basant was shouting, 'You know what? That lab assistant Hari committed a blunder. He had given a reduced dosage of chloroform. With less sedation, they were a confused lot, and were flying such.'

The lab was closed for ten minutes, till the poor insects were caught, fully sedated with another dose and were brought under control. And, then we started the procedure.

Over a period of time we had to dissect prawns, snails and cuttlefish (those disgusting ink-filled creatures!). I often wondered at the usefulness of those futile exercises, but I couldn't have charted a different course. Getting into a medical college was my ambition. So, like many of my contemporaries, I had to undergo similar travails. I had to complete my second year, and try again for MBBS entrance.

Winter arrived. The university gardens were again flooded with colourful blossoms of various hues, on cradles of tender shoots; among green leaves. Among tall trees and lush green grass, such picturesque surroundings would reinvigorate my resolve for realising my ambition.

Winter gave way to spring. March brought the same ordeal of college examinations, and in no time I was appearing for the competitive exam with the aim of fulfilling my long-cherished goal. I estimated that I had done well.

But again neither Neelima nor I could make it to the medical college. But why couldn't we? There were no answers—sometimes we get no answers for certain occurrences and events in our life. We have to just leave it to God.

But that is easier said than done. When the end result is the only barometer of your intelligence and hard work, failure does cause heartburning and frustration. And, in reality frustration leads to bitterness, despair, and unhappiness. If we keep on thinking about failures, our progress is impeded.

At night, I could not sleep. I was left wondering about the possible causes. I analysed all the episodes, dissecting them to their bare details, but couldn't figure out why I had failed. Each analysis indicated no dearth of effort.

I conjured up Shama's image, my only respite, and wept silently before her, '*Shama, at least you know the truth of my efforts, please do not desert me, ever. I would try my best to realise my ambition. Then I would come to you, seeking your hand.*'

I needed her in my dreams, in my thoughts, and in reality. In my mindscape, Shama smiled and cupped my face in her hands. She wiped my tears, kissed my brow, caressed my head and face affectionately. Her face was radiant, innocent, and pleasing. She spoke, her voice mellifluous and charming, pouring into my ears like drops of honey, 'How can I leave you? I too love you, but you are so shy that you never looked at me nor have you tried to meet me. How can a girl come and express her love? And now you cry. You summon me when you feel like. You invoke me only in your dreams. What about me? Have you ever bothered?'

And then I saw Shama proceeding to leave, apparently moving under compulsion. I followed her, entreating, 'Please don't go away Shama.' I found myself standing beside a river bank and Shama standing all alone in a boat, floating on the water stream, driven by the currents with her arms stretched out, soliciting my embrace. She was singing:

Aaja reeeeee…Pardesi,
Main to kab se khadi iss paar,
Ye aakhiyan, thak gayee panth nihaar

She was slowly receding from my view, her voice dimming. I kept calling out her name, 'Shamaaaaaaaaa, Shamaaaaaa.' She disappeared, vanished into thin air. I fell on the ground: desolate, unconscious. I was woken up by chirping sparrows, followed by the cacophony of the customers vying for buying milk at the Delhi Milk Scheme's dairy that was in front of our house. Just a dream. I woke up to another day…

Selection of a few more friends into the medical colleges caused more heartbreak. The process of ruing over the past continued for a few more days. Then I plunged into the grind for another year, with the same resolution and ambition.

Third Year comprised study of the vertebrates: fishes, amphibians, reptiles, birds, and mammals, including human beings. I enjoyed only human physiology and biochemistry as they gave the feeling of being in a medical college.

Practical classes in the lab included dissections of innocent animals sedated with chloroform; many were like butchery. Only singing sessions would be cathartic, to overcome the guilt of pointless slaughters of pigeons, frogs and the like. Interestingly, those sessions germinated in the dissection lab only: Once during the absence of a lecturer, someone mooted the idea. It was Savita Dheer first. In her melodious voice she sang a popular song. People enjoyed and egged her on to sing one more. She obliged. 'Rohit now you sing,' beseeched Sonam, seconded by Komal. I was always ready, singing being my second love. I sang a ghazal by Shaharyar, imbued with pathos, from the movie *Gaman*:

Seene mein jalan, aankhon me toofaan sa kyun hai,
Iss shahar me har shaqs pareshan sa kyon hai,
Seene mein jalan...

With my eyes closed, my voice deep and pregnant with pain, I sang under a magic spell. Hardly anyone could know the cause for such anguish in my voice. I sang for—Shama—my heartthrob. I finished with a resonating note and my eyes opened to loud applause. Such singing sessions became a regular feature during free time. My singing prowess made me popular in my class. While singing I would envision Shama, her beautiful and charming face, smiling and aglow, feeling that she was listening to my entreaties. I would sing from different movies, of various singers, portraying varied moods and emotions, precisely capturing the sentiments and depth of lyrics. At home too I would listen to the radio and try to remember the lyrics, tunes and, above all, the emotive appeal of the songs and their music. This would make me forget the drudgery of studies, the stink of the lab, and the butchery of the innocent animals!

During those days came an emotional and sensitive movie with teenage love story as the subtext: *Akhiyon Ke Jharokho Se*.

The movie and especially its title song in the voice of singer Hemlata deeply moved me:

Akhiyon ke jharokho se maine dekha jo sanware
Tum door nazar aaye, badi door nazar aaye
Band karke jharokho ko, jara baithee jo sochne
Mann me tumhi muskaye,
Mann me tumhi muskaye
Akhiyon ke jharokho se...

That song would drive me crazy, giving me hallucinations: of Shama, in a garden, innocently smiling at me; her eyes pristine and pure. I would sing that song daily in the bathroom, or whenever alone at home.

Cricket fever in those times had intensified. Kapil Dev with his sterling bowling and batting had infused new life into Indian cricket.

One after another Australia and then Pakistan were defeated in India by the Indian team. It was an inspirational performance and the whole country was gloating over his superlative efforts. In college, I would enquire from Sonam about cricket scores, and she would readily oblige.

But one day, like the explosive batting of Kapil Dev, an explosion occurred in my life too. Sonam had come dressed in a beautiful white salwar suit, printed all over with lovely orange and yellow polka dots. All the girls were praising her. I observed and overheard their comments while passing across. She was really looking very nice. On a few occasions I looked at her; but that was merely a glimpse of appreciation without any covert intentions. I felt that she had noticed my gaze. We had three continuous lectures that morning followed by half an hour break. I stayed back in class as I had to complete copying some notes from the blackboard. The entire class was leaving and so did my friends.

'Hey Rohit; not coming to the canteen?' Manmeet and Malik asked.

'Yes. I will join you in ten minutes. Order a coke and samosa for me.' I replied. They left, and I got absorbed in my work.

'Rohit, how am I looking in this suit?' I was surprised to hear Sonam's murmur, almost after five minutes. The lecture theatre was empty. I lifted my head and looked in her direction. I was startled to find her seated beside me; her eyes, straight, expectant and inquisitive, her face suffused with oodles of innocence. I was speechless. I didn't know what to say.

'Rohit, I asked you something,' she implored.

'Aaaah, yeeeeeah, youuuuuuuareeeelookkkkkkinggoooooood,' I stammered.

'But why didn't you say it on your own,' she countered.

'Sooooonam, I dooooon't understand what you are saying? How can a boy just get up and tell things like that to any girl?' I replied, vainly trying to control my stammer.

'But for me you are not any other boy, Rohit.' Her voice had pain.

'I just don't understand what you are saying, Sonammmmmmm.'

'Don't tell me Rohit that a boy of nineteen doesn't understand what a girl of his age is trying to convey,' she said sharply.

'Oh, really, Sonam, I am unable to comprehend what you are trying to convey.'

'Just tell me Rohit, am I not a good person? Am I not good-looking? Don't you like me? Don't you have any feelings for me?'

'Yes, no doubt, you are a good person. In fact you are too good and decent. You have grace and elegance. And, of course, I like you, but I like you as any other good person, and as a good classmate. That's all. But please don't read too much into this. I don't know what feelings you are referring to,' I asserted with a firm voice.

That was the trigger. In a doleful tone she continued, 'Don't you miss me if you don't see me or if I am absent for a day? I miss you everywhere. I feel like seeing you always.'

I felt very sorry. So my apprehensions of the last one and a half years were correct. She loved me. Those were the only words that remained to be said. And Suddenly, I was awakened to the reality. I didn't have any special sentiments for her. Shama was my universe, my life. There was no space for anyone else. So, the time had come to remove the haze and illusion. 'Sonam, I think you have misinterpreted my conduct. I like you, I repeat. Let me make it clear, for me you are a very nice and decent person. I respect you. But I would not be honest if I say that I miss you or your absence. I don't have any other feelings or sentiments for you except as a good friend. Please forgive me if inadvertently, my mannerisms or my conduct has conveyed anything else.' I now had to look directly into her lovely eyes. I was upset to find deep agony, dejection and some tears desperately trying to remain in their confines.

She looked innocent and pure. And, I, for a moment, felt if Shama had not sneaked into my life and senses, I would have accepted Sonam. Perhaps, in my past incarnation she was my soul mate. But in this life, though she had discovered me, I, despite recognising her, was not mentally prepared to accept her. She may have to wait for a few more lives, maybe yes, maybe no. Still at that moment my heart went out to her. I took out a paper tissue from my pocket and offered her. She took that tissue, and with a lot of effort wiped the corners of her eyes.

'But I wish to share something with you. Sonam, I have been in love with a girl; for the past three years; someone whom I worship ardently, who is part of my life and my psyche.' I spoke with a lot of hesitation and with a heavy heart. It was difficult to share my intimate secrets with a girl.

'What Rohit? You and in love! That too for the past so many years! You never told me,' Sonam uttered in surprise. She was taken aback at my revelation.

'How could I? I can't advertise my love.'

'Now I understand why you sing so passionately? By the way, what is her name? Does she stay in your locality? Is she studying somewhere nearby? Can I meet her?' Sonam erupted.

I then told Sonam about Shama, about the time when I was hit by Cupid; that I had never expressed my love to her; that since her leaving our locality we had never met; that I hardly knew what she was doing; and about my commitment of meeting her after my achievements.

'Rohit, you are impossible. You love and worship a girl and have not expressed your love to her! And, you have never met her since she left your locality! How do you know whether she loves you or she would be waiting for you? It is purely a one sided story. You are clinging to a totally uncertain relation. I wish you were more realistic. Here I am, totally in love with you; and you, you are pursuing a mirage.'

'Sonam, please forgive me. I am deeply sorry. I do appreciate your feelings, I profoundly respect them. But, for me, you are only a good friend, nothing else.' Her throat was choked, and so was mine.

With a very heavy heart, I extended my hand, smiled and said, 'Friends?'

She too reciprocated, 'Yes, friends,' and smiled, a forced smile.

Both of us left the class together, though in different directions—she towards the toilet, to unload her emotional overload, and I, to the canteen to quench my thirst and settle my hunger pangs. But on the way, I found my eyes were moist. I pulled out my handkerchief, and wiped them.

Winter arrived. Colours of beautiful flowers instilled a new passion—for plants and flowers. I would be enamoured of the lovely hues and shapes of roses, chrysanthemums, asters, nasturtiums, and dahlias. They reminded me of the innocence and beauty of Shama, in all its freshness and vivacity. One day while returning from college I spotted a plant seller, carrying a basket of green saplings and flowers on his head. Lovely saplings laden with flowers were sashaying to his steps in the mild breeze. I was smitten by the thought of buying a few.

'Let us go to your house and assess the requirement,' said the vendor on finding my interest. Mummy protested initially, but later yielded to my desires; a few plants were purchased. This was only the beginning, as my love for plants increased with time. Slowly, our empty courtyard was full of a variety of plants. It became my hobby to buy pots, tend to plants, and water them daily. I would be happy to see them grow. Blossoming of a flower would fill me with a new zeal. It was a new obsession that would further increase my sensitivities.

Dissections, studies, songs, cricket and the love for gardening kept me busy. The clock's hands kept on chopping time into seconds, minutes and hours, and the rising and setting of the sun marked the passing of days and then months. Time is dynamic and fleets like the water of a running river. There was the same sequence of annual exams followed by the entrance exams for the medical colleges. This time I was confident and agog but waited for the declaration of the results with bated breath.

Lady luck had decided against my becoming a doctor. I missed again by a few marks.

I felt the ground beneath my feet slipping fast. All my dreams of becoming a doctor were shattered. Life came to a standstill with no further path in sight. Engineering, I had never planned to pursue, though I was good in Physics and Chemistry and loved Mathematics. What would I do? I thought of the toil of my parents. I could not live up to their wishes. On the way, I met R. Kumar, one of the best students of my class; he too had not qualified. I found an ally in similar distress—distraught with the system and not able to understand as to why we had met such a fate.

On reaching home scenes similar to those of previous years were enacted—same sequence of sobbing, sympathetic hands and consolation from Mummy and Nalini. The biggest issue before me, at that moment, was my future. I was neither interested in doing Masters in Zoology nor would I have got it anyway because of the low percentage in graduation level.

Like many of my friends, I decided to pursue Law. I applied for both the morning and evening colleges. And, based on my percentage I got shortlisted for both. But, suddenly, a sense of responsibility for my family seeded the idea that I should earn and augment my family's income. I sacrificed the morning course and took admission in the evening college. I decided that I would go for a job in the morning. And, the easy job at that stage appeared to be that of a medical representative or a sales representative. I kept on applying for various vacancies as and when I saw an advertisement in the newspapers. Papa started guiding me.

But, then we got a bitter-sweet news in September. Papa, after a long wait, got his promotion, but with a posting to far-off Bhubaneswar. It was a shock. When Papa left, we realised the problem of running two establishments. The financial position became precarious. Papa, who had been my guide and great support, was not with me at a critical juncture of my career. As I was not having any job, I started giving tuitions to some students at home.

Pilani Detour

Then one day in the middle of November …

I got a message from Om Mamaji that my paternal grandfather wanted to talk to me urgently. In those times landline connections were rare and a privilege; Om Mamaji had one. I rushed to the nearby booth, and when connected, grandfather enquired, 'What are you doing nowadays?'

'I am studying Law, part time.'

'Meet me in my associate's office in Kirti Nagar; we have a plan for you!'

'Okay, Grandpa; I will come.'

I didn't know what it all meant. Mummy allowed me to visit my grandfather to have an idea! Grandpa stayed separately with my step-grandmother and my two unmarried aunts, one six years older and another three years older than me, in Kirti Nagar. He, after Papa's birth, had some compatibility issues with my real grandma. It ultimately culminated in a divorce. He, I had learnt, didn't re-marry till my father was eight years old. He had six children from his second marriage: a son and five daughters.

My real grandma, I had been told, was a simpleton, lacking sophistication while my grandpa was a man of refined tastes. He was the Head Station Master at New Delhi Railway Station even before India was partitioned, and had a big railway bungalow and servants. He didn't like his first wife as she was neither good-looking, nor well-read. She would, unmindful of his stature, go to the neighbours' homes and perform all the small chores which a servant would do. And there were many such and similar things that greatly annoyed him.

Grandpa on the other hand would dress up tastefully in European style. He was well-read, had interests in fine arts like music—he himself played the flute very well. In a nutshell, he was an aristocrat and my grandma a plebeian.

In olden times in India people would have their children married off as soon as they attained youth without bothering much about matching the qualities or ensuring compatibility. Marriage, in those times and to some extent even now in villages or small towns, is the mode of providing biological partners for the sole purpose of propagation of the family. It was a widely held belief that the man without a woman or vice-versa does not have any identity. People should establish homes and have families.

We would visit our grandparents off and on. Grandpa and my aunts were proud of me, and always keenly followed my academic performance; although of late there was nothing significant in my achievements.

After his retirement, Grandpa had dabbled in many ventures, and then settled down with one Mr Bhutia, a Marwari who was dealing in non-ferrous materials and had one branch office-cum-residence in Kirti Nagar. I had seen that office in the past but was not aware of the kind of business they ran.

Grandpa's call brought me to that office. They asked me, 'What are you doing nowadays, and what are your plans for the future?'

'I am studying Law and am also on the lookout for a job.'

'Why job? Why don't you think of setting up your own business? You are a science graduate and quite intelligent. You can be self-employed, and in fact, have salesmen and staff working under you. But, you may have to be away from Delhi. We feel that you can start your own factory of copper sulphate at Pilani. Come on, do one thing, we are going to Pilani the day after, you can join us. You can come over in the morning at around nine. We shall proceed by car,' the gentleman said.

'Okay, you can discuss with your mother and revert to us by tomorrow evening, and confirm over telephone if you wish to go,' he said on finding me confused.

At home, Mummy was initially at a loss to decide. 'Your father has gone to Bhubaneswar and now we are on our own. You have two tuitions and you are yourself studying Law. Let me see. I need to discuss the matter. It's not so easy.' Then she consulted few of her friends who could be banked upon. 'People say, although uncertain, the proposition is not bad considering the job market. Business, if successful, would kick-start your career; and money, no doubt, is very important, especially when we are feeling the crunch. In this world people go for jobs as they don't have capital or they don't have someone to support them in their ventures, but in this case you are being offered help unasked. I think this will be a good opportunity for you,' Mummy said.

Thus, with one suitcase and a bag I set out for the journey to a town which regularly boasted of the best school band in the republic day parade. The car—a white ambassador, started finally at ten in the morning. Mr Bhutia was driving and we had two other gentlemen as companions. Going through Punjabi Bagh, and seeing those two adjacent bread factories of Britannia and Modern on the Ring Road, I was reminded of the many journeys that I had undertaken since my childhood to visit Rohtak, where my cousins lived. Now, it was for a different reason.

The car was now running on the Rohtak road and in no time it reached Bahadurgarh. An hour and a half's journey brought us to Rohtak, and my child-like heart craved to visit my aunt there. But I had to grow up. I was on a different course that day. I had to show maturity. We had some tea and snacks and then proceeded to Pilani. On the way I saw dust-laden roads facilitating a variety of traffic: buses, cars, trucks, tempos and different types of cart, being pulled by oxen or bullocks or horses or camels. The scene was anything but glamorous. The car, on finding the open road, gained speed.

On reaching Pilani in the evening, the town appeared eerily calm, the roads dustier and houses very sparse. The industrial area—which was almost at the end of the city—looked even more deserted with huge industrial sheds, each with a lot of open space around them; hardly any people around. We entered the factory complex, and after parking the car came into the main shed. It was big and spacious inside, with five work stations with different types of machines. Around ten workers were drawing copper tubes through different machines, and processing the same for the manufacture of television antennae. There was a small office on one side, and the other side had a kitchen. The toilet, I learnt, was outside in the open. Besides, near the gate there was another room where three cots had been laid down.

We all were quite hungry. To my utter surprise, Bhutia ji and the other two gentlemen themselves started cooking. I observed with keen interest how they kneaded the dough, washed and cut vegetables, cleaned dal by segregating stones and dirt, and then commenced cooking on the kerosene stove and a local *chulha*. After the dal was boiled, it was mixed with ghee and spices that had been heated separately. The food was served while we all sat together on the floor. The day's journey had lit a fire in our bellies and the food was really delicious. It was a different ambience altogether. They chatted, and then before retiring for the night started playing cards. It was a game of 'sweep'. I had observed my parents and relatives playing it too. I too had tried my hand and knew the rules but I was not very adept. I expressed my inability but Bhutia coaxed me, 'Hey, grown up, and afraid of playing? What would you do in life, if you can't even play cards?' I gave in. While playing I wondered, '*How these people, who were away from the comforts of their families, were enjoying wholeheartedly. I too may have to attune my mind and heart accordingly.*' The game continued till eleven thirty at night, and then weary after the long day, we fell asleep.

We returned in two days. And, I didn't understand much out of the whole episode.

Next day I visited Grandpa's office for a little more discussion on the issue.

'You see, setting up of a factory will require time. First of all you will be going to Pilani to gain some experience in running our present factory. After three or four months you shall take over completely from the foreman. In the meantime we shall prepare and submit the project report to the bank for getting the loan sanctioned. Once the loan is granted we will establish your new factory,' Bhutia ji explained with his eyes dancing behind his spectacles.

Grandpa, in all solemnity, nodded in agreement. It was a grand intoxicating idea for a young man of twenty!

'And, you see, in the process, you will be earning a decent salary; much more than what you have been getting from your tuitions,' Grandpa supplemented. 'Now, you fetch a sample project report from Okhla. We will study that and then shall formulate our own project report.'

In the evening when I left office, while standing at the bus stop, I felt intense pain in my heart, it was not a heart attack but heartache; I was filled with a feeling of emptiness. Shama's memory and her image were haunting me. I was filled with a queer feeling. I boarded the bus. My heart was craving for her. 'I would be going away from Delhi after sometime,' I wondered, 'When will I meet Shama? Already more than four years have elapsed and despite being in Delhi, I have not come across her even once!' It was true that I had not taken any active steps towards reaching her. But that was a pact I had made with myself: I would not pursue her till I became something in life, that I would meet her only if God ordained. So far God had not been benevolent.

While I was lost in my thoughts, I found the bus was approaching the stop near the Jhandewalan temple. All of a sudden, I noticed a girl with her back towards me, and standing near the driver's seat, planning to get down. My God! It was Shama! The same slim torso, similar jet black wavy hair, fair complexion, and when she turned slightly, I recognised the same oval face. I couldn't control myself. Involuntarily I got up from my seat, and in no time, wading through the bevy of passengers standing in the aisle, I reached her. I was yearning to see her face but it was not possible as she was facing the exit door with her back towards me. She was trying to figure out whether her stop had arrived. She was desperately attempting to balance herself in the midst of the persistent undulations of the bus.

The stop arrived and she got down, and started walking. I followed suit, as if under a spell. I must have followed her for five minutes. There were many people walking on the road. She was thus unmindful of my chase. She stopped at a tailor's shop. Perhaps she had given something for stitching. There was a stationery shop besides that. I stopped there to buy a ball pen though I didn't need any. While purchasing, I kept track of her movements in the other shop.

She was arguing with the tailor, 'What masterji, you have made the border of my kameez very wide. I wanted it sleek. What about the two embellishments which I wanted on the shoulder?'

'Madam, I am so sorry; I will definitely put them. But, I thought a wide border would look good.'

'No, No, masterji, please alter it. Now, I will have to come again. Janakpuri is so far, and it is so difficult to come here time and again.'

Even her argumentative voice had melody and sweet jingle.

'Okay, Madam, I will change it. Give me a week.'

She nodded and turned. I was standing and pretending as if I was waiting for someone from the other side of the road. The moment she turned I got an opportunity to see her closely. I waited with bated breath to have a complete view of her face. She turned further, and for a moment I felt that my heart had skipped a beat. She was Shama! My beautiful and charming love, my red butterfly; her splendour much more pronounced. God had been generous while endowing her beauty. She looked exquisite.

It was a full moon night. One moon shining majestically in the sky, and my moon was on the ground, sparkling and unnerving me. I deliberately came from the opposite side on the footpath so as to be face to face with her. She was stunned when I came close, the moment she saw me. We looked at each other, transfixed. Four years was a long period to bring changes in our appearances. Both of us had gained height and she had become a little plump but not fat or stout. Her eyes evinced that she had recognised me. I spontaneously smiled … my winning Libran smile. She too had to respond … but her smile was restrained.

I didn't want to lose that moment, the way I had lost four years back because of my shyness. Now, having been in college for three years, I was no longer nervous in the company of girls.

I gathered courage and said, 'Excuse me.'

She stopped, expecting me to say something. She was not scared, but only a bit perturbed, her face luminescent in the street light.

'Yes; did you address me?' She asked, her tone soft but firm.

'Yeah; were you not staying in block no. 2 at Motia Khan almost four years back; and then later shifted to Janakpuri?'

'Yeah,' she nodded, and I saw a vagrant wisp of her hair waving - with the breeze that commenced suddenly—and covering her eye. She raised her hand and settled it.

'Don't you recognise me?'

'Yeah, I do. My brothers and sister used to study in your mother's tuition centre.'

'How are they?'

'Fine, doing well.'

'And, how are you people finding Janakpuri?'

'It's fantastic. But what about you people? Are you not staying in Motia Khan now? My siblings wanted to meet Auntie ji once. But we learnt that you had shifted.'

'Yeah, We shifted almost two years back; to Vijay Nagar.'

'And … how do …?' I uttered in muted voice.

'Did you say something?' She asked.

It appeared the breeze got imbued with the fragrance of *raatrani* flowers; and there was melodious music being played in the background … with the magical notes of the sitar and violin.

'No … nothing?' I mumbled.

I wanted to lay open my heart to her. But something prevented me. That thought, whether it would be appropriate, held me back. I wished time would stand still. I wished she would open up and say something. But it appeared her lips too were sealed. I was expecting something from a girl, which, I a boy was hesitant to utter.

'Ah … um … Come home sometime. Mummy would love to meet her students,' I said meekly. She nodded … a noncommittal nod of a shy girl.

'Okay. Bye, see you,' she uttered with utmost civility and softness.

She turned and started walking. I just stood there, frozen in time looking at her receding figure. I wished I could shout, 'Shama, I love you. Please stay back. Come on, talk to me. I miss you so much.' But those words coming from my heart couldn't escape my throat. I saw her boarding a bus for Janakpuri. I could see her faint contours through the big glasses of the DTC bus. And, I just stood there …

That chance meeting with Shama, after momentary happiness, now caused more depression and desolation. I felt sad and helpless. 'Should I go home and spread more unhappiness?' I brooded. 'No.'

I saw the lights of the Jhandewalan temple from a distance, decorating the skyline. I heard the soothing sound of temple bells and evening prayers emerging from the loudspeaker. Under a magnetic pull, my feet moved towards the temple, and in no time I found myself before the idol of Goddess Vaishno Devi; who appeared to be looking at me in all resplendence and benign grace, showering benevolence and assuring that I would find the best in my life. I closed my eyes and touched her feet and lay prostrate before her. Then, I visited the cave where Hanuman's Idol was there. I opened the top three buttons of my shirt. Then with a lot of affection and faith I applied sindoor on the spot where rested my revered Shama, where rested her memories, in the heart that throbbed for her! I got a feeling that my day too would come, I only had to keep faith till then, to have patience.

I got up, infused with life and vigour to face the challenges of the world and to wait for my Shama ... till eternity.

The following day, with a lot of enthusiasm, I reached my grandpa's office to present the project report that I had painstakingly procured from National Small Scale Industries Corporation, Okhla. They all applauded my efforts. I felt elated.

'Okay, we will study the report. You may have to wait for a few days. We'll let you know when you have to go to Pilani again.' This bland statement dampened my enthusiasm. I spent sometime in the office, and then with their permission went home.

Nothing was heard from Grandpa on the issue.

The whole of December just passed by; luckily I could appear in my semester exams of Law.

In the first week of January, 1981, we got a telegram:

'Reaching Delhi tomorrow evening.

Papa.'

We were all ecstatic. The moment Papa got out of the auto-rickshaw the next evening; I passionately hugged him, and carried his luggage inside. Under the fluorescent tube light, I discovered that he had pulled down a lot. Was it because of the long journey of almost thirty hours or otherwise? His face had lost the aura. He seemed to have aged.

Papa was enthusiastic about my setting up of business. 'Let your Law course be secondary,' Papa opined, 'You know such opportunities are rare, and one should grab it with both hands and make the most of it.' Incidentally, my brother Subhash will be arriving from Canada next week. He is getting married. My sisters have selected a good match for him,' Papa further informed. I knew that the process had been going on even during the period of my visit to Pilani.

Next day morning we went to Grandpa's office. Papa got into a huddle with Bhutia ji and his son. They had animated discussions for an hour or so. Papa was elated when he emerged from the meeting. Bhutia ji declared, 'After your uncle's marriage in January, you have to leave for Pilani.'

'She is a convent educated, good looking girl. The marriage has been fixed for 19th January. You know, the girl is just nineteen, and the family is decent,' my aunts revealed in unison when we reached Grandpa's house. Their voices were enthusiastic.

I was disturbed and shocked, 'My God, my aunt is twelve years younger to my uncle and six months younger to me!' But I concealed that and gave a genial smile instead.

'We are not taking any dowry,' Grandpa announced, 'instead the girl's parents shall be hosting the marriage in Hotel Ashoka, that five-star hotel in Chanakyapuri. And, we will host the engagement ceremony in Hotel Akbar on 17th January. It is close to Hotel Ashoka.'

The engagement ceremony was lovely and elegant.

On 19th January, my uncle's *baraat* started from Hotel Akbar. He was in the traditional Punjabi dress, on a mare, his face covered with a veil of flowers dangling from his crown. Gaiety and fervour pervaded amongst the *baraatis*. People were dancing and I too joined them. Clad in dark brown corduroy jeans and a light brown suede jacket, I danced with gay abandon. Whenever people asked me about my vocation, I would reply, 'I am planning to establish my own business.'

After dinner commenced the *phere* ceremony: the bride and the groom were to tie the nuptial knot and take seven rounds around the holy fire to the chanting of mantras by the priest, besides performance of other rituals. While keenly watching the proceedings, I chanced to look at the innocent face of my would-be aunt. 'Why a girl of not even twenty, agreed to marry a man of thirty-two?' I wondered. My uncle was quite handsome and gentle in his appearance and conduct. Still I felt it was a mismatch. Suddenly, I was struck by an uncomfortable thought, 'In India it doesn't matter if a young girl is married off to a comparatively elderly man, as the first priority is to get married and have a home. Could this also happen to Shama?' I looked around and observed the melee of guests and relatives enjoying the event. My discomfort increased, and I left the arena; on the pretext of going to the restroom. The outside temperature had fallen considerably with an intense chill in the air; but I felt my heart burning like a hearth. In the vacant corridor, I kept looking into the darkness, into the blank spaces, and I found myself very lonely in the razzmatazz. A few lines of an old emotional Hindi song echoed in my mind:

Yeh mera diwana pan hai, ya mohabbat ka suroor,
Tuna pahchane to hai ye teri nazaron ka kasoor.
Aise viranne me ik din ghutke mar jaayenge hum,
Jitna ji chahe pukaro ...

My eyes welled up with tears. I felt like shouting, to spew out all the tension built up inside; but what emanated was a whimper! I stood there in a lonely corridor, sobbing for some time. After feeling a little better, I went to the restroom. In the mirror I saw my eyes: wet and red. I felt sorry at my plight. I saw Shama's lovely face in the mirror beside me, and said, 'My tears are my only offering to you–my goddess. Please don't leave me; meet me soon; I am very lonely without you.' It was only a hallucination. I washed my eyes. I tried to sport a smile, and came to the marriage hall.

I found Nalini staring at me with probing eyes. I just tried to avoid her gaze.

'What happened Rohit? Are you not feeling well? You seem to have wept a lot. Your eyes are red. Has someone told you something here? A few moments back you were fine. Why do you look so sullen? You are looking so handsome with your jeans and jacket. But your face has lost the exuberance it had a little while ago. Tell me, why are you so distraught?' Nalini's questions and observations were relentless.

Siblings are after all siblings with strong filial bond, and it is difficult to hide anything from them. The secret of my love for Shama, which I had briefly shared with Inder Arora, was now squirming to find a vent. I had thought that my tearful outburst in the lonely toilet was enough to regain emotional poise. But Nalini's avuncular intervention had now upset the balance. I wilted. I moved to a lonely foyer. Nalini followed me, and again asked, 'What is this Rohit? You have been avoiding my questions. Please tell me, I am getting worried. Should I tell Mummy?'

'Please don't involve Mummy. I beg of you. Also don't tell anyone else what I am telling you know,' I pleaded.

'Okay, then speak up. I am dying to know.'

'Nalini, my sweet sister; I appreciate your affection and concern. I have never tried to hide anything from you but for the one secret which I have been able to conceal for the past four years. Now I find it's just not possible.'

'Come to the point. Mummy must be worried,' Nalini chided.

'Nalini, do you remember Shama and that letter I had written to her five years back when I was just sixteen,' I said. Nalini's eyes became attentive and she nodded.

'You know that day I denied it vehemently, and luckily Mummy took it lightly because of her faith in me. But Nalini I have not forgotten Shama. I have been deeply in love with her. She has been the beacon of my life. It doesn't mean that I underrate my affection for you all. Her love has never made me lose my focus in life. Actually, that one ray of hope has allowed me to bear all the vagaries so far. And, her pious image is consecrated in my heart. Nalini, I don't know whether you would appreciate my position; still, having come of age now, I feel that you may. And, I must tell you, that even though I could never convey my sentiments to her, I have made a pact with myself and her soul—to propose to her when I find a good job and am settled in life.'

Nalini asked, 'Do you know if she loves you and is inclined for a lifetime union with you?'

'I just don't know. How could I? I had never spoken to her. One day when she had come to our house, I out of hesitation had moved to the other room. But, I feel, she would wait for me.'

'It all sounds so wishful. Anyway if it all has to happen in future, why be so flustered now and in tears?'

'You know, our to-be aunt, Uncle Subhash's bride, is younger to me by six months, and I am being haunted by a thought that Shama too under her family's pressure may agree to marry anyone. It depresses me. But Nalini, it can't happen to us. She is mine, I invoke her every time. She comes into my dreams; I feel that she will never leave me. That she will wait for me,' I said while wiping my tears.

'You are mad Rohit. What kind of a pact have you made with yourself? It is so nebulous with so many ifs and buts. Still, my dear brother I am proud of you. You are such a nice, pure soul. I pray that God will listen to your deep prayers and Shama too will wait for you. After leaving school I never met Shobhana. You know I could have tried if and only if you had disclosed it to me earlier. Then it would have been so easy to know Shama's mind. And things would not have remained so uncertain.'

'What to do Nalini, I am shy, timid and an introvert.'

'Okay, now be a good and mature boy. What would people think if you move around with such a face? I am your dear sister. You can take my word that I will always be with you, always on your side.'

We moved towards the marriage pandal.

The ceremony was almost over; the groom and the bride were taking the last *phera* around the holy fire. I had an illusion that I was taking those rounds with Shama, and people around were showering flower petals on us. The priest was declaring, 'Now you are husband and wife.'

'Come, we have to go home,' I heard Mummy's voice. I came to my senses as if woken up from a dream. The wedding was over, and the hall was being vacated. I went to my aunt and uncle and touched their feet, and wished them a happy married life.

I had found an aunt who was younger to me!

After my uncle's marriage, I went to Pilani as decided with dreams of becoming a young entrepreneur. I harboured the notion that soon I would set up a factory, have a number of people working for me; that I would be sitting in a plush office; that I would be financially well off in no time; and I would be worthy of seeking Shama's hand.

We reached Pilani late in the evening, and like last time cooked our meals and satiated our hunger. Drained by the day's journey, I fell asleep the moment I hit the bed. Soon I was haunted by nightmares. First, I saw myself getting down at a railway station to buy some fruits. Suddenly, the train started and vanished at a great speed with my luggage. And, I was running and shouting, 'Someone please stop the train. My luggage is inside. How will I go to Delhi? It is so far and I don't have much money too.' No one paid any heed; they all looked at me as if I was an alien. I rushed to the Station Master. He said, 'Our telephone lines are out of order. I am sorry. You may have to wait at the platform the whole night as the next train is in the morning at four. I will try to place you in that.' 'Buttttt my luggageeeee!' I was in tears. 'That I can't guarantee. Give me your seat number. I'll send a telegram to Delhi. Let us see if they can keep your luggage in safe custody.' I was tearing my hair in desperation ... and just then I woke up. I was sweating profusely.

I had another dream. I saw a weird old man—long white hair and long white beard.

'Why have you come, leaving your family, to this place? There is nothing here for you. All this is only an illusion,' he thundered in a baritone voice.

'I have come here to set up a business,' I said.

'Business! They are all playing with your future. Go back. This is a mirage.'

Before I could ask, the old man started retreating from the scene, laughing in a queer and sarcastic manner; his laughter resonating. I woke up sweating! I prayed to God and consoled myself that it was merely a bad dream. But its impact remained in my mind, lurking in a corner.

In the morning I wondered, *What would happen to me? Was that old man right?*

Then I banished all negative thoughts. *I hoped everything would be fine*.

Bhutia ji left me the next day with the foreman named Siyaram giving him instructions to train me.

Siyaram was good natured and experienced. I got good exposure of the factory. I picked up many things from him. I learnt the production process, how to control the labour and handle other issues in running the factory. Pilani was a very small town with hardly any sign of excitement or glamour. I was pursuing a dream in the sandy terrain, away from my family and missing the city life of Delhi. Although I seamlessly gelled with the people over there yet I always felt empty deep inside.

Almost every evening I would take out time from the factory schedule and from the huge open area of our factory compound, watch the sun set in the far horizon. The sun's golden rays turning red and shooting behind the clouds would be mesmerising. Scores of cumulus clouds would appear like lumps of yellow glittering coals suspended in the air. Clouds and rays of different hues would present many exotic formations. There would be a few birds hovering in the sky, trilling and returning to their nests after their daytime forays. There would be a few butterflies too: yellows, cabbage whites and blacks. But I would remain enamoured of the red butterfly with black and white striations. In the serene ambience all around, I would hear the rustling of leaves swaying to the soft breeze. Stray dogs would bark sometimes and cows would moo. I would glimpse the blank winding road occasionally ridden by some vehicles. Remembering my family and Shama, I would hum an emotional song from the movie *Anand:*

Kahin door, jab din dhal jaye,
Saanjh ki dulhan, badan churaaye, chupke se aaye,
Mere khayaalon, ke aangan mein,
Koi sapanon ke, deep jalaaye, deep jalaaye

There would be irrepressible illusions of Shama, standing far away—with her lovely face, twinkling eyes and captivating smile, her arms open, inviting me; then transforming into a red butterfly, fluttering and gliding into faraway horizon. My voice carried entreaties and supplications to her to remain with me forever.

A month passed.

I got the instructions to return to Delhi. I was so excited. I would be meeting my family. While returning by bus, a journey of six hours, I had a yearning: *May I never go to Pilani again*!

I found deep solace in the warm embrace of my family. It was the first occasion when I had been away from them for one month.

Next day, I reported my Pilani experience to Grandpa and Bhutia ji.

'You may take a break for a few days till we are through with other formalities. We will let you know when you have to visit Pilani again,' Bhutia ji's eyes betrayed ambiguity.

During the period of my stay at Pilani, Papa had remained in Delhi on leave. He kept my tuitions going which I resumed on my return. There was no call from Bhutia ji for ten days.

Raj Mamaji, my elder maternal uncle had been closely following my academic as well as Pilani pursuits. One day, he remarked off hand, 'Rohit, I have known you since your childhood. Though you are planning to enter business, I feel, a good government post will be far befitting your personality. You must try for the Civil Services. I wanted my children to appear for that but they didn't have the diligence and aptitude. I wish to see you as an IAS or IPS officer—it sounds so prestigious.' Since I always wanted to become a doctor, I hardly ever thought of the Civil Services. I just ignored Mamaji's remark. *I was bitten by the business bug.*

Almost twenty days passed since my return from Pilani. I resumed my Law classes as I had my semester exams scheduled for May. There was no call from Bhutia ji. There was thus no clarity regarding my future. One day Mummy had an intuition, 'I don't know why I am not comfortable with this Pilani venture. Let us go to your grandpa's office tomorrow.'

Next day coincidentally Bhutia ji was not there in office. Mummy spoke to Grandpa, 'The setting up of business seems to be taking a long time. What we need is an urgent source of income–he can help by giving tuitions. Moreover, since his father too is out of Delhi, it is becoming difficult for us to maintain three establishments. Hence, I strongly feel we must, for the time being at least, drop the idea of going to Pilani.' Grandfather's jaw dropped. He was shell-shocked at the monologue. By chance, Bhutia ji's accountant too joined the discussion. I had met him there on a number of occasions, but he had always remained quiet. And, that day he spoke for the first time, and spoke a lot. 'There is nothing in this project. It is certainly better if your son stays in Delhi, completes his studies and looks for a job elsewhere,' he said. 'What you are saying is not correct,' Grandpa protested feebly. There was a little more discussion on the issue and Mummy politely said, 'We will think it over and then decide.' We got up to leave.

When we were out on the road, the accountant addressed us from behind, 'I am going home for lunch. My house is nearby. Please come with me. I wish to have a word with you. You are not aware of many things.' We agreed. He then lifted the veil over the entire business. He disclosed, 'The factory presently running in Pilani is in the red. They are not going to start the project they have promised. Your grandfather's money is stuck and Bhutia ji is giving false assurances of recovering the losses if your father too invests in it.'

The whole thing was stark naked; crystal clear. I had to chalk out a fresh course. On the way I found relief on the comforting shoulders of my mother. I said, 'Mummy, as always, you were right. I love you very much.'

The Turning Point

The aborted Pilani venture bestowed five benefits upon me: One. I reunited with Mummy and Nalini; two, I could now help Nalini in her preparations for the impending Secondary School Certificate Exam and also accompany her to the examination centre; three, I was able to continue my Law studies; four, I would be in Delhi, the city I loved; and five, I would have the opportunity of meeting Shama—my heartthrob.

The old routine started: waking up at five fifteen in the morning; going for jogging and some physical exercises in an open public gym, that charged a nominal sum of just two rupees a month; watering plants in the veranda on return; after getting ready scanning newspapers for any vacancies for the positions of salesman, medical representative and other office jobs and selecting possible opportunities for applying; teaching Nalini for long stretches and also carrying on with my studies; teaching my students in the afternoon. In the evening I would go to Law College. Late at night, I would again concentrate on my own studies. My youth allowed me to accomplish so much in a day.

Nalini's examination centre was near Connaught Place. I would accompany her in a DTC bus, and on the way and after reaching there would keep reading out the notes for her. Once she was inside the examination hall, I, in order to kill time, would roam about in Connaught Place.

Days passed and Nalini's exams got over. Then came my exams and I did reasonably well.

On the commencement of summer vacation, Papa came to Delhi and took us to Bhubaneswar. I didn't know that the journey was going to change my life forever.

The thirty four hours journey by Neelanchal Express was long but exciting. The passage through a number of states: Uttar Pradesh, Bihar, Madhya Pradesh, West Bengal, and Andhra Pradesh provided us glimpses of different people, diverse lifestyles, cultures and traditions. Hawkers at each station would bring eatables having distinct flavours of those states. Nalini and I were like little children again—joking, chit-chatting and enjoying every moment.

Bhubaneswar was a sprawling, green, clean, and planned city, just like Chandigarh, the city of my childhood. Tall trees of palm and coconut were in abundance. Our house was in Shaheed Nagar, a beautiful place. There were rows of big bungalows with spacious verandas and backyards teeming with tall trees, herbs, creepers, climbers and other potted plants laden with flowers. A lovely sea breeze welcomed our arrival. I fell in love with the city. No hustle bustle, unlike Delhi; tranquillity prevailed and serenity ruled. Our home was on the first floor, and the window provided a beautiful view.

After we freshened up, Papa took us to his office, in the next lane, hardly five minutes walk. The landlady of the property, staying in the next bungalow, brought us tea and snacks. We enjoyed them while sitting in the common room of the office as Papa introduced us to his staff. Papa was the Head of the regional office of the Project Evaluation Organisation, an arm of the Planning Commission, entrusted to evaluate the efficacy of various government schemes.

At home, in the evening, Papa introduced us to Darshan, his roommate. He was a fair-complexioned young man in his late twenties, from Jammu who worked in 'Save Grain Campaign', a government organisation. The bookshelf in the drawing room was arrayed with a fine collection of books: literature, geography, history, politics, music, cricket, general knowledge, etc. I was awestruck.

Seeing me mesmerised, Darshan said, 'Rohit, it seems that you are a bit surprised.'

'You have so many books and all on diverse subjects!' I said with excitement.

'Well, I read them for the Civil Services and other similar competitive examinations.'

My curiosity was aroused.

In a matter of two days, Darshan became very close to our family. We would discuss lots of things, including family matters, during dinner or when we all went out together.

'I wanted to become a doctor, and have ended up pursuing Law. I am totally disoriented. I want to take up a job, but barring the job of a sales or medical representative, there is hardly anything that an ordinary graduate like me can do,' I shared my dejection with Darshan one day.

'Don't be disheartened! You have unlimited potential and lot of opportunities awaiting you. Just motivate yourself and work hard. Make up your mind and start looking for vacancies in the government, semi-government and banking sectors. Don't worry about the level or grade you apply for. Each entrance exam is going to build your confidence. Accept whatever service you get and then aim for the higher ones. Your aim should be to earn and learn. Don't stagnate; keep on striving for higher goals,' Darshan advised in all earnest.

It all sounded very lofty and idealistic.

'How do I prepare for competitive exams?' I asked innocently.

'Build up your General Knowledge (GK); improve your General English, hone your letter and essay writing skills; brush up your matriculation level Mathematics; and prepare for IQ tests. So many guide-books are available in the market. GK is an important part of the Civil Services Examination. Read newspapers, magazines, and read books on science and social sciences that are prescribed for schools of secondary and senior secondary level. Cultivate the habit of reading good literary books too. All this would entail time, hard work and focus; no shortcuts. Gear up,' Darshan was didactic; and me spellbound.

Darshan became a friend, philosopher and guide. His exhortations stirred a passion in me: a burning desire to prove that I had the mettle to fight and become something; yes something of worth for getting my Shama. The motivational editorials and essays in some career magazines prodded me, and inspirational quotes started resonating in my psyche:

STRIKE THE IRON WHILE IT IS HOT;
NOTHING SUCCEEDS LIKE SUCCESS;
NONE BUT YOU HOLD THE KEY TO YOUR FORTUNE;
YOU CAN BECOME WHAT YOU THINK YOU CAN;
FAILURE IS NOTHING BUT A STEPPING STONE TO FIND AN ALTERNATIVE PATH TO REACH YOUR GOAL

Darshan gave me one GK book, and said, 'This would be your basic book for preparations.' Although, I had been a science student, I developed immense interest in Humanities within a week. I started enjoying varied topics in the newspapers and magazines unlike earlier, when the sports section alone interested me.

Seeing my interest, Darshan gave me *Oliver Twist* by Charles Dickens. Initially, I found the text difficult; later, I took it as a challenge and finished it in a week. I also started applying for whatever competitive exams I was eligible for. Assistant Grade's Exam to be conducted by the Union Public Service Commission for recruiting Assistants in the ministries and departments of the Central Government was slated for October along with a few others. I became so fond of Darshan that I accompanied him on his official tours.

Darshan's organising skills were fascinating. Despite his ordinary background and effeminate voice, he had tremendous confidence. For me, he was a role model. I was grateful to God for my Bhubaneswar visit which occasioned my meeting this inspirational personality.

Bhubaneswar also provided me with an opportunity to understand the culture of Odisha and its geography, history, and architecture. Bhubaneswar got its name from Tribhubaneswar, the Lord (Ishwar) of the Three Worlds (Tribhuban) i.e.Shiva. It is also known as the 'City of Temples' as it houses many Hindu temples, which span the entire spectrum of Kalinga architecture. And, together with Puri and Konark, it forms the Swarna Tribhuja (Golden Triangle). I had read about the Lingaraj temple and Rajarani temples of Bhubaneswar, and temples of Jagannath Puri and Konark. Chilka Lake, Asia's largest brackish water lagoon famous for Oliver Ridley turtles, is also situated in Odisha.

Papa took us to all these places on Sundays, and we were enchanted by the sheer grandeur of the temples, and their art and architecture. The congregation of devotees at Puri temple and the mass of people revelling on Puri beach were sights to behold. It was fun to see the belongings of tourists getting swept along by the waves of the Bay of Bengal. Faraway, waves would rise slowly and then disappear into the sea; tides would intensify insidiously and ripple towards the beach with a huge momentum; inundating stretches of shining sand, making people hop. Then, in a few seconds the waves would recede, exposing vast expanse of glistening sand under a radiant sun. People would again rush back to enjoy the wet beach and wait for the next wave to enact its dance.

Suddenly it occurred to me, '*Life is also like a sea beach, People make their plans like the sand castles; the waves keep coming and going, destroying them. Still, despite being fully aware of their likely fate, people instead of crying over their labour gone in vain, continue to build and enjoy the whole cycle. In real life too, people work hard and build their fortune, their careers, and harbour desires. If only they realise the evanescence of everything, likely to be swept aside by the vagaries of fate, life would be simple; no one would rue over the loss. One has to just put in efforts and leave everything to God's will: when to reward, how much to reward and for how long to sustain the reward.*' Those thoughts imbued me with a new resolve and a new confidence.

The Bhubaneswar visit was the turning point in my life giving me an aim, a focus and a purpose. It also manifested a rainbow of Indian communities and cultures. Papa, with his simple nature, had endeared himself to a large number of officers working in different government departments, public-sector undertakings, banks and private companies. The common bond of their friendship was their being North Indians who initially felt somewhat alien in the new environment, Odisha being a state in the east. There were people from Bihar, Rajasthan, Uttar Pradesh, Madhya Pradesh, and Jammu and Kashmir. Slowly the group expanded taking into its fold the people of southern states and West Bengal. It did not remain parochial, and in course of time, developed healthy and close social interaction with the people of Odisha. I observed that the natives of Odisha were very sober, peace-loving, and hospitable. The tranquillity pervading the overall populace had, in fact, impelled many outsiders to settle down in Bhubaneswar as it was very accommodative and assimilative.

Evenings were full of social interactions with families paying visits to one another's homes. Papa was an adept singer and was popular for his melodious renditions. I too was encouraged to sing. Amongst the receptive and appreciative audience, I would sing with the passion of one lost in the ocean of love and pining for his heartthrob. My renditions were effusive: vividly enacting the agony, the turbulence, the bliss and the zeal of one absolutely in love. Everywhere I would see my Shama—my omnipresent and ubiquitous goddess of love. When someone would enquire about my academics and future plans of my career, I would reply, 'I am doing Law and aspire to be a civil servant.' My subconscious mind had its eyes now fixed on that single dream—the bridge to attain my Shama.

In my private moments, during sleep, I would talk to Shama, sharing with her my new ambition. Time was fleeting and I was trying to read as many books adorning Darshan's shelf as possible. In between one day, one of my father's friends working in a private company advised, 'You can take up the job of a salesman in my company, Shourie Duplicators, at Delhi. They manufacture cyclostyling machines.'

As I wanted to take up any job due to the economic condition of my family, especially when we had to run two establishments, I agreed. He gave me a recommendation letter.

In a few days, when we were leaving for Delhi, Darshan patted me on my back saying, 'Nothing in life is difficult. Just put in your whole-hearted effort.' Papa also gave me a few words of encouragement, 'Don't worry, I will take a month's leave in September for helping you in your preparations for the Assistant Grade Exam.' We left Bhubaneswar with heavy hearts. I was indebted to the city and my guide.

Doctor to Salesman!

It is true that we have all kinds of things, people, and situations around us but only such things appeal to us and grab our attention in which we are genuinely interested.

During our return journey my eyes would rest only on those magazines and books that were important for the competitive exams. My eyes got riveted onto the photographs of the space shuttle 'Columbia' that had successfully returned after its lunar mission. I was on a new course of life, on a new journey…

I chalked out a time table for focusing on improving my physique, knowledge and intellect. I started visiting a lending library in my locality. I would browse the newspaper thoroughly, jotting down important information and also scan advertisements for any vacancies suiting my educational qualifications. The prevalent economic situation of my home impelled me to vigorously look for a job. My students were on vacations. I was free. I visited the office of Shourie Duplicators along with my bio data and the recommendation letter from my father's friend.

Shourie Duplicators' factory in the Kirti Nagar area was a bit intimidating; for a moment I was overawed by the imposing exteriors. I somehow mustered courage and entered the office of the personnel manager. He was a middle-aged gentleman. 'Sir, I am Rohit Sharma. I have been recommended by Mr Mathur, Branch Manager of your Bhubaneswar branch for the post of salesman,' I blurted out. 'How do you know him?' 'Sir, he is my father's friend.' I replied with cultivated confidence. 'Okay, let me see whether we have any vacancies. You would hear from us in a few days, if there are any.'

I did not have any choice or scope to ask anything in the face of the blunt and curt dismissal. On my way back I wondered whether I would get the job at all as the response was in sharp contrast to the assurances.

Two days later, I got an interview call from Shourie Duplicators.

Shourie Duplicators' registered office was on the ninth floor of Surya Kiran building on Kasturba Gandhi Marg in Connaught Place.

Mathur Uncle had suggested, 'You should wear plain trousers, plain shirt, and your hairstyle should be simple with the hair slightly oiled and neatly combed.' I borrowed clothes from one young man known to us, working in a private company. On the D-day, I reached the office of Shourie Duplicators on time. I was excited at the prospect of getting a job. In the elevator, I had the occasion to appraise myself in the mirror. I adjusted my ruffled hair; set the crease of my shirt, the pleats of my trousers, and the alignment of my waist belt. My appearance gave me confidence, and I felt that I was not nervous.

A number of private offices were housed on the same floor. Locating Shourie Duplicators was not difficult. There was only one entrance-cum-exit door. The entrance was graced by a good-looking receptionist of short stature. 'Good morning, Madam. I am Rohit Sharma.' I handed over my interview call letter. The lady put me at ease with her genial smile, and pointed to a vacant sofa, 'Be seated; you would be called.' I dutifully obeyed, suffused with excitement. I displayed all good manners and civility, and kept on smiling at whosoever my eyes met with. It was a small office with one big table lying beside the desk of the receptionist, and around the same, in eight chairs, were seated salespersons involved in some discussion. They all looked at me amiably. There were hardly five cabins.

I waited. After almost half an hour, the salespersons seated in front of me finished their discussion, and prepared to move out for their field duty. I smiled at them. A few of them looked at me with curiosity and amusement, one or two with indifference, and two of them returned genuine smiles. That relieved a bit of my tension. It was peak summer and I wiped the sweat on my brow. I heard a buzzer, and saw the receptionist picking up the phone. Immediately she called, 'Mr. Rohit, you may kindly go to cabin number two.'

In the cabin, behind a large table was seated an amiable Sikh gentleman on a large executive chair.

'Good morning sir,' I wished after summoning all courage.

Mr Arora, the gentleman, reciprocated warmly. He asked me preliminary questions about my family, my father's occupation and also whether I had a scooter. Encouraged by his demeanour, I divulged all the details.

'Why do you want a sales job?'

'My father's posting to Bhubaneswar has put enormous pressure on the family finances; getting this job is so important for me. I assure you, sir that I will put in sincere efforts.'

My simplicity and Mr Arora's generous nature struck a resonant chord. His countenance indicated that the scales were in my favour. The interview session extended to almost forty-five minutes, and as the time progressed, I felt more comfortable.

Mr Arora asked, 'Do you have an idea about the mechanics of running the pedal of the cycle? When the pedal is moved initially why does one have to apply more force?"

'May be to break the inertia sir; and the friction of the tyres with the surface,' I answered.

'And, why doesn't it move in the reverse direction when you reverse pedal?'

I didn't have any idea.

'Sorry sir, I don't know.' My honesty perhaps impressed Mr Arora. I saw a glint in his eyes, and had the intuition that I was almost through.

'Okay, you may go now. We will let you know in due course.'

I emerged from the cabin ebullient. I smiled at the receptionist.

She said, 'Hope to see you soon.'

Two days later, I got the appointment letter requiring me to join them on next Monday.

I joined as salesman with a lot of enthusiasm. I had thought that along with the job, I would be able to study for my Competitive Exams besides pursuing Law. I was given one briefcase.

Initially I was put on one week's training in the office itself; to understand company's background, the product details and learn practical functioning of the machine. I grappled with the literature and whatever other materials had been provided. The company's technician taught me to take out neat cyclostyled copies and also to fix minor faults. I evinced keen interest and dedication. *I had metamorphosed from an aspirant of medicine to law student and now a salesman.*

On the receptionist's insistence, I used to join her for lunch: the lunch which we used to bring from our respective homes. On the third day, she was also joined by a friend of hers, Poonam. Poonam was almost my age. She was very genial and beautiful. I felt comfortable in their company when I was introduced. We had nice chit chat. She left after lunch.

Poonam's departure initiated consternation in my mind and my heart. She revived memories of Shama. Shama was all over my senses. A stray thought crossed my mind: 'When will God be kind enough to grant me a glimpse of my beloved?' I could visualise Shama's face on the body of Poonam. I wished if I could be near Shama, see her resplendent face, sense her intoxicating scent and immerse in the sparkle of her presence. My hands felt like touching her. But, alas! I was to wait much longer for that moment to arrive, if ever it would arrive. I found the literature and catalogues of duplicating machines superimposed by images of Shama, Shama staring from everywhere like pictures of Sharmila Tagore's eyes pasted on all the walls of Rajesh Khanna's room in the movie *Safar*; with its song echoing in my ears:

Jeevan se bhari teri aankhen,
Majboor karen jeene ke liye, jeene ke liye …
Saagar bhee taraste rahten hain,
Tere roop ka ras peene ke liye, peene ke liye…

What could I do? Shama was an intrinsic part of my life, and I, having come of age, was craving for her, to express my love, my feelings, my emotions … I wanted to be near her, I wanted to hold her. But what was I holding instead? Brochures, literature and stencils for cyclostyling … the stencil was there to take out the copies, but my own heart carried the indelible imprint of only one image … my Shama. Her image was there in all iridescence, which only I could see. My financial and societal condition at that moment, as also my career ambition had made me refrain from embarking on any plan of pursuing her. I had chosen my own path and perhaps rightly so.

Life as a salesman was tough. I had a long arduous schedule with sleep of hardly five hours. I would spend long hours in the field with a briefcase in my hand and with my neck in the grip of a necktie. From one office to another on foot, in the bus or sometimes even in a cycle rickshaw, I would be constantly on the move, exploring the assigned area, coaxing and cajoling people to buy our machines. I had to steal time for my studies. Whenever, I got the opportunity, I would read my study material for optimum utilisation of time. Lunch would be at any place on the way: in any roadside stall or where I could sit peacefully. Sharp at 6:00 pm, I would leave for home, walking to the bus stand, jostling in the crowd. Totally drenched in sweat, weary from the day's strenuous efforts, I would board the bus; my eyes always focused on my watch, calculating the possible hours I would get for studies. While walking, I would calibrate my speed to reach by a fixed time.

It is true that time is really valued by people who are running short of time.

Mummy and Nalini gave me due support. We would have dinner sharp at 8:30 while watching TV, enjoying our favourite programmes. I would share with them the day's experiences. My future was uncertain, but there was a ray of hope. I was doing my best to realise my dreams. Night would bring more energy, zeal, focus and exertions: I would study with a lot of interest till late at night up to 1:00 am. Then, completely exhausted, I would retire to bed, slip into my dream world suffused with memories of my Shama. With my heart aching and pining for her, I would count those moments for something equally uncertain like my future, wondering if at all I would get her.

When conjunctivitis struck Delhi's populace, I too couldn't escape. But, after a day's rest, I came to office with zero power spectacles. In the evening, on my way back home, while I was proceeding to the bus stand in Connaught Place near Allahabad Bank, I saw a familiar face. It was Sonam wearing a skin colour salwar suit with her trademark boy-cut hair. There was hardly any change in her personality.

'Rohit,' she shouted, and I stopped beside her.

Before I could even wish her, she smiled, and asked, 'What are you doing here? Are you still continuing with your studies? Where do you stay? Never heard from you since we graduated!' Although bamboozled by the barrage of questions, I controlled my nervousness and replied calmly without facing her, 'I am studying Law. And, I am working as a salesman with a company dealing in cyclostyling machines. I am also preparing for some Competitive Exams.'

'Are you having any problem with your eyes?' she asked.

'Conjunctivitis.'

'Oh that is why you are not looking at me. You are looking good in spectacles, but a bit serious too. You were never so serious in your outlook though you were quite serious in your studies while in college.' she said and then rambled on, 'Are you in touch with other classmates? Any idea what they are doing? How do you commute? How much does this company pay you? What are the job prospects? What have you planned for the future? How many brothers and sisters do you have? What are they doing? What does your father do?'

My replies were in monosyllables.

'And, what happened to your love interest? Do you meet her?'I could feel pain in her voice.

'No, I haven't made any efforts so far. I have to build my career first. Then I will try,' I said.

'You haven't changed Rohit. You are still pursuing a mirage.'

Her remark was like a pleading. In spite of fully understanding her thought process, I pretended incomprehension, and behaved as if it was a routine exchange. I could fathom tremors in her voice, and from the corner of my eye, I could see pleadings in her facial expressions. She was restrained by her modesty to make any proposal for a private moment in a coffee shop or in a garden as such proposals normally come from the menfolk. She stood there waiting—waiting for one encouraging step from my side, but to no avail. I felt very sorry for my behaviour yet showed as if I was not at all affected, as if everything was normal. Ultimately, she cleared her throat—she was choked with emotions, but didn't want to show them in public—and said, 'Okay, goodbye. See you sometime later.'

'Oh sure,' I said without exchanging my address or contact number or making any specific commitment for meeting her in the future. I turned around and took a bus. While returning I was quite disturbed. I was wondering at the plots of the almighty.

Those whom we love and desire for, are either not available or they don't reciprocate, and those who love us cannot get our reciprocation. There is needless pain in God's designs, but why? Deep in my heart, I felt that I had caused anguish but, perhaps it was right, so as not to keep Sonam under any illusion when I had never harboured any special feelings for her.

In a few days, I got fed up with the salesman's job. I discovered that I was not able to do justice to both my studies and my job. And, I could not attend Law College too. Slowly, the desire to quit started brewing. But loss of salary was quite intimidating. I would leave but not before I got two shocks.

One day, Mr Arora directed, 'Today you have to visit Maulana Azad Medical College on Bahadur Shah Zafar Marg. They have expressed interest in our colour duplicating machine. You may contact the purchase manager in the college, and make a presentation about our product.' 'Okay, Sir,' I consented.

Reaching there at 11:00 in the morning, I was filled with a strange feeling. Memories of my coming there three years back to collect the application forms for MBBS entrance exam were revived. I wondered, 'What dreams I had then of becoming a doctor: stethoscope dangling around my neck, running around in the hospital, attending classes, going to the library, and rushing to attend patients in distress. But where has destiny brought me? Today, I am here, with a neck-tie dangling from my neck instead of a stethoscope; a briefcase containing pamphlets and literature of duplicating machines instead of medical books or the case records of the patients.' Reality dawned, and I met the Purchase Manager Mr Aneja, 'Good morning sir,' I greeted him and presented my card and started off with my regular sales pitch and usual spiel.

I found Mr Aneja was positively inclined, 'Okay, we will revert to you soon after the decision by the competent authority.'

'Thanks a lot sir,' I packed my briefcase and proceeded to the main exit, wading through the maze of alleys and corridors of the college. I moved at a brisk pace lest I may encounter anyone known to me.

'Hi! Rohit,' I heard a familiar voice, and had to perforce turn around. To my delight and discomfiture, I saw Rajiv Malik, looking at me with equal surprise. He had put on a little weight. I was seeing him after two years. He had the same naughty looks but satisfaction on his face. I had to stop and explain my present role and future aspirations, my Civil Service ambition. I thought Rajiv must be inwardly laughing at me and my predicament.

People value you not for your struggle but for your achievements.

'I shall be free in half an hour. Please wait for me in the canteen. We will sit and talk. Jaideep too would join us,' Rajiv held my hand and said.

'Okay,' I replied.

I waited for five minutes, but then realised my position. *What I had to show them or speak about? I would just be an awkward spectator in the conversation of medical students.*

I felt dejected and tears rolled down my eyes. *No, you cannot afford to be so weak and show yourself in such a shameful manner in full public view.* My inner voice cautioned me. I immediately collected myself. I took out my handkerchief promptly, and wiped my brow and eyes at one go, giving the impression that I was merely wiping my sweat. I hurried out of the college lest I may be seen by any other familiar person. Once outside, though with tremendous emotional overload, I walked fast halting only after ten minutes. And then, after identifying a desolate spot under a tree, I broke down, reflecting over my past and my uncertain future. Looking up at the sky, angry and helpless, I questioned God, 'When will I be able to tell my earlier classmates and my relatives that I am worth something?'

Another day, it had rained in the morning. The weather was quite pleasant. As per the directions of my superior, with my office briefcase in my hands I had gone to Chandni Chowk to collect some outstanding payment from a client. After finishing my work, while walking I happened to pass across Arora Saree Emporium. Just involuntarily, I saw the same mannequin. She was clad in a red saree with black border and long black and white striations running all over. I kept on mulling over it. Oh! She was so much like my red butterfly … my Shama! A strong urge to see Shama rose in my heart. *If I could have the fortune!* I heaved a sigh.

A few minutes later, I came to my senses and moved ahead. There was hardly any crowd in the morning. When I happened to pass by Sisganj Gurudwara, I just stood at the gate, and bowed in reverence. When I lifted my head, my eyes caught the casual glimpse of a young girl coming out. Her head was covered by a black dupatta. Suddenly the cool breeze blew. Her dupatta slid from her head, exposing her face. I was startled. It was the face of my lovely Shama: doe eyed, innocent and glowing. Her glistening black waist length hair was ruffled by the wind. My God! She was in a red kameez and black salwar. It was a new dress of slightly lighter shade, but the shirt had very fine white and black striations near the border. Her face, despite the glow, had an element of sadness. I was stupefied. I couldn't move. My yearning had materialised. She was going to the shoe section outside to collect her sandals perhaps. And, I too found myself near that place. She chanced to look at me. Her face showed recollection. When she came near, she was equally perturbed. I don't know under what spell my lips curled and my face broke into a smile. She too was compelled to reciprocate. My eyes conveyed that I was a harmless creature. And, to my surprise, she didn't pass across but stopped.

'You! How come you are here?' she asked.

'IIIII.................'

Before, I could reply she saw my briefcase, and enquired, 'Are you working somewhere? Have you taken up a job?'

I became nervous at such a probing question.

'Yeah; I am working as a salesman for a cyclostyling machine company,' I replied honestly.

'But, I think you wanted to become a doctor.'

'Yeah; but I couldn't get through the entrance exam. Now I am doing Law part time, and this job.'

I glimpsed pity in her eyes and a frown on her brow. The expressions then transformed from despair to something bordering on disdain.

'Actually this job is just temporary. I am preparing for Competitive Exams for government and bank jobs,' I clarified as if pleading not to change her opinion about me. It seemed that I was being viewed as a picture of failure.

'Are you trying for clerical positions or officers'?' she asked. I was not prepared for such a direct question.

'I am trying for all. But my aim is Civil Services. I wish to be an IAS or IPS officer.'

'But, that is a long, difficult and uncertain process. When do you expect to succeed?'

Shama seemed to be very practical and restless.

'One can't say. But I am trying hard.'

'What are you doing?' I asked.

'I finished my graduation in political science from Janki Devi College. I have taken admission in MA, but I don't know how long I will continue.' Her voice had some agony.

Before I could ask her, I heard a voice, 'Shama ... what are you doing there? I have been searching for you.' I saw her elder sister coming out of the Gurudwara. Her sister didn't notice me.

'Oh, I just came to collect my sandals,' she said.

They collected their sandals, wore them quickly, and walked. I moved ahead and then from a distance kept on looking at them. After around thirty seconds, Shama looked back. Our eyes met. But what was in those eyes, I couldn't make out. Still I thought there was something in her mind for me; *after all, she had spoken to me and then turned back to look at me*.

Still like those moments of five years back, a lot still remained unsaid, unexpressed and unresolved.

They disappeared from my view. And, I found a wave of pain rise in my heart. My eyes were again moist. My red butterfly had met me and then vanished. I wanted to caress her, possess her, and love her. I felt like throwing the briefcase aside.

I was to appear for Assistant's grade exam in the first week of October. I was finding it difficult to cope. The twin shocks I got prompted me to sacrifice the myopic charm of salary from that salesman's job. But Papa in his letters didn't want me to. I expressed my difficulty to Raj Mamaji.

Papa came from Bhubaneswar in the first week of August. I opened my mind while he was still unpacking his bags. 'Papa, I don't want to work there anymore. You see, my exams are approaching and there is hardly any time left for preparations.' I persisted in my narrative and continued filling Papa with details. Papa was half-listening as he was weary with the long and arduous journey of almost thirty-six hours, 'Uh! Ah! Hum, Ooh! Is that so? Oh really?' The things were partly registering in his mind. When he found it difficult to imbibe further, he said, 'Okay, we'll discuss it tomorrow.' I found a ray of hope and felt that at last my burden would be over soon. I embraced my father tightly.

The next day was Sunday. Raj Mamaji came to our house. After exchanging pleasantries and after enquiring after my father's welfare and details of the journey, things veered towards my affair. Papa said, 'Rohit himself wanted to work, and after a lot of effort I got him this job. It will be really embarrassing for me as well for Mr Mathur if Rohit quits. Besides, it will affect us financially too.' I was now emotionally charged and almost in tears. I pleaded and persuaded. Mamaji could sense the situation well, and, 'Let us look at it from a long-term perspective. Since he is emotionally and mentally inclined to make a serious attempt for the Competitive Exams we must give him a chance. After all, it's a private job and he will get many opportunities in future. Expediency demands that we don't bother about embarrassments. He would earn much more by imparting tuitions. Let him try and realise his dreams, when he is passionate about them. I am sure that you won't regret this decision.' Such sustained and enlightening persuasion as well as my pleadings rendered Papa speechless. He gave in, and I was tearful with delight. I touched Mamaji's and Papa's feet, and said in a very passionate tone, 'I will not let you all down.'

Late at night, I consulted Papa, and wrote a resignation letter in duplicate using a carbon paper. In the morning, I carried that in my office briefcase. I was to carry the briefcase for the last day! My walk that day was brisk, my body, light and my mind, euphoric. I felt as if it was the dawn of a new day. The world appeared different: the sunshine brighter; the horizon gilded; canopies of trees with golden edges; birds flying in the sky with gay abandon. These things had never appeared so beautiful in the past two months!

Tasting Triumph

Papa had taken a month's leave to give me moral support and also to fine-tune my English. I would discuss things with Papa. I became so much obsessed with general knowledge that I would talk about it nonstop. One evening while attending a marriage function in our neighbourhood, I kept on posing questions to Papa, 'You know what the capital of Lakshadweep is? Who wrote the *Train to Pakistan*?' Papa was indignant. 'Have you gone crazy? When you have come to a function, enjoy it. Learn to balance things. Don't allow the obsession to travel along with you; people will think that you have gone mad.' *This reprimand was merely superficial. Papa was delighted that I was on the right course and was now living my dream!*

Time flew on its wings and on the day of my exam Papa accompanied me to the examination centre. The first paper was English essay which was to be completed in two hours. Among the choices available I found the topic—'Middle East, the time bomb of the world' very interesting. I wrote from all that I had internalised in my mind from the regular reading of newspapers and magazines. I attempted the rest of the papers with the same flourish. When I narrated my performance, Papa was exultant and tearful. At last he was seeing a ray of hope. Shortly thereafter, he left for Bhubaneswar with words of encouragement.

Paulo Coelho has very aptly postulated in *The Alchemist*: 'When you deeply desire something the whole universe conspires to help you achieve it.'

In the winter break that followed my third semester Law exams, I chalked out my plan for preparations for the Civil Services Examinations with renewed resolve. And, with the dawn of the New Year, I started pursuit of my goal in all solemnity. I developed a set routine.

Each day now appeared to be full of positives. I was now a man possessed with a tremendous reservoir of energy. The passion for achievement and success made me forget the day's toil.

And, Shama's love and memories remained the leitmotif of my venture as always. Shama ruled my heart and the flame of her love inspired me. My desire for success was ultimately linked to finding my love too. I always wished that some day she would stumble upon me or I would bump into her—per chance. In the course of my visits to the university library too I would contemplate fortuitous meeting with Shama. But the days passed and my wishes never materialised.

I appeared in the Preliminary exams of Civil Services, in June with full vigour and confidence. A month and a half later, I qualified. And ten days later, I emerged successful in the Assistant Grade's exam which I had taken a year back. A government job was now in my pocket. The guidance of Darshan, Raj Mamaji's advice and my family's faith had been honoured. I could finally taste success, albeit a small dose. And this small dose was, perhaps, a prelude to more!

On reaching home I shared the news with elation and ebullience. *Of course to one's near and dear ones, one is not merely an object but a real person with love, emotions and feelings; and one's near and dear ones are able to appreciate one's state of mind.* I touched my mother's feet and hugged Nalini. 'Get some sweets, beta,' Mummy said with misty eyes and heavy throat. I rushed to the market, and with my chest swelling with pride, said to the *halwai*, 'Give me a quarter kilo of the best *burfi*.' We celebrated the happiness which God had bestowed after a long time; the last time being father's promotion before his departure to Bhubaneswar and earlier when I had got my higher secondary results.

Imbued with enthusiasm, I now clothed my persona in all earnest. I was seriousness personified. I followed a stricter schedule and started spending more time in the Law library. Civil Services, I had learnt, besides providing financial security, guaranteed prestige, power and status. Subconsciously, I began cultivating attributes expected of a civil servant. I tried to inculcate the traits of diligence, perseverance, organised effort, systematic studies, and above all the value of time. For me there were no avenues open for higher studies or the pursuit of any other professional career. Selection in Civil Services or as a Bank Probationary Officer was my opportunity to prove my calibre and mettle. It was a stark challenge that had to be surmounted at any cost. With such a status only could I pursue my cherished desire to seek my Shama–my heartthrob!

Time passed on and with that my enthusiasm, zeal and efforts kept increasing. Spending long hours in the library and executing my plans became my daily routine.

In the library, I found many serious students of my ilk. There were many others who were preparing for their Law exams or also preparing for their masters course in Law—LLM.

In the Law library there was a separate section for the senior students, pursuing LLM course. I would go and sit there, immersing myself totally in studies. But, slowly, I became aware that a pair of beautiful eyes would lift whenever I would enter that section or when I would get up for going out after regular intervals. I had the occasion to see the owner of those eyes: a lovely lady with a round well-chiselled face and fair skin. Her hair was jet black and tied up in a ponytail. She had good height, 5 ft 4 inches perhaps. She would always be elegantly dressed in salwar suits or churidar and shirts. A look at her could sway anyone. But she was reticent. She hardly interacted with anyone except one or two girls. The boys around would never approach her; such was her aura. When a few had tried, they met with curt responses and rebuffs.

There were many occasions when our eyes met. And over a period of time I learnt her name— Padmini.

My reflections in the mirror had apprised me of the fact that now my personality had acquired a distinct attractiveness and it did cause some disturbance around. Something that could not be blamed, something which in fact was the hallmark of youth—*youth, which brings with it vivacity, vibrancy and colour and perforce brings a magnetic attraction between opposite sexes; that which is the combination of the hormonal changes and symptomatic of distinct chemical composition of the different sexes*. It adds vitality, joy and glee in the world, to create equilibrium. Else, there would have been ennui. Sexual dimorphism adds colour and music, gives the artist and the litterateur the material for creation.

Sagacity dictated utmost restraint. I had to remain insulated from such forces; I had put blinkers on my eyes; I wanted to follow a straight and focused course with one unwavering aim—studies, studies and only studies. I was in the library to pursue and further that aim and nothing else—no distractions.

Whenever I would enter the library, my sharp eyes could locate her position from a distance and I would look at her; but when in my vicinity, I would ignore her as if she didn't exist at all. This art of exhibition of nonchalance I had perfected through constant and consistent training since the time I had acquired youth or since I became aware of the existence of the tender gender. This art I had honed in my college, and I could develop into a strong individual, never perturbed by the presence of enchanting beauties. Deep in my heart I had started enjoying it: teasing the tender gender by paying scant attention to them. But it caused me immense pain too; the pain of eschewing the privilege of beholding nature's creation!

Life is a complex journey! And, God has his own grand design that is beyond human comprehension. We meet certain people in this world as per our destiny: some people are with us for a short period; while others may be for a little longer; and a chosen few are with us for the whole of life, and maybe our lives get so much intertwined that we may continue to be with them for many more incarnations. We are destined to develop some relation with them in life, or we are related to them in the past or we may get related to them in a future incarnation. Thus the whole cosmos, the dance of nature, and the whims and fancies of God can never be understood. Such phenomena—the occurrences and the events—are unpredictable.

One day, after I had finished taking notes on the Constitution of India, I took out my Mercantile Law book and was going through the chapter on Negotiable Instruments Act. Suddenly I heard, 'May I have that Constitution book if you don't need it?' and looked up. I was surprised. Padmini was standing beside me and looking directly into my eyes. Her eyes were beautiful and black; their glow disconcerting.

'Oh sure,' I said politely while picking up the book and passing it to her.

'Do you study here in the morning Law course?' She asked in a whisper while standing there.

'No. I am in evening college. Law Centre I.'

'Are you studying for the IAS?'

'Yeah; I have qualified the Prelims.'

'Your good name?'

'Rohit, Rohit Sharma.'

'Well I am Padmini. Padmini Bhardwaj. I am in LLM first year.'

'Oh,' I replied.

She waited for a moment, waiting for further initiative from my side. But, I looked at her blankly, despite understanding the turbulence her eyes conveyed.

'Okay, All the best,' she said, and moved back to her seat.

Since we had got introduced, I, everyday on seeing her, would wish her by nodding my head and with a restrained smile. Padmini too would respond similarly. But, I also discovered that whichever book I would finish, the same was required by her. So, it was not merely borrowing the books; much else went on in her heart and mind! But, I always gave the impression that for me it was just casual; nothing special and nothing amiss.

After every fifteen to twenty minutes of continuous studies, I used to take a break of five minutes looking into vacant space just like that without focusing on the book. But Shama and her memories would not leave me, her sweet image, would be spread over the texts of Mercantile Law, and like my red butterfly fly into the Indian Constitution, and the Indian Penal Code provisions, amongst pictures of human physiology, the references of cell biology and articles of current affairs. Her face would be smiling at me, reminding me about the times when I had seen her in flesh and blood. Those memories would take away all my tardiness and tiredness. After all Shama was my motivation to slog and achieve my aim.

But during such unintended lifting of eyes, if my eyes chanced to meet Padmini's eyes, I would give an innocent, casual and blank look. I was sure in my heart that I didn't want any dalliance with her. My heartthrob was and would always be Shama. Even after a lapse of six years since the ever-callous destiny separated me from Shama, I still yearned for her. Shama, with whom I wished to live my life and realise my emotional dreams. Amidst all the toil of the day, Shama's innocent and lovely visage, though virtual, was always with me. So, how could Padmini encroach on Shama's pious territory–my heart?

My preparations were in full swing. God had bestowed upon me faith and confidence. Despite the exam being one of a highly competitive nature and the course being too vast, I was surging ahead with a positive affirmation that I would succeed.

-o-

During that period came two famous movies. One was *Umrao Jaan*, in which actress Rekha touched the pinnacle of her career. The film based on Mirza Ruswa's eponymous novel, was an absolute masterpiece—fine and crisp script, fantastic acting, and above all beautiful lyrics woven into melodious music. This song in the voice of Asha Bhonsle was the most popular and heartrending:

> *Ye kyaa jagah hai dosato, ye kaunsaa dayaar hain*
> *had-ye-nigaah tak jahaan, gubaar hee gubaar hai...*

It was the tragic tale of a girl kidnapped in her childhood, who by quirk of fate becomes a nautch girl. Ironically, she loves a Nawab, who is already married. In the end, she happens to meet her mother and brother; but she is not accepted in the family fold for being a nautch girl.

The story touched my heart and reinforced my feminist instincts. I had a special place for women in my heart. I always held the opinion that women needed to be respected.

Another movie that touched me was *Prem Rog*, Raj Kapoor's masterpiece starring his son Rishi Kapoor and actress Padmini Kolhapuri who had graduated from a child artiste to a heroine. It was a typical Raj Kapoor film with fantastic, melodious and emotionally rich musical score.

The movie had love as subtext where a plebeian boy and a patrician girl grow up together. The girl, oblivious of the boy's love for her, gets married to another patrician, becomes a widow and after undergoing a lot of trauma returns to her home. The boy learns of her sufferings; she in turn is able to learn about his love for her; and after a lot of drama and violence they unite.

I pondered, 'I didn't try to fall in love with Shama; love just happened naturally without my realising anything, and now it was an integral part of my life and psyche.'

During those times in 1982, India was hosting the Asiad Games. Delhi was under the tremendous spell of renovation and beautification. New infrastructure, flyovers and stadia were being constructed. Zest and energy pervaded the air. My preparations were also resonating with similar zeal and passion. However, the onset of October brought an ill-fated break. Something for which I was not prepared … Delhi was engulfed by a deadly viral disease spread by mosquito. In those days it was called dengue, though it is disputable whether it was dengue. But infected people would be bed-ridden for at least a week. The fever would be very debilitating.

Unfortunately, I too contracted the same. First I did not realise and went to the library for a day. But I found the slog unbearable and had to return home. Then I was down and bed ridden; not for a day but for a week. My whole rhythm was upset. I didn't know how to make up for the loss at such a crucial juncture when I had to revise whatever I had studied so painstakingly. Whenever I ruminated over the situation I felt more sullen and morose, and tears would roll down my eyes. I could only pray and wait; biding my time till God showered his benevolence and relieved me from that ailment, and my strength came back.

Anything that is beyond human comprehension has to be left to the Almighty's judgement. God has his own designs. Bhagwad Gita advocates performance of one's karmas to the best of one's abilities and forsaking thought about the results, as the results would be commensurate with your karmas. Karmas are not merely the deeds of this life but they are the cumulative total of karmas of our past lives as well as the present one; the human body may be belonging to only this life but the spirit that resides therein is in continuum residing in various bodies whether human, animal or even plants. But the results should not deter us.

I heartily prayed and started recovering after six days; but the whole process took almost ten days. On the 11th of October, I realised that only twenty days remained before the main exam. But my faith in God carried me through without much worries. I found that my hair had grown quite long; I decided that first of all I needed a haircut. I didn't give any specific directions to the barber, and left the affair to his judgement. He cut my hair a bit short. Later I had a bath, and while drying my hair, I thought of trying a new style. I was very fond of John Travolta's hairstyle after the success of his movie *Saturday Night Fever*. I started backcombing and was surprised that it stayed, revealing my broad forehead. While I was having breakfast, Mummy remarked, 'Rohit, your hairstyle is looking good.' I appraised myself in the mirror, and was elated with my new looks; it had accentuated my personality.

And, with that new look, I cast aside any worries and negative thoughts. I became a picture of confidence, hope and positive attitude. *I, after having put in hard work in the last one and a half years, should not let that ten days' indisposition make me lose my momentum.*

The next few days sped by like a dream. It was time to consolidate and do my best. Before leaving for the exams I would pray to God, and Mummy would be standing at the gate with a steel tumbler containing water in which I was supposed to see my face; she would be carrying one dish plate containing little curd and sugar; she would put a spoonful in my mouth; and also apply it as a tika on my forehead. That ritual my mother had been following right since my childhood whenever I would go to appear in some major exam; that was supposed to be an auspicious ritual. It was suffused with Mummy's love and her faith in my abilities and calibre.

'Whatever one may say, there is power in prayers,' Dale Carnegie has said in his famous book, How to Stop Worrying and Start Living. *Even doctors after doing their best say at one point of time, 'Now we can only pray for the best.'*

Thus armed with my mother's blessings and the power of her rituals, and with a firm belief and hope I went out to appear in a major exam. I boarded the bus to UPSC, and throughout kept on poring over the notes that I had so painstakingly made.

In the examination hall, I discovered that the paper was unlike my higher secondary or graduation level exams. It was an entirely different cup of tea. It was expansive requiring knowledge of many fields. So, it was not possible to attempt all the questions. My pen was initially slow but gained speed. I could summon things from my memory bank. I calmed myself rationalising that my plight might be like most of the applicants as nobody can be an expert in a variety of fields. I just gave it my best.

On reaching home I found Raj Mamaji waiting for me with my mummy and Nalini, eager to know about my performance. The review started over a cup of tea. He listened, and gave me an encouraging pat, 'Although it has been your first attempt, I think in the given circumstances you have done quite well. Don't feel dejected; focus instead on your remaining papers. God willing everything will be all right. You have the capability and you have put in earnest efforts,' Mamaji spoke with a twinkle in his eyes; perhaps happy with his disciple's performance.

I pulled up my socks and summoned all my energy reserves for the rest of the period. The tiredness entailed by the dengue fever was forgotten. One after another the papers got over in a span of two weeks. Though I felt satisfied, yet with so much of competition around, involving so many candidates from a number of academic fields, and the vast course, I didn't know how to rate my chances of success. My experience with the Medical Entrance exams had laced my natural optimism with a tinge of pragmatism, and I was conservative in my self-evaluation.

A fortnight after the exams, I appeared for the State Bank of India's Probationary Officer's Exam, a highly prestigious exam in those times. SBI, which in the British Raj was known as the Imperial Bank of India is still the most important bank in the public sector. Then, the salary of a Probationary Officer of SBI was 400 to 500 rupees more compared to Probationary Officers joining any other nationalised banks. The experience of Civil Services Exam had instilled loads of confidence. I performed very well in objective-type GK test as well as the English paper, and exceptionally well in the mathematical ability and intelligence tests. The most unexpected performance was in the essay and letter writing part. With the experience and vast knowledge on a variety of subjects that I had gained from the Civil Services Exam preparations, I could write an essay on 'Rural Development as I see in India'. I could recall all the schemes of the Government of India including the '20-point Programme' of Mrs Indira Gandhi for poverty alleviation. Those three hours in the examination hall were exhilarating. I came out elated and ebullient. It was in stark contrast to that episode just two years back when fresh from graduation I had not been able to perform well in the clerical exam of the same bank!

I reached home and narrated my experience to Mummy and Nalini.

The dawn of next day brought sad news while I was still savouring the exuberance of my performance of the previous day. A messenger from my mamaji informed that my paternal grandfather had expired. We were to reach Rajouri Garden as the funeral procession had to start. Since my father was at Bhubaneswar and Subhash Uncle in Canada, I was the one who would have to perform the last rites at the crematorium. On reaching there I was deeply moved and in tears. There lay my grandfather on the pyre; he had harboured visions of my becoming an entrepreneur! But later when that didn't materialise, he too had wished me to become a government officer.

Law exams got over and I filled up the application for the next attempt at Civil Services. I resumed my visits to the Law library in January. And I maintained my rhythm of regular studies. I also had one more Bank Probationary Officers' Exam for the Western Region scheduled for the next year. I would come across Padmini as usual, and my interaction had the same pattern. I could sense special feelings in her eyes. They had a twinkle, they were lively and they had a craving. My eyes on the other hand evinced deliberate blankness, no feelings and no emotions. My blank looks would contrast with her intense gaze.

One day, I happened to meet her near the college canteen where I had gone for a cup of tea. She was sitting all alone beside a table. The moment I entered, she looked up accidentally. Our eyes met. Her lips widened into a refreshing natural smile. I smiled and nodded in veneration, and prepared to move to another table. 'Why don't you join me Rohit?' She said with an inviting gesture.

I had to relent, and with some reluctance reached her table. My heart was constantly rationalising what people around would think.

'What happened? You were not to be seen for long,' She asked.

'Yeah, actually in the first week of October I was down with dengue for almost ten days. Later I became so weak that I preferred to study at home. Then I was busy with my Competitive Exams and the term exams,' I said in one go.

'How did you fare in your IAS exam?'

'It was my first chance. And, there are lots of ifs and buts. I did my best. Let's see.'

'You are such an intelligent boy. But you don't understand certain things,' She remarked.

'What? What do you mean?'

Her eyes were on the table. She scratched something meaninglessly on the table with her index finger. I had the occasion to see her fingers for the first time. They were lovely. Her nails had been well manicured and painted with soothing red nail polish. Then she lifted her head, cleared a vagrant wisp of her hair, which had got disturbed by a swish of sudden breeze, and looked into my eyes directly. I tried to shift my eyes in an evasive action, but heard her barely audible but melodious voice, 'Rohit, have you ever fallen in love?'

Her candid question surprised me. And, I knew what was in the offing. I didn't want the Sonam episode to be repeated. At that very moment Shama's lovely face danced before my eyes and my heart said that I should reveal my secret. 'Yeah; I have,' I replied with a deep voice and in a whisper.

She was taken aback. The rosiness of her cheeks segued to bloodless white. Her face contorted with pain.

'Are you joking,' She laughed. I could sense the hollowness of her laughter. She had not expected that.

'No, I am serious,' I replied.

'When? Where? With whom?' She shook while asking; her voice betraying the consternation of her heart.

And, then I narrated, very briefly, the circumstances, events and duration of my love for Shama.

'You say that you last met her about a year and a half back. Do you think she will wait for you,' she gave a look of disbelief, 'Rohit, you are queer, and you are chasing a mirage.'

'But, I am comfortable with the mere thoughts of her. I am what I am, I can't change,' I replied.

I was surprised by my interaction with a perfect stranger.

Finally, with laboured effort, she said, 'Okay, nice to learn about your love. I thought you were a novice in such matters. And, since you are a decent boy, you needed to be tutored by a senior.'

I laughed, my natural laughter, without making her realise that I understood her sentiments.

Then we got up. She didn't allow me to pay the bill. Something was understood though not stated. That our emotional paths ran parallel but would never cross. I had not left any scope for that.

In the last week of January, I got a letter from the Ministry of Steel and Mines, Department of Steel, Udyog Bhawan, Delhi that I had been appointed as Assistant. I filled the necessary forms and sent them. Later, I underwent a medical fitness test at Ram Manohar Lohia Hospital (then Willlingdon Hospital).

Now, my antecedents had to be verified by the police. When told about the police verification by one of my friends, I wondered what it meant, 'Will it mean I have to visit the police station and will I be subjected to uncomfortable questioning as I had seen in the movies? Movies generally depicted how a policeman, with enormous power, treats a commoner. How interrogation leaves one gasping and praying when the tribulation would be over; how the prey wishes to escape the clutches of his tormentors. What will happen to me? But what I actually encountered was an anti-climax. One fine morning in the second week of February while I was reading the morning newspaper, sipping tea in between, I heard someone calling, 'Rohit Sharma!'

'Who is it?' I asked on seeing an ordinary looking man on a bicycle; wielding a laathi.

'Well, I am from the police department.'

'Oh, I am Rohit Sharma,' I replied incredulously.

'Cleared Assistant Grade exam? Get me your ration card,' he ordered, his authority not befitting his appearance.

I was excited and immediately rushed inside, and brought the family's ration card.

He read it, 'So, you are Rohit. Okay! Is everything alright?' He returned the card and winked. 'So everything is okay?' he winked again.

'Yeah, everything is fine,' I replied innocently. The man repeated the question yet again with a wink but I couldn't understand its import. The man went away with some incomprehensible murmurs. I, instead, was fantasising that soon I would be getting the call from the Ministry to join. Little did I realise the blunder I had committed. Although my identity had been verified, the verification was not complete as the greedy palm had not been greased. I had to wait for almost two months to get the call letter from the Ministry. After all, a person remains unidentified till his police verification report reaches the Ministry. When I didn't get the intimation for more than a fortnight since that episode, I learnt from one of my friends what those incomprehensible murmurs of that man meant. Mummy, perturbed by my situation, approached some acquaintance in the police narrating the episode. The matter got expedited, and in a span of one week the report was prepared and despatched to the Ministry. Almost after one and a half months later, one fine day, in the first week of April I got the call letter to join in the second week.

Things meanwhile had taken a very interesting turn. As usual, I went to the library near my house for scanning the newspapers and magazines. While going through the paper, all of a sudden my breathing stopped when I found the title in bold: 'Civil Services (Mains) Results.' Then my breathing became faster and my heart raced. First I thought I should not see it as there was not much scope for me in my first attempt. But, I had to see, although I was almost sure my roll number would not figure in the list. After all, it was the most difficult and uncertain exam. I knew my roll number and repeated it in my mind. Then with curiosity and anxiety I started going through the list; for a moment my heart missed a beat and my brain numbed, my finger had stopped on a number which turned out to be mine—I had made it to the list of successful candidates who would be called for an interview! I was staring at it. The reality was not sinking in. Then I shrieked; attracting the attention of the person sitting next to me. I hardly used to interact with people in the library. The person became very curious, and on an impulse I informed, 'I have cleared the written exam of Civil Services,' and got glances of appreciation. I was ecstatic and impatient to rush home and break the news. On the way, I met Kuldeep, one of my friends, who had also aspired to be a civil servant. 'Rohit, how are your preparations going on for the Prelims?' Kuldeep asked. I was desperate to share my joy. 'I have cleared the Mains this year,' I told him riding on cloud nine. Kuldeep, who was just a beginner in the world of Competitive Exams, was equally thrilled; and accompanied me home. On seeing Mummy, I fell at her feet.

Mummy was confused, 'What happened?'

'I have cleared the IAS Mains,' I said tearfully.

Mummy was moved. She said, 'You had to; after all, you have been working so hard.'

Kuldeep interjected, 'Auntie you are privileged to have such a son, and so am I to have such a friend. I shall take his study table; I am sure that it would prove lucky for me too.'

Tears were rolling down my cheeks; but not of sorrow or loss; my happiness was pouring out of my eyes.

'Now, go and get us sweets,' Mummy said.

I got half a kilo of sweets. We all had it. Coincidentally, Om Mamaji also came to meet us. Mummy could not contain herself and shared the news. After all, for a middle-class family in India it is one of the greatest events. Om Mamaji was dumbfounded for a moment. Despite the element of jealousy pervading in the family that had always affected our relationships, he was glad and said, 'At last we can also proclaim with pride that someone from our family has passed this prestigious exam. Go and meet Neelima; she would be extremely happy to hear this.'

My joy now knew no bounds. I had finally got my moment of glory; though the final selection still hinged on a lot of ifs and buts. I rushed to their house. Mamiji hugged me and held me close to her for a while, moving her hand affectionately over my head and showering loads of blessings. Neelima too embraced me. Even though she, in the past, had criticised and doubted my course of action, that day my success silenced that critique. Our combined happiness was all-encompassing and worth remembering for the rest of our lives. I was no longer a loser or an underdog. The canvas of my achievement had enlarged!

I learnt that my Khalsa College friends, Prashant and R. Kumar, who were pursuing Law, had also got through the Mains. Now, I was in an elite group as many other students who had got through Mains became my friends. All of a sudden, those very people, who would cursorily glance at me, were taking notice.

Padmini too wished me with a broad smile, 'Congrats. You are a studious guy. You had to succeed.'

Despite the arrival of April, it was still chilly in the mornings. So, I reached Udyog Bhawan dressed in dark brown corduroy jeans, dull grey shirt and light brown suede jacket, to join my new posting. Udyog Bhawan's imperious structure in Dholpur stone and its many entry gates, floors and labyrinthine corridors appeared intimidating; evoking awe.

After some efforts and enquiries, I could reach the assigned room.

'Mr P. Rangarao, Section Officer, Establishment', read the dull brass name plate. The ambience in the room was equally dull: ten persons, mostly middle aged, cramped in a small space, behind as many tables. One of them was a lady. Barring the lady and a young typist all were in dull, apparently old clothes. There were files and papers everywhere: on the tables and in open racks.

A smart and fit man in his mid-thirties, with a genial face and ready smile, had the biggest table that lent him an aura of authority. He was the Section Officer; of medium height, wheatish complexion and well-combed black hair. He belonged to Andhra Pradesh.

'Good morning Sir, I'm Rohit Sharma. I have come to join as Assistant.' All eyes turned towards me, in interest.

'So, you are joining today. What happened to the Civil Services' result?' he asked.

'I got through sir,' I replied with enthusiasm and to everyone's surprise. The eyes, I felt, were now filled with awe. Mr Rangarao too didn't expect it.

'Are you through with the interview?'

'Not yet sir, I haven't got the call letter so far.'

'What were your optionals? Was it your first chance? What has been your field of study? What does your father do?' Rangarao rapid-fired a volley of questions. I replied with equal zest.

Gradually, I got introduced to the staff around: two assistants, two upper division clerks, two lower division clerks, one typist, one daftary and one peon.

'Sir, would you allow me to study in the office till my interview?' I innocently asked.

'No problem; it is not going to be cumbersome here,' Rangarao said cheerfully.

Despite those dismal surroundings and the presence of old, unenthusiastic people I felt a ray of hope. 'How contrasting an atmosphere compared to Shourie Duplicators,' I mused.

Later, Mr Rangarao took me to meet the Under Secretary and the Deputy Secretary. The Deputy Secretary, an IAS himself, enquired about Civil Services' result. Learning that I had qualified and that I had also appeared for two bank exams, he directed that I may be kept in the Establishment section only, under Mr Rangarao.

We returned to the section. I was allotted a table cluttered with files. I cleaned up the things, and made the space presentable by neatly stacking the files and the papers. As no work was allotted to me, I spread out my newspaper and started reading seriously.

I was not allotted much work. So, I could utilise my time for preparing for the interview. That government job, although providing me economic security, had robbed me of the freedom I had as a student. So I had to try and utilise the maximum time that I could steal. I would avoid the usual chit-chat and just respond with a benign smile.

Luck too had a benign disposition towards me now. A fortnight after joining, I got another surprise. While I was flipping through the morning newspaper during breakfast, suddenly a headline 'Results of State Bank of India Probationary Officers' Exam,' caught my eye. For a moment I was nervous; it was a small list of almost 170 candidates with the roll numbers relating to Delhi region only. With bated breath, I scanned it with very little hope. I was stunned; I had been shortlisted for the interview! Unbelievable! Two years back I had failed in the clerical exam of the same bank. My mentor Darshan's words were ringing in my ears: 'Hard work seldom goes waste.' It was the fruition of my efforts.

With tearful eyes, I went to the kitchen and fell at Mummy's feet.

'What's happened beta?' she asked, perplexed.

'I have got through the SBI written exam.'

'I am not surprised. You are my intelligent and hardworking son,' Mummy responded.

I was jubilant, but in the office kept quiet about it. It was around noon when Muthuswamy, the typist, while going through the newspaper disclosed, 'Sir, results are out; I couldn't make it.'

'Muthu, how can you unless you work really hard,' Mr Rangarao said.

'Which exam's result are you referring to?' I asked.

'SBI PO's. Had you appeared in that?' Muthu asked.

'Yes, I got through,' I declared calmly.

'Whatttttttttt? And you are sitting there so calmly?' Rangarao boomed.

'I was about to tell you,' I stammered.

Rangarao was impressed. He was enthusiastically updating all the visitors to my room about my success. I became an object of admiration, curiosity and envy. And, in my heart, I had mixed feelings: one of elation and the other of a complex that I did not belong to the place.

It was a big occasion for me when I appeared for the Civil Services' interview in the third week of May. Attired in my new black trousers and a light pink shirt I reached the UPSC at 8:30 in the morning. It was a huge exposure as there were many candidates who were already well employed. One was from the Indian Space Research Organisation and another from Engineers India Limited. They were busy in animated discussions. It didn't take me long to become friendly with them. That helped me in remaining calm and composed.

'Rohit Sharma,' I heard my name, and in no time was guided to the interview room where five members were sitting behind a big table; a big window covered with long diaphanous curtains behind them; bright light illuminating their visage. I was unnerved for a moment, then auto-suggested: *everything will be fine*.

I greeted them with utmost humility. They smiled genially.

One of the members began with a question on punishment of juvenile offenders and then moved to abetment of murder, surrogate mothers and their status. Suddenly he asked, 'Where is the International Court of Justice? Has any Indian judge ever been appointed on its bench?'

'Sir, it's at The Hague, Netherlands. Dr Nagendra Singh from India has been appointed recently.' He was apparently pleased.

There were a barrage of questions from other members on a number of topics; but their tone was friendly. I could answer most of them.

The interview ended on a happy note. I started dreaming of getting a high rank in the merit list.

While returning I had to change three buses. It was the peak of summer; but neither the heat nor the swelter bothered me. I was on a song, and reached home euphoric. I hugged Mummy.

'I have done very well; hopefully, I should be through.'

Mummy was ecstatic and kissed my forehead. 'Now our days will change for the better.'

We had a nice lunch together. A day later, I had to appear for the medical check-up at the Safdarjang Hospital; it was a compulsory medical examination for all candidates who had appeared in the interview.

The day at the hospital was quite hectic and it took full five hours for the entire process. It was commotion all along as we were herded from one room to another at different floors and departments. The delay on certain occasions was irritating. A few of the candidates got so annoyed that they took up the matter with the hospital authorities. They had already started feeling as powerful bureaucrats who deserved to be treated differently from the commoners!

Suddenly, I came across a familiar face amongst the doctors—Chawla, yes, Sunil Chawla who had got selected in the first year itself. He recognised me and said, 'Hi Rohit, how do you do? I think you have also come for the medical test? That day during discussions with R. Kumar and Priya, I learnt that you too have succeeded in the Civil Services Exam.'

I was elated on my being the talking point at last. It was hardly thinkable two years ago when I had met Rajiv Malik in Maulana Azad Medical College as a struggling salesman, selling cyclostyling machines, with my future bleak and uncertain.

Now, Sunil Chawla, with apparent envy was saying, 'See *yaar*, it's good that you were not selected for the MBBS. Soon you will be a big officer while we would be taking so long to establish our career.'

I downplayed the whole thing and said, 'But it is not the final selection as yet.'

Still deep in my heart I was appreciative of divine justice…

Next day, in the office, everyone was inquisitive about my performance. My account of the whole episode evoked reactions of both exuberance and envy.

A week later on learning about the declaration of results, I went to the UPSC in the afternoon. A huge crowd had gathered there scanning a list of almost 850 successful candidates. I discovered that my name was there though much lower in the merit list: 705th rank. I had made it, though not with flying colours. I was a little desolate when I spotted that guy from Engineers India who had secured 300th rank and was hopeful of getting into Customs or Income Tax Service. When I revealed my rank, he sympathised and philosophised, 'Oh man, you are too young and have two more chances to try. If in the very first attempt you have made it to the list, you can always hope for better in your future attempts.'

A little dejected but still happy at my achievement, I returned to my office and shared the news with Mr Rangarao. 'So, from today onwards you are at least a Section Officer,' he said congratulating me. Deep in my heart I did not like his comment but that was the truth. I had desired becoming at least a Group A officer.

The news of declaration of the results had spread like wildfire. In the evening when I reached home I found Raj Mamaji waiting for me with my parents. I presented a morose face, and after touching their feet informed, 'My rank is 705, and I am likely to get a Group B service.'

'Great! You have made it to the merit list of this prestigious exam! Why such a morose face? You will be a gazetted officer in the Government of India at such an young age, and in your very first attempt. How many are so lucky? It is a matter to rejoice; we are so proud of your achievement. You did your best despite having fallen sick at the critical juncture. You can always improve in your remaining two attempts,' they boosted my morale.

I hugged my parents and appreciated the glow on my father's face. He, after a long time, had got something positive. For an ordinary government servant who had risen from the ranks such an achievement by his son was a big accomplishment! 'Papa, you are right,' I said, 'I will certainly try harder in my next attempt.' I cast aside my glum facade and enjoyed the moment with my family: Mummy and Papa who had done so much for me; Raj Mamaji who was my guide; and Nalini, my dear sister who loved me so much.

I motivated myself that my initial success was a stepping stone for the battles ahead where I would, by sheer grit and determination, attain success. I had to project a picture of confidence and not anguish.

Almost a week later, I got a postcard from my old buddy Inder Arora. Just a long sentence ran from top to bottom:

'Congrats my dear friend,
May this be the springboard for more success in future!
Love,
Yours Inder'

I was in tears. I remembered the day when we had parted on his selection in medical college; he had boarded the bus and I had been left stranded. I had come a long way since then.

In the third week of June, I got the interview call for the State Bank of India for an interview in the first week of July. On the D-day, I, attired in black trousers and the same light pink shirt, reached SBI's Local Head Office, the building next to the SBI's main branch at Parliament Street. I was wearing shining patent leather shoes that were a fad during those times, and had been purchased for Raj Mamaji's daughter's wedding. With my nice puffy hairstyle, and childlike winning smile, I was at perfect ease with myself.

It had started drizzling when I entered the imposing building.

A number of candidates were waiting anxiously. My name was announced after half an hour's wait. I was ushered into an imposing and palatial room where five members of the interview board were seated in a calm and composed manner. 'Good afternoon madam and sirs,' I wished with my customary pleasant smile. I had come with the notion that I had nothing to lose. *Such a mental state removes any kind of nervousness.*

Their first question was regarding Civil Services' result. When I disclosed, they enquired if in spite of my selection in the State Bank I would strive for Civil Services. I revealed honestly where my preferences lay. There were mostly general questions including those about my job as an Assistant. They were intrigued as to how I couldn't qualify in the clerical exams of State Bank. They seemed to have no question about my capability. Their only concern was the probability of my remaining in the Bank. But I was honest and categorical.

When the interview got over I didn't know. But I knew I was unflustered.

I returned home laughing.

'Mummy I don't know if I would be selected as I had been honest in telling about my preference in pursuing Civil Services.'

Mummy remarked caressing my head, 'Don't worry. You have a job now and sooner or later you will get a call from the government on the basis of your selection in the first attempt. You can certainly focus on your exams.'

My star was on the ascendant closely following the Indian cricket team's rise in the limited overs World Cup that was held from 9–25 June 1983. Indians led by Kapil Dev were branded as Kapil's Devils, and winning the World Cup changed the complexion of the game and the power equation in world cricket.

My mental tenacity was goading me to move ahead with my singular goal but my soul was lost in the thoughts of Shama as that was my emotional and spiritual goal. My pristine love was clamouring for her. In so many years no one could tinker with that image; instead of blurring it had sharpened even more, become clearer still. Time had not dampened the flame of passion for Shama; it had only intensified it…

Each Hindi song touched the Shama chord in my heart, and I would imagine her while humming or singing it. I saw the movie *Woh Saat Din*, and found the resonance of my true and unadulterated love for Shama in that. Shama was there in the innocent face of the heroine Padmini Kolhapuri and, I found myself reflected in the simplicity of the hero Anil Kapoor. I felt that like that hero, I too was uncomplicated and, emotional. I genuinely missed my soul mate and wanted to seek her hand only with her consent and not with any intent of imposing my will on anyone. And, I had got entangled and ravelled in her love not with any design or machination. I had long before realised that love cannot be planned but it just happens. One song from the film encapsulated my state and my sentiments thus:

Pyaar kiyaa nahin jaata, ho jaata hai,
Dil diya nahin jaata kho jaata hai...

I replayed that scene and song in my mind, and hummed it many times over and over again in the bathroom while taking a bath. Despite being far removed from Shama in time and space I felt her proximity.

With my studies continuing, and my mind and heart suffused with her love, time simply flew past. I qualified the Prelims for Civil Services in 1983 as well. I planned to take leave from the month of September. Suddenly, somewhere in the first week of August, I got another surprise: the morning newspaper revealed that I had qualified the written exam of Probationary Officers of the Banking Service Recruitment Board (Western Region) for which I had appeared in March that year. I had scaled one more peak. A week later I got the papers from the Board intimating that I was to appear in an interview on 30th August in Mumbai (then Bombay). I wrote to my cousin Naresh who lived there. Once getting confirmation that I could stay with them and that he would be booking my return ticket, I left for Bombay on the 28th reaching there on the morning of 29th. Accompanied by my uncle, I attended the interview at the Express Towers, in the Nariman Point area. I faced the interview board with confidence. The questions were mostly general and also regarding the current events. I could answer them with ease and coherence wondering how each opportunity was helping me in refining my skills. The interview was over in no time and I learnt from other candidates that the results of State Bank of India's exam had been declared and they had been published in *Times of India*. Uncle got me a copy.

I rummaged through the paper and slowly went through the pages. One, two, three, and then my eyes lit up on finding the desired information on page seven. The next phase was of anticipation and nervousness whether my roll number figured there. The chances were fifty-fifty as in my interview I had been very candid about not being very keen about the bank job. I scanned the rows of numbers and then all conjectures were over, my roll number was spotted.

My joy was limitless. After the moderate success in the Civil Services Exam it was a big day—selection as a Probationary Officer in the biggest and the most prestigious nationalised bank! I was longing to reach Delhi and break the news to my family and relations. Raj Mamaji's prophesy and his encouraging words rang in my ears, 'One day you will succeed, it is only a matter of time ...'

The very next day I boarded the Delhi-bound Deluxe Express.

The train started and with it also started a train of thought in my mind. I now had about two months remaining for my Mains exam. On the way I took out my competitive exam magazines and got engrossed in the same. When almost two hours passed I found people around were looking at me keenly, curiosity writ large on their faces. One of the elderly ladies asked, 'Are you appearing for some exams.' 'Yes, I am trying for some competitive exams,' I replied. 'For what posts?' I enlightened her about my attempts and successes thus far. My answers generated a fair bit of awe and admiration amongst the fellow travellers. Their reaction gave me joy.

I was dying to reach Delhi to reveal my success to my family and relations and share the joy and excitement

The train reached Delhi at around 11:30 am the next morning. I picked up my luggage and walked out of the station to get a bus. With my mind in the seventh heaven, I found the commotion of Delhi beautiful and exhilarating.

Time had acquired wings, and soon I was home. I plonked my luggage and flung myself at Mummy's feet saying, 'I have been selected as a Probationary Officer in the State Bank.' While saying so tears started rolling down my cheeks. Mummy held me in her tight embrace and I wanted to remain locked like that forever.

'Look my son; I always had a strong intuition that one day you would succeed and would succeed with flying colours. You have, made us proud, enhanced the prestige of our house. Now I can, with my head held high, face all the people who had questioned your commitment. People used to say sarcastically, "your son keeps on appearing in one exam or the other, but when will you ever be able to give us the news of his success."' Nalini hugged me, 'Oh, bhaiyya, you are a role model for me.'

After taking bath, I brought some sweets from the market, and offered it to the Almighty—for showering his benevolence. I wrote to Papa and Darshan, pouring out my joy. Later in the evening we went to Raj Mamaji's house to share our happiness and also to express our gratitude for his timely motivation and guidance during my trying times. Mamaji jumped with joy; he hugged me with affection and said, 'See, I told you that you were meant to achieve something big. It was just a question of time. May God bless you with many such successes in future and develop you into an enthusiastic and confident individual!'

The spell of merriment continued when I joined office the next day and distributed sweets and burst the bombshell. My selection at such a young age in my first attempt in Civil Services and as a Probationary Officer in the most prestigious bank in India was unbelievable. Wherever I went in the office I could sense awe and admiration.

In the evening that day, with a box of sweets, I visited Om Mamaji and broke the news. My cousins Neelima, Neerja and Shailja gave me warm hugs. I touched Mamaji's and Mamiji's feet. They held me tightly and affectionately caressed my head, 'So, someone from our family has become a bank officer. We are proud and our happiness knows no bounds today.' We were all tearful.

'Give Neelima some tips,' Mamaji said, 'she is still a clerk in SBI.'

'It's only a matter of time; she too will become an officer. She is more intelligent and diligent than me,' I replied lightly.

After a week I proceeded on two months' leave including leave without pay ready to bear the financial loss to scale higher peaks. So it was back to Law library and strenuous studies.

Now, I had a strong urge to go and find Shama. But I realised that I had climbed only the first few steps on the ladder of success. My task ahead was uphill and the path tortuous. I had to redouble my efforts to run the last lap. *But I could spare a day at least,* I thought. *Should I go alone? No, I didn't have the courage.* So, I revealed my turbulent mind to Nalini on a Friday evening. She listened intently and agreed to accompany me. We planned that we could go to Janakpuri on Saturday on the pretext of going to Nai Sarak for buying books. Nalini would accompany me as she had a holiday on Saturday.

'Mummy, I have to buy some important books for the forthcoming exams. I need to go to Nai Sarak; I will have an early lunch,' I announced in the morning while Mummy was cooking.

Suddenly, Nalini also intervened, 'Mummy, I am feeling bored. Can I go with Rohit, if he doesn't mind?' Mummy didn't have any problem and agreed to our request; she did not sense anything amiss.

So after an early lunch, we set out in Shama's pursuit, and boarded a bus to Janakpuri.

'Which block?' The conductor asked while vending tickets.

'B block,' I said.

We took the tickets and got seats. On the way Nalini said, 'I thought you had forgotten her. I didn't know you still wanted her in your life. We are going to meet her. But have you ever expressed your love to her? Do you know whether she also loved you?"

'Nalini, I have not disclosed to you earlier. In fact I chanced to meet her twice since she left Motia Khan: once when I was dabbling in the Pilani venture and later when I was working for Shourie Duplicators. On both the occasions she talked to me. Especially when I bumped into her at Sisganj Gurudwara, she spoke to me at length. The arrival of her sister disrupted our conversation. But, that time I was only a salesman. She did appear to be in some distress. But I didn't have the courage to elicit anything from her. Now I have gained in stature. I think she will accept me,' I spoke more in expectation than in reality.

'Even now things are still nebulous. What kind of person are you? In life we can't just expect that if we love someone that person also loves us. Love has to be expressed. Love is a two-way process. We just can't presume and assume things,' Nalini laughed.

Nalini's laughter pinched me. But what she said was true.

In half an hour, the conductor announced, 'B Block, Janakpuri.'

We got down. Janakpuri in those times was a newly built colony: wide roads; well planned localities; greenery and parks. Unlike present times there were hardly any cars. Vehicular population in those days was scarce and scant. DTC buses, two wheelers, three wheelers and cycle rickshaws were the prevalent modes of transport. It was amazing. We began our quest. B 56 was the address I remembered. We sought directions from a few residents. I recollected Shama's father's name was Shyam Arora. Yet it was not as simple as we had thought of. One well mannered middle aged gentleman seemed to understand our predicament. He was quite helpful, but asked a counter question, '"B 56?" But which pocket. In Janakpuri you just can't say a simple A, B, C or D block. First of all you must tell is it B1 or B2 or B3 or B4. Then you have to tell the pocket also. Is it BA or BB or BC or BD or BE or BF?'

The question was baffling. I just asked, 'Which is this block?'

'This is B1. My dear this way you may take the whole day to figure out. Anyway you may try. Otherwise I would suggest that you just call up those people and find out the exact address.'

My jaw dropped. I just said, 'Thanks a lot sir; I think we would call them up.'

We took his leave, and moved ahead. I looked at Nalini. It was a blind chase.

'Okay, Nalini, I don't think we have much time. Let us search for an hour or at the most an hour and a half. We'll see if we are lucky or we'll keep it after my exams.'

We started with B1 block. We walked for some time and found the first destination BA 56. With lot of hope, I looked at the name plate: *Mr Suresh Bhatia*. We sighed in disappointment.

Then we proceeded to pocket BB 56. The name plate read: *Mr Rajinder Saldana*.

It was difficult to walk now. So we boarded a cycle rickshaw, and reached BC 56.There was no name plate. We deliberated and decided to knock. A decent young lady opened the door.

'Is it Mr Arora's place,' Nalini asked.

'Yes,' the lady replied cheerfully. 'I couldn't recognise you but, '

'I am looking for my school friend. Have you people shifted from Motia Khan?'

'No. We used to stay in Karol Bagh earlier.'

'Oh, we are so sorry. Actually I don't have the exact pocket number,' Nalini said.

We took leave. 'Okay, this will be the last try,' I said, but with little enthusiasm.

We were perspiring profusely. There was a fellow selling *jal jeera* in a big earthen pitcher on a small hand cart. The pitcher was draped in a wet red cloth and its neck garlanded with bunches of fresh mint leaves and limes. We bought two glasses. It was so refreshing and energy replenishing. Quenching our thirst we resumed our pursuit in a rickshaw.

Our eyes twinkled when we saw house no. BD 56 and the name plate Shyam Arora on the door. *That must be the one*. We thought. We rang the bell and an elderly lady opened the door.

'Excuse me auntie. We are coming from Motia Khan. I wanted to meet my friend Shama. Is she there?' Nalini said politely while I smiled.

'Shama! Which Shama? There is no one named Shama in our house. And, moreover, we never stayed in Motia Khan. I think you are mistaken.'

'Sorry auntie,' we said in unison, 'actually we don't know the exact block number.'

After leaving the house, my head sagged in despair. Nalini saw my condition and put a comforting hand on my shoulder. 'Rohit don't' worry. We'll try again after your exam.'

I couldn't speak. My throat was parched. There was so much in my heart and mind. But my vocal cords couldn't give shape to my thoughts. I controlled myself and said, 'Let us quickly go to Nai Sarak and buy the books. Otherwise Mummy will smell a rat.' Nalini agreed and we quickly finished the round of Nai Sarak and boarded the bus back home.

We returned with heavy hearts. 'I will certainly go in pursuit of my Shama after I finish the Civil Services Main Exam,' I decided.

Journey to a Goal

Just before my last paper, when I returned home, Raj Mamaji handed me a letter with a mysterious smile, 'Your appointment letter from SBI.' I was shocked on reading it. I was allocated to the Bhopal Circle! I was required to join at Kutchery Branch at Raipur in Madhya Pradesh on 9th December! The euphoria of having been selected in the SBI evaporated.

'Madhya Pradesh! Raipur—a place never heard of! I had the notion that I would get a posting in Delhi,' I expressed deep resentment. All the dreams that I had woven, of staying in a good house with Mummy and Nalini at Delhi, vanished like smoke in thin air. The vortex of my wishes and desires was rising sarcastically in the sky. After merriment it was a bolt from the blue.

Raj Mamaji and Mummy consoled me. I was in a fix: the call for the Group B post from my first attempt was not expected before May/June next year; I was selected as an officer in one of the most prestigious banks of India. But my posting was so far away from Delhi; and in Delhi I was holding a non-executive post of Assistant in the Government of India. I now had to weigh all the pros and cons. I needed advice from people from different walks of life.

Two days later, on resuming office, I learnt that Raipur was almost near the Odisha and Andhra border; that it was a 26-hour train journey from Delhi and only one train plied daily between Delhi and Raipur. *Now Chhattisgarh has become a separate state and Raipur is its capital and a fast developing city; during those times the area was hardly heard of*. From my geography books I had learnt that the Bastar district which was near Raipur was totally inhabited by the tribal population, and it was bigger than the state of Kerala! For a Delhite the word tribal population brought the vivid scenes of Hindi movies: tribals with cannibalistic propensities; with weird apparel; untouched by civilisation and singing strange songs and dancing wildly. They evoked images of underdevelopment, dust and grime. Neither Raipur nor Kutchery Branch appealed to me.

Papa, on learning about my posting, was also not very enthusiastic. He dissuaded me by writing a letter almost daily, saying it was a tribal area. He advised me to remain in Delhi and wait for a call on the basis of my selection in the Civil Services. But the tag of SBI PO was too tempting. In such a predicament I got advice from a seasoned couple. The gentleman was a senior officer in the State Bank while the lady was an Assistant Commissioner in Delhi Police. They advised me not to let such an opportunity slip and to enjoy the job.

'So the time for flight from the snug nest of my family has arrived,' I mused. Papa too had to leave Delhi and move to Bhubaneswar to take a promotion. With the cobwebs of confusion removed from my mind, I felt as if a heavy load had been lifted off my shoulders and heart. '*Life is on a predestined course*,' some wise person had told me long ago, '*we have to go to the places God has ordained and also meet the people, the actors of our lives' script as per the directions of the Director of our lives—the Almighty*.'

I booked my ticket for 7th December by the Chhattisgarh Express. I also took two references, one of a distant relation from my mother's side and another of my father's branch office there to ensure some help in the event of encountering any difficulty. I got a bank draft of ₹1000 in the name of the SBI which was mandatory as security deposit; I also carried ₹500 rupees in cash and ₹500 in traveller's cheques to tide over the period till I would get my salary.

As the day of my departure for Raipur was nearing, I was getting a queer feeling of losing something. I was going to leave Delhi for a future so uncertain! Time and again this thought was piercing my heart.

Besides, losing the smug and snug nest of my home, where my mother and sister had ever nourished my emotional self with their love and care, I was going to lose something equally precious. My star was on the ascendant as regards my career graph but what about Shama? I had carved a temple of love in my heart and Shama was my 'love deity', whom I had passionately consecrated with all my emotional outpourings; worshipped her with my cravings and tears. She was always with me: in my moments of sorrow and despair, in my happiness and ecstasy. Apart from my career I had the deep desire of pursuing her and kneeling before her and her parents, seeking her hand for an eternal nuptial alliance–the embodiment of our true love. In Delhi, there was a probability, of coming across her—at some place, be it in DTC buses, markets, tourist places, cinema halls or some mall. 'What designs does God have in store for me? Are we destined to meet and unite or not?' I reflected upon the promise I had made to myself. 'I have not become an IAS officer; but I have got some significant successes. Shouldn't I try to meet her at least once before I leave Delhi? Shouldn't I try and find out whether she loves me or not? Whether she too misses me like I have missed her for so long? There were so many questions that needed answers. *What was to be done? But my innate shyness prevented me from being proactive in this area. I still thought I must achieve some more, something more concrete*.

Mummy announced on my return from office one evening, 'Your father's cousin Virender had come today. His daughter's marriage is on 2nd December. You are leaving on 5th December. I think we can make it. It would be a nice outing before you go to Raipur. Your father is not here. At least we all can go and enjoy one last function before you leave.'

'Yes, Mummy, we can go. I will come home early that day. By the way, where is the wedding?' I asked casually.

'I think you have forgotten. Virender stays at Janakpuri. The marriage will be held at the community centre of B block, Janakpuri.'

'Janakpuri!' I was startled as the familiar name struck my ears.

'What is the matter? Do you have any problem?' Mummy asked.

'Not at all. It's fine. We can certainly go,' I quickly covered up.

I felt an electric current running through my body. Visiting B Block, Janakpuri had opened up the possibility of something that I had long cherished.

Like the orbital in the structure of an atom where there is maximum probability of finding an electron, B-block, Janakpuri too was an orbital, where there was maximum probability of finding my Shama. But unlike an atom where the electron moves around a central nucleus, here Shama was the nucleus of my love, and I had been roaming like an electron in a far off orbital, always craving and desiring that with my achievements and career growth, I may become capable enough to gain entry into the innermost orbital, close to my Shama; and that one day, I may lose all my nomadic proclivities and unite forever with the nucleus of my love—my

Shama. I don't know why that day I felt a very strange inner rumbling as if Shama was calling me; as if she wanted to tell me something before I left for Raipur. On that day, after a long time, my sixth sense indicated that, perhaps, I might have the long-coveted glimpse of my Shama. Maybe that invitation to Janakpuri was an invitation from Shama. Although, Shama had always been pervading my thought process, I was getting illusions. There was certainly a very high probability!

Two days just passed like that. I was very busy in making preparations for going to Raipur; discussing with many people, getting my morale boosted and also reassuring myself that everything would be all right, consoling myself that I would always have the sweet memories of Shama to help me surmount all obstacles and eventualities.

It was my last day in the office. As a send-off gesture, the office arranged a small tea party at four in the afternoon. I too thought of entertaining them and got some pastries from Connaught Place. Mr Rangarao said some good words and wished me all the best in life. Two other staff members spoke; and they spoke with heavy hearts about my leaving them so early. The moment was overwhelming and touching. When I proceeded to finally take leave, I bowed and touched the feet of all the seniors. They were not prepared for such a gesture from my side. But that is how I am. I have imbibed those values from my parents. I never felt that such an act would belittle my stature. I had always learnt that one should remain humble.

I returned home early in the evening. All of us were exultant. We were going to attend a marriage function. I was dressed in my favourite brown corduroy trousers with a matching suede jacket, time and again appraising my wavy bouffant hair in the mirror. Our faces were radiant, reflecting our inner happiness. We, a middle-class family, had something to flaunt now: my achievements along with my prime youth and personality were enough to project me as an eligible bachelor.

We reached the venue at around eight. It didn't take us long to trace the community centre of B block. It was quite large and had two big marriage halls. The marriage season was in full swing. Though at that moment both the halls were well-decorated, there was only one floral signboard that read '*MINU weds RAVI*'. It tallied with the details of our invitation card. Huge tables covered with white cloth had been laid out in the hall and many chairs lined up in its centre and around the walls. The floor was nicely carpeted. The venue was embellished with lovely colourful lights. Garlands of fresh flowers: rose, marigold and jasmine were galore; their varied scents wafting, lending heavenly freshness to the ambience. A Cassette player with powerful speakers was playing numbers from the latest Hindi movies. There was gaiety, enthusiasm and fervour. We met many of our relatives. Mummy was introducing me with pride, 'My son, Rohit.'

'Oh, yes we know him; but he is all grown-up now. What is he doing?' people enquired.

'He is in a government job. But he is going to join as a Probationary Officer in the State Bank of India.'

'Wow, PO in SBI!' I must have heard at least twenty people exclaiming, sending waves of elation down my spine and tingling my nerves with joy. We got lost in conversation while enjoying the snacks. The time simply passed. Two songs from the movie *Betaab* were being played time and again.

Jab hum jawaan honge, Jaane kahan honge,
Lekin jahan honge yehi fariyaad karenge tujhe yaad karnege…

Baadal kyon barasta hai, dar kuchh aisa lagta hai,
Chamak chamak ke lapak ke ye bijli hum par gir jaayegi

Initially I was enjoying the songs. Suddenly my mind grew restless. I felt very uneasy. The lyrics and musical notes of the songs were reminding me of Shama. I was feeling suffocated. I needed fresh air. 'I am just going out for some fresh air Mummy,' I said. Then I moved out, all alone. Lost in thought, with the piercing lyrics of the song following me, causing continuous consternations in my mind and heart, I moved towards the other hall. I started appraising its decoration and lights. A fresh breeze wafted across and I felt a strange fragrance pulling me.

Far away, I saw, the bride in the other hall being escorted to the stage. And then, I felt a thud. I couldn't believe the spectacle. I rubbed my eyes, and saw again. The bride was dressed in a sparkling golden lehenga and magenta choli, ornate with filigree, artificial pearls, glass chatons and sequins, her hair black and shimmering, and her face resplendent like the sparkle of many stars. Her arms and neck were adorned with lovely jewellery. She was of medium height. But her face was oval and her eyes doe shaped and bright. For a moment it appeared as if she was Shama! But could that be so? My heart missed a beat. Something magnetic pulled me to her side. And, then at the entrance of the hall I saw another well-decorated floral signboard: '*SHAMA weds RANJEET*'.

End of the Reverie

'Oh my God!' I whispered. But still my heart didn't want to believe it. It was doubtful. After all, Shama was mine. I went a little ahead to have a clear view of the bride, and I recognised her distinct face, that innocence, that naughtiness in her eyes—she had not changed much. But in that bridal make-up she was looking very beautiful; stunning. Although, I was feeling very dejected and miserable, I still harboured doubts. But I could distinctly hear those jingles in my subconscious and musical notes of sitar in my heart. She was my heartthrob, and my heart was pining to have a full glimpse of her.

There was a constant debate going on between my heart and my mind. Is she the one? My heartthrob, the deity of my love temple, my most precious possession; but my mind didn't want to believe any of it. 'How can this be possible? Shama had to wait for me, she is mine; we had a pact. She had promised me so many times in her appearances in my dreams. I had to seek her hand for a nuptial alliance. She had to be my life partner. It is just not possible.' while I was lost in these thoughts, I heard Nalini's voice from behind. 'What are you doing here Rohit?' I turned around caught unawares and perhaps red-handed. A girl was standing beside her. 'Do you recognise her?' Nalini asked. I tried to figure out. Her face appeared familiar. I made a laboured effort, and expressed, 'No, I can't.'

'She is Shobhana, my school friend, remember? She has come here to attend her cousin Shama's marriage. Do you remember her? They were in our locality for a few months almost seven years back,' Nalini had smartly concealed and suppressed her agony and was willing me to do the same, as only a sister can.

'Oh, yes, I remember, faintly though' I replied, with an air of pretended nonchalance.

Only I knew what efforts I had made to keep up the facade. Deep within, I was devastated. All my dreams of pursuing and attaining Shama came crashing. My heart was broken; I felt for the first time how fragile hearts could be. I could hear its distinct sound. If someone had put an avuncular hand on my shoulders at that moment, I might have broken down.

'Coming for dinner? We are getting late,' Nalini prompted.

'Oh, yes, you proceed. I will go to the washroom and come,' I replied.

Nalini vanished with Shobhana. I stood there; still, like a rock, for a while; my limbs heavy and my eyes welled up. I took out a handkerchief, and desperately wiped my cheeks, not allowing anyone to have a whiff of what I was undergoing. That fated day in June when Shama had left our locality almost seven years ago came to life. I made a last attempt to capture that image of my Shama which I had to savour forever. I saw her in all her bridal splendour with lot of passion, constantly taking care that I was not being spied upon. I wished to remain standing there for aeons and epochs waiting for that one incarnation when I would get the companionship of my soul mate—my Shama. I had an illusion that my Red Butterfly had flown! I was just looking at her flight helplessly.

Just as I came out of the washroom, removing traces of my misery, Nalini was waiting for me. She alone knew the facts. With a few hurried words, she consoled me and helped me regain my composure.

We returned to our section of the hall. Mummy thankfully was busy conversing with a relative and our long absence had not registered with her. It was getting late. We commenced our dinner. But that night the taste of the food didn't matter to me. I ate as if in a trance, and like a machine drinking oil—without any senses.

At home, late in the night, I sobbed in my bed, all alone, for a long time. On that winter night, I must have emitted one mugful of tears, with my hand on the spot in my heart where Shama's name was deeply engraved. My heart throbbed. But there was pain. This time, the pain, compared to the one I had felt seven years back, was much intense. Seven years back, I had some hope; but now everything was lost—just everything. It was utter catastrophe. And, I was afflicted by the feeling that I lacked courage. I wondered if Shama had accepted that marital alliance happily or was it a compromise, like many marriages in India. Those were all my conjectures and surmises. But my love, though pious and divine, had failed. I don't know when I slipped into the cosy world of dreams with the radiant image of Shama in her bridal attire. She was smiling, perhaps, at me! After all, she was my soul mate!

Next morning, Nalini asked me, 'Are you all right brother? Hope you have got over the trauma. I know what you must have felt on seeing Shama. I wish I had known about her marriage earlier. I could at least have warned you. It seems to me yours was a purely one sided love story.'

I didn't say anything; but streams trickled down my cheeks.

'Brother, I understand and sympathise with you. But, seriously, you will have to forget it and start your life's journey afresh. One more thing, you must take inspiration from your pious love. And make a promise to yourself that if in your life you ever come across true love, you will honour it and accept it. At that moment never falter like you have done in this case.'

Nalini's voice broke down and she too had tears streaming down her cheeks. Her words lightened my load to some extent. I also realised that her advice was sound and mature. My little sister had grown to a little woman any man would be proud to cherish! I promised Nalini that I would keep her advice in mind to set her mind at rest. But deep down I knew what she asked of me was going to be next to impossible; I knew it was difficult to forget my Shama—my first love.

In Search of Greener Pastures

I had to catch the train for Raipur in the morning from Hazrat Nizamuddin station. Raj Mamaji stayed at our home overnight so that he could accompany me to the station. I got up early and readied myself. We left in an autorickshaw at the pre-planned time, and reached the station well in advance. I settled down in the compartment comfortably and discovered that I had good co-passengers. When only five minutes remained for the departure, I found Mummy and Nalini on the platform. It was not at all planned. I was surprised to see them. Mummy had brought along some fresh fruits, bread and parathas and passed them on to me through the window. She went on giving me instructions so that I may not face any problems. It was, after all, a mother's heart! And, I could feel its parting pangs and concern. I got up and came out of the bogie near the door. Nalini hugged me, and whispered in my ears, 'I have penned some good wishes and advice for you. Read it when you are comfortable.' While saying so she quickly pressed a small folded envelope in my hand and closed my fist. My eyes became moist, and through the misty envelope I saw them crying and waving at me. The train now started moving slowly. I got into the compartment and stood at the door, and started waving back. The train chugged, and with that Mummy and Nalini too moved a few steps, passing me instructions to take care; and then with the train gaining momentum, it became difficult for them to keep pace. Slowly they started moving away from the ken of my vision. Far away I could only see their hands in the crowd, and then those too merged in the sea of humanity at the platform. All of a sudden, I had a feeling that I had lost many things precious: the company of my mother and sister that had sustained me through all these years; and of course the irreplaceable loss of my heartthrob … my Shama. My heart felt very heavy and I could not leash in my tears when the images of Mummy, Nalini and Mamaji disappeared from my visual range.

I stood at the door waving emptily, in the faint hope that I was visible to Mummy and Nalini. Then I took out my handkerchief. The surge of emotions was profound, and I found myself in an embarrassing position. I didn't want the people around to see me in such a state. I stood there for some time and then entered the toilet. I cried there for a full five minutes. Later with the weight of emotions slightly reduced I washed my face and wiped it with a hanky.

I was eager to read Nalini's note. I quickly unfolded the paper, and started reading:

'Dear Rohit Bhaiyya,

I had seen your condition after we returned from that wedding. I love you bro and am concerned about your welfare. Let me share a secret. After our Janakpuri venture, I happened to meet Shobhana in Karol Bagh market. She had come with Shama; but at that moment Shama had gone to some other shop and she was alone. I tactfully probed her regarding Shama, on the premise of making casual enquiries. Then, after around fifteen minutes Shama too joined us. She had recognised me. From their discussions I could make out that Shama was likely to get married, and for that reason only they were on the shopping spree. Shama appeared to be excited and ebullient, seemingly awaiting the event. Although I mentioned your name, I could elicit no reaction. I could not make out whether she loved you too, despite the fact that I kept bringing up your name and your achievements. In fact she kept on telling me that she had seen you when you were working as a salesman.

Rohit, I think you were indeed chasing a mirage; it seems to me yours was purely a one sided love. Moreover you hardly ever tried to meet her to reveal your heart and your feelings for her. Here I agree it was necessary as you had to build your career and could not foolishly endanger the reputation of two families by any rash act of yours. You behaved like a boy of good breeding and as a thorough gentleman would. Maybe she was not ordained for you. But please don't let this embitter you. Don't turn your back on true love when it knocks at your door. Your heart will tell you. And God will show you the way. Please Rohit, don't think I am being precocious and despite being younger to you sermonising. But bro, you are too much of a gentleman and sometimes seem to spurn the overtures of women because of your innate decency and upbringing. Don't ask me how I know, sisters always do. They too watch over their brothers just as brothers watch over their sisters. Till now Shama was your goal, your soul mate; so not letting other girls touch your heart was right;

it was very decent on your part. But now, don't let her image chase other girls away. Keep an open mind please. I want the best for you so please, please don't misunderstand me.

Lovingly yours,

Nalini'

I ruminated over the note. Nalini was right to some extent. But thoughts of Shama were rekindled. She was my soul mate. How could I forget her?

I had a vision that Shama was standing far away in the horizon, beckoning me with her arms extended, assuring me, 'My soul mate, we shall certainly meet in some other life. It was not destined to happen in this one. But I shall remain forever in your heart, in your memory, in your psyche; we can never be separate.'

The title track of the movie *Akhiyon Ke Jharokho Se* was reverberating in my ears along with that scene from the movie and Shama singing for me:

Ankhiyo ke jharokho se, maine dekha jo sanware,
Tum door nazar aaye, badi door nazar aaye,
Band karke jharokho ko, zara baithee jo sochne,
Man me tumhi muskaye...

Now her memories alone would be my constant companion!

I came to my seat and closed my eyes.

I embarked on another journey of my life...with my aching heart.

My mind was still wandering. Just the previous day I had mentally prepared myself for going to Raipur. But when reality dawned on me, I could comprehend the enormity of the problem, the amplitude of loss and the feeling of melancholy that had now gripped me. My fellow passengers in the compartment appeared to be good, but it took me at least an hour to come out of the microcosm of my thoughts and the memories of my family standing on the platform and waving me goodbye.

'Are you going out of Delhi for the first time all by yourself,' I heard a young man of almost thirty addressing me. He was with his mother and seemed a decent person. 'No, not exactly, I have travelled earlier too all alone; but this time I am going to join a job,' I replied, trying to portray a semblance of confidence.

'Where?'

'I've been selected as a Probationary Officer in the State Bank and I am to join at the Kutchery Branch at Raipur; do you have any idea where is this Kutchery Branch?'

'Well, Kutchery means court, and this branch must be in the court premises; it is a famous place in Raipur; not difficult to locate; after all Raipur unlike Delhi is not very big; and the people are very helpful,' he replied in a reassuring tone.

Comforted by his reply, I felt encouraged to ask more. There were so many queries. I didn't want to show desperation. The journey was long and there was enough time to get other details.

'Are you from Raipur?' I asked.

'Oh no, I am from Delhi only and am working in Bhilai; I am an engineer and shall be getting down at Durg station; that is the nearest station for Bhilai,' he replied.

The word Durg sounded very banal; although from my general knowledge book I had learnt that for building the commanding heights of the economy, government had built steel plants at Durgapur, Rourkela, Bhilai and Bokaro; the first one with British, the second with German and the last two with Russian collaboration. But still the words Bhilai and Durg did not raise my spirits unlike the names Bombay or Kashmir would. 'How is Raipur?' I asked.

'Well, it's a small place. You can't compare it with Delhi,' he said. I felt depressed. But, to keep the conversation going and to understand the topography of the area, I enquired about Bhilai. 'Oh, Bhilai is beautiful and well-planned.'

'Is it like Chandigarh?' I asked expecting if I could find something like Chandigarh which had always been the city of my dreams, where I had spent my childhood.

'I would not say as beautiful, but it is planned and most of the city looks the same as you will see the houses made on the same pattern; in fact they are all part of the Bhilai Steel Plant authority and have the same design; you can say that it looks like a government colony. But its marketing complexes and other avenues are well planned. The city is green and roads are wide, there is no congestion at all. You get all the facilities which a modern city should have; there are good educational institutions–schools, colleges and institutes,' he enlightened me.

'Don't you feel like leaving Bhilai and going back to Delhi?'

'Why? I have already been here for the past eight years and am well settled; I have got my job, my colleagues and my home here only; once in a while I go to meet my relatives.'

I felt embarrassed at having asked such a question.

'Once you start living in a particular place you start adapting to the situations and liking it. After all the whole of India is ours,' a tall, elegant Sikh gentleman in his late twenties interjected.

I felt those words very encouraging. It crossed my mind that army personnel too have to leave the cosiness of their native lands and have to work in difficult terrains and inclement environs, just because they are imbued with the spirit of patriotism, for defending their motherland and countrymen.

As I had got over my initial reservations, I asked them, 'Which would be a good hotel near the station at reasonable rates? Are there good places for food around?'

'Oh, there are so many. You don't have to worry much. Since you are a Punjabi, you can go to one Satkar. It is safe and quite reasonable. And, North Indian food is served at almost all the places.' The name Satkar appealed to me and also registered in my mind. With such assurances and facile conversation, the journey became easier; and I didn't realise till Durg station came the next morning. The engineer got down with his mother. Now I was left with that Sikh gentleman and waited for my destination–Raipur. Reaching Raipur, I alighted from the train, very much wary of the fact that I was new to the place. Soon, I was surrounded by a few coolies; I became circumspect whom to trust. Mummy had advised me not to pay people whatever they asked as it would indicate that I was a simpleton and also flush with money. I had to tread cautiously, and portray that I valued money. I bargained with them to settle at some reasonable and fair sum. I had three pieces of baggage: one bed roll, one large hand bag and one suitcase. As my money, certificates and traveller's cheques were in my suitcase, I preferred to carry the same myself and told the coolie to pick up the bag and the bed roll. We walked some twenty steps on the platform till we reached the exit gate. 'Ticket please,' I was accosted by the TTE at the gate. I stopped to take out the ticket which I had securely kept in my front shirt pocket. It took me some time to take out the ticket as I was obstructed by the tightness of my sweater. In the process I became totally oblivious to that coolie's trail. Once finished with the TTE, I looked around. But, goodness gracious! The coolie was nowhere in sight! I became nervous and panicky. I went out, but couldn't find him. Then I went back to the platform, but in vain. My mind got bombarded by stray thoughts, 'What if I don't find that coolie? Most of my clothes, chappals and another pair of shoes were in the bag and the bed roll. I will be in an utterly hopeless position with my baggage lost.' I felt like crying. At that time I saw that Sikh passenger.

'What happened? Are you waiting for something?' he asked.

'No nothing … nothing,' I tried to hide my embarrassment.

I thought, *'If that gentleman comes to know about my loss, he will laugh and may think that the man who is going to join as an officer in the State Bank is so irresponsible that he can't even take care of his luggage!'*

After the gentleman left, I came out of the station wondering what I should do. 'Should I report the matter to the police and see what comes out or should I forget the loss and move ahead?' I closed my eyes for a moment in contemplation, remembering God. I thought of going out and hailing a rickshaw. While passing through the narrow corridor, my mind made up, to my utter surprise, I saw that coolie standing with my bag and bed roll with a very innocent smile on his face.

'Where were you sahib? I've been waiting for you for ten minutes. I could have got another passenger after finishing with you, but now it doesn't seem possible,' he said, all one breath.

Bewildered; yes bewildered I was. But I kept my face expressionless and pretended as if everything had been normal. 'Oh that TTE took time. I thought you would wait for me there; but you came out faster;

you were perhaps in a hurry to get another passenger; hard luck. But don't worry I will partly compensate you for that loss,' I told him in a composed manner.

I thanked God for his benevolence, and also felt good that in such an unknown place my first encounter was not bad. I had found an honest coolie. The worries that I had harboured a few moments ago evaporated. Instead I felt a soothing assurance that my mother's blessings were with me; that I had the protective cover of God. The coolie dropped my luggage near the rickshaw-stand, and also fixed a rickshaw at a reasonable rate. I paid him some amount over and above what had been decided earlier. But deep in my heart I was full of gratitude for him. I patted him on his back with affection as I had seen my father doing quite often. The coolie returned a simple smile.

First Impressions

Having recovered from the initial hiccups, I reached hotel Satkar in ten minutes. The first impression of Raipur was not very encouraging. The city appeared dull and dirty, with narrow roads; like the surroundings of Pahar Ganj side of New Delhi Railway Station. The faces of the people around totally lacked appeal. They appeared tired and frail. Perhaps I was yet to encounter the better gentry of Raipur. I found shops lined without much attraction and glamour, mostly selling goods of day to day needs: cycle shops, tea stalls, sweet shops and a number of small shops selling paan, bidi and cigarettes. The body language of the people in the market and those slouching on the road was languid; no urgency at all as if they had all the time in the world. Unlike Delhi, the weather despite the second week of December was not cold.

The hotel was of medium range. At the reception, I was greeted by one Sardarji. It comforted me. So there are some Punjabis too in this city. I heaved a sigh of relief. 'I need a single room without any attached bathroom or toilet facility. What is the rent?' I enquired. '₹15 per day,' said the receptionist. For me ₹15 per day was a princely sum in an unknown place when I would be getting my salary after one month and the amount brought along with was too little. But I had to take it. One attendant took my luggage and ushered me into a small room with one bed and a chair. I appraised the room, mulled over my overall position and felt very lonely and low. Somehow, I collected myself and proceeded for cleaning my system, shaving and ablution. I even washed my clothes and spread them around at a place suggested by the attendant. I got ready in my favourite attire: blue denim jeans, light pink shirt and light brown suede jacket. I wore black half boots. I was well aware that I looked good in that dress. I knew that despite my wiry frame of 5 feet and 10 inches, weighing merely 65 kilos, I had a proportionate physique: tall and straight. My gait had elegance; though on occasions bordering on haughtiness.

Half-heartedly I filled myself with some bread and jam that Mummy had thrust into my hands while boarding the train. Though I was required to join the Bank on 9th December, i.e. the next day, I decided to visit it that day itself to have a fair idea of the route, the location and the set-up of the bank. I hailed a cycle-rickshaw.

On the way, after almost ten minutes of drive, the road became less congested and even the area around was quite spacious. The city, however, resembled a small town like Rohtak which I had visited on a number of occasions in the past. The more I saw, the more depressed I felt. Then I consoled myself, 'I am here to just gain some experience and enjoy an officer level post which people crave for. I will be here for another three to four months, and once I get the call from the government on the basis of my first attempt I would leave the bank and this place too.' With such thoughts I passed by a medical college on the way followed by another significant building—the Raipur Jail. Then I reached the Court or the Kutchery. I looked for the SBI branch inside but was guided by people to go to the opposite side. The rickshaw stopped in front of a building which was neither shabby nor appealing. 'State Bank of India, Kutchery Branch' was written prominently in Royal Blue Colour against white background on a big board on its front. And, it also had the big logo of SBI of the same hue. I got off the rickshaw and after paying the fare, entered the compound through missing gates. The compound had barren ground without any layer of cement; no trees nor any grass; a cow was ruminating beside a window of the main building and there were some puddles of water too. It was totally unglamorous; in stark contrast to the Local Head Office building at the Parliament Street, New Delhi where I had been interviewed. Whatever little enthusiasm I had harboured, ebbed. With heavy steps I entered the building and found: lot of people; lot of activity; everybody busy in work. It was unlike the scene on the road where things had appeared to be moving at a snail's pace. I found myself in the front portion of a big hall with a continuous row of counters and staff manning them. They were all dealing with the public. At one point the counters ended and there was entry to the inner flank. I entered through that and found to my left a large wooden and glass chamber of the Branch Manager. But the option of straightaway meeting the Manager appeared too intimidating. I was in a fix: whom to approach? As I moved ahead inside, I found a few desks where the staff were not surrounded by public. I looked around and then spotted; bent on a desk beside a pillar, one female figure clad in a brick red saree. My feeling of desolation was momentarily replaced by naughtiness.

I moved to the lady who appeared to be the only lady amongst the whole staff. 'Excuse me, I have been selected as Probationary Officer in this bank and am supposed to join tomorrow. I am new to the city and do not know anyone. Whom should I contact? Can you guide me?' I rattled off. The lady, who appeared older than me, was befuddled by such fast speech and the appearance of a total stranger. She couldn't understand my purpose, and pointed towards a young colleague sitting next to her. Then I faced that boyish colleague. I thought perhaps the lady and other people were not much comfortable in conversing in or understanding English. I repeated my question in Hindi. The young boy was equally flummoxed by my presence. He, however, regained his composure and said that he would take me to the proper officer. I was taken to one Mr Shukla, a very amiable person. I again introduced myself. Shuklaji immediately struck a resonant chord and took it upon himself the task of introducing me to the entire branch. I was taken around to almost thirty officers and staff. I felt comfortable. There were a number of sections handling different items of work that sounded all Latin and Greek to me. I could get only half of their names and very little of their job profile. Then I was introduced to the ladies: one handling issuance of 'Demand Drafts' and another 'Transfer scroll'. Finally it was the turn to meet the lady who was the first one I had encountered in the branch. I learnt that her name was Mitali and that she too had joined that branch a few days back. In fact Mr Shukla too had not met her earlier. From close quarters she looked younger than what I had thought earlier. The reason of the earlier impression was perhaps her wearing that saree which in North India only married ladies used to wear. She appeared charming: with beautiful shapely eyes; long jet black hair and good complexion but not very impressive as per my experiences in North India. Social dignity prevented me from looking at her for more than the reasonable duration.

Then I was taken to the Branch Manager, Mr Ganeshan who was a Tamilian, with a wide forehead and neatly backcombed salt and pepper hair. He would have been around forty-five. His visage had a glow of contentment, peace, and control. He was coolly chewing paan. I was put at ease by his affable demeanour and it also reduced my depression.

'So you hail from Delhi. What does your father do? How many family members? How far have you studied? Have you come out of Delhi for the first time? Don't worry, you are safe. It is an enjoyable job. Don't be anxious about your stay. All things shall be taken care of. That Hotel Satkar is not very good. You can shift to another Hotel,' Mr Ganeshan went on, 'You know one more probationer, Raghavan, will be joining tomorrow. He came to the branch yesterday.'

The prospect of company lifted my sagging spirits. I also learnt that there were two other officers in the Branch who were from the Probationary Officers' channel of direct recruitment. One Mr Malhotra was the Manager in-charge of loans, advances and small business finances; another Mr Anthony was a Field officer under him. 'So things are not as bad as I had imagined,' I said to myself. I was introduced to one Mr Ashok, the Head Clerk who possessed an Engineering degree. Such information further assuaged my apprehensions. Now my main concern was to get another accommodation as ₹15 per day for a hotel room was too prohibitive. Mr Shukla assured me, 'Don't worry. Some arrangement will be made.'

I decided to proceed to meet my father's colleague in Shankar Nagar. After taking necessary directions from Mr Shukla regarding the location, I boarded a rickshaw. Another twenty minutes and I was in Shankar Nagar. It was a neat and clean area unlike the chaos, congestion, and filth at other places I had seen thus far. After seeing a board which indicated the possibility of the number I was searching for, I abandoned the rickshaw and started on foot. But that was a mirage as the house number was not visible. I kept on walking in the broad sunshine for almost thirty minutes enquiring in between, but the search became tedious and agonising. I was hungry and sad, almost in tears. Then all of a sudden I could see the Board of the 'Regional Office of the Planning Commission' at the second floor of a building at the rear entry. My eyes moistened and heart was agog. I hastened and in no time was in the office. The Regional Project Evaluation Officer, Mr Khandelwal, appeared to be a familiar face and he could recognise me as I bore a lot of resemblance to my father. Still the encounter was not such as would evoke some sense of comfort.

'Have you had lunch?'

'No, I didn't find time as I had been searching for your office.'

'Oh I see.' Khandelwal said and cleverly swept aside the issue with the rings of smoke rising from his cigarette. 'Have some tea.'

Tea was laboriously made by his office peon over a dim electric heater, and was served with two biscuits. I craved for more but was restrained by the norms of decency. Khandelwal had a long chat with me but did not evince much interest in helping me to find an affordable accommodation. Although he was kind enough to give a suggestion of getting sumptuous meals at ₹6 a thali at Geeta Bhojnalaya—a small eating joint in the vicinity of Hotel Satkar.

I thanked him and moved out, sure in my mind that I would never meet Khandelwal again. I boarded a rickshaw for my hotel. On the way I looked around insouciantly: the traffic and the people moving on the road. Suddenly, two young girls passed by, giving amused and appreciative glances, whispering something to each other, dropping all the hints that I was a good specimen. I felt elated. I gave a restrained and lazy smile and went on.

After reaching my hotel, I picked up my washed clothes that had dried up in the warm and dry weather of Raipur and to my relief had stayed put there safely. I took two slices of bread with jam and then sat aimlessly surrounded by incessant thoughts crowding my mind. Two hours I spent in that condition were like aeons. Memories of my family and the images of my past played like a motion picture. With hunger pangs becoming unbearable, I came out for dinner at 8:30. My hunt for Geeta Bhojanalaya succeeded after a few enquiries. It operated from a house. I ordered a thali and waited with my rumbling, hungry stomach. Luckily it arrived in five minutes comprising rotis, two vegetables dishes, dal, curd, some salad, pickles and sweet kheer. It was the most sumptuous, homely and delicious food I had since my departure from Delhi. In my heart I thanked the cook. Since it was unlimited, I ate like a glutton—like a camel who could store water and food in his stomach, unsure when he would find the next oasis in the desert.

I was tempted to buy a sweet paan from a nearby paan vendor. He, a young man of around twenty, was also chewing a paan, with a

Hindi film song from the movie *Taqdir ka Badshah*, playing from the radio. With the paan melting gradually under the action of the saliva, the melody of the song soothing my nerves and pleasing my heart, I was reminded of an old adage: '*Happiness is just a state of mind*'. Far removed from my native place, away from my family's protective fold, in a totally unknown terrain, I felt at ease and without much effort on my part—happy. My future there being uncertain and shrouded in mystery, my mind and heart apprehensive; yet for a moment there was a spark of hope; of the company of another probationer in the bank.

On my return to the hotel, I hit the bed weary and drowsy from the day's exertions, I remembered my parents and Nalini—and as always I remembered Shama whose thoughts were always a glimmer of solace ... slowly I retreated into my world of dreams—dreams of Shama beside me, smiling at me with the same innocence and sparkle that had got etched deep into my mind almost seven years ago.

The warble of sparrows woke me up at dawn. I got ready in no time. But the bank was to start at eleven. I used the intervening period to catch up on my reading. Around ten I came out with all the relevant papers, went to Geeta Bhojanalaya and ordered for meals as that would sustain me for a long period. Again filling myself to the brim I embarked on the journey afoot. The benefits were twin as I would be saving the rickshaw fare besides getting a clear idea of the city's topography.

I could reach the bank in exactly half an hour. I met Mr Shukla and the Branch Manager who gave me a warm welcome and introduced me to Raghavan, my fellow probationer, a Tamilian. He appeared to be simple and friendly. After completion of formalities of joining, the Branch Manager asked Mr Shukla, to take us around in the branch for familiarising ourselves with the staff and the work. The process of introduction started again but now it involved Raghavan too. For me all the introductions were perfunctory, except Mitali's. I got an opportunity of looking at her from close quarters. She had a charming smile. *Another source of interest for sustenance in that mundane city and the bank!*

In the afternoon Raghavan took me for lunch to the Indian Coffee House; it was going to be an important place for me. There I was introduced to two other probationers, Ram Mohan and Balasubramaniam, who were a batch senior to us and were also Tamilians. They were posted at the Main Branch of SBI. For the first time in my life, I had South Indian style meals served in a thali comprising rasam, rice, various chutneys, some vegetables, sambar and some rotis. It was so different! I had decided to forgo lunch, but the prospect of budding friendship made me change my decision as it would reduce my sense of loneliness.

'You know, before coming to Raipur, I had asked a couple of friends about the places for boarding and lodging; Being a South Indian I had to make special efforts,' said Raghavan while slurping rasam, 'luckily I have met a few South Indian friends here.' Though I didn't like the meals very much, I decided that I should try to get accustomed to all kinds of food.

Raghavan told me that he was staying in Hotel Natraj in the Tatyapara area, and in the opinion of the bank officers and staff it was a better place. Though I was entitled to stay at Satkar for half a day more, Raghavan's company was tempting. I decided to shift in with Raghavan. In the evening Raghavan accompanied me to Satkar. I settled the dues and packed my things and we got on to a rickshaw with my luggage. It was an amazing sight: we were chatting animatedly while my bags were dancing to the vacillations and vibrations of the rickshaw; we had to hold the side bars firmly as our bodies too were acquiring the undulations with every possibility of our being catapulted onto the road in the eventuality of the rickshaw encountering a bump. However, we managed to reach Hotel Natraj in one piece!

The three storeyed Natraj hotel, located along the wide Grand Eastern Road leading to Bhilai, with its well illuminated facade, appeared majestic. But, such grandeur was illusory as I discovered on gaining entry into the rooms. In upkeep and maintenance it left a lot to be desired. Raghavan, after some deliberations with the receptionist, managed to get a double room. I helped him in shifting our luggage and belongings. The room was atypical; as every average room in a hotel in Indian cities, low on aesthetics or cleanliness. However I heaved a heavy sigh of relief as I would not be alone during my stay in those dull locales.

⊸o⊷

Life in Raipur slowly followed a set routine. The Kutchery branch's timings were eleven in the morning to six in the evening. We were supposed to be there fifteen minutes before opening time. Public hours were till three in the afternoon. It mostly handled government accounts, government salaries and pensioner's accounts. We would start from our hotel at nine thirty in the morning walking, and after breakfasting at the Indian Coffee House on the way, would reach the bank in the nick of time. South Indian dishes like idli, vada, dosa, etc. which were delicacies for occasional consumption in Delhi, became the staple diet. I also started liking the aroma of hot coffee.

We were initially posted to the introductory counter which besides being the information desk also handled Recurring Deposits and Gift Cheques. Slowly, we graduated to Savings Accounts and Current Accounts counters. We were trainees, so we had to only learn the work under the able guidance of experienced staff. But in a few days we picked up the work and started manning those counters independently. And, we would realise soon that although training policy desired our exposure to all the sections, we would be used as per the expediency.

In the span of four days I got introduced to a few other persons, mostly Tamilians, through Raghavan. Bala and Ram Mohan were staying together at Tatyapara in Mr Bakshi's house, an officer working in the Main Branch. He used to let out a two room accommodation along with attached bath and toilet in his own big kothi to Probationers who would come to Raipur for a few months in various phases of their training. It was close to Natraj hotel. Bala had earlier been working in the Ministry of External Affairs as a Section Officer.

'Sir, why did you leave that job for the SBI?'I asked him out of curiosity. Bala moved his hand thoughtfully over his face and said, 'For a dynamic life in the bank.' Bala would be mostly engrossed in tomes of Robert Ludlum. *How people could read such big novels!* I would marvel.

I got introduced to Hariharan and Jayaraman who were in clerical cadre in the Andhra bank. They were quite affectionate. Over a period of time there was more affinity between Hariharan and I; and Raghavan and Jayaraman. And then I also met one Delhite, Kishore. He was a PO in Oriental Bank of Commerce. He was tall and handsome with a very pleasing personality. All of us, in Raipur, far away from our native places, formed a wonderful group replete with bonhomie.

Raghavan was a moody person and a voracious reader. He would always be absorbed in some book, magazine or newspaper. Raghavan's company taught me that reading should not merely be only for academic excellence or for getting a job; that one should read widely and extensively for one's evolution and personal growth. Raghavan was an idealist and a great fan of Arun Shourie, who had earned a good name in investigative journalism, and would quote him quite often, 'Arun Shourie says that in this country we only worship mediocrity; we only go on with "all is well syndrome" and no one tries to change things. He says that to bring about change someone has to bell the cat.' We would discuss many things: the injustices in the society e.g. how a rickshaw puller does not get enough to even replenish the energy he expends while ferrying able bodied, calorie laden people; the all pervasive inequalities in the society and country's lop sided development.

One day Hariharan brought one cricket set, presented by one of his customers. And a little fun with the kit on the first day made it our regular affair though with all improvisations, unorthodox approach and unconventional rules. Almost every evening we would play on the terrace of their two room top floor rented house in the main market area, near Sharda Cinema Hall. We would play with a tennis ball with the wall as wickets. Only slow spin bowling was allowed. To add spice to the whole affair, Hariharan would bat while wearing a lungi. Howsoever, one may try to beat him, Hariharan's third line of defence, his lungi, besides his bat and pads, would come to his rescue. His tantrums would make everyone laugh. Raghavan would spin the ball dragging Hariharan out of the crease and getting the ball around his legs and lungi to hit the leg stump. It would be fun to get him out!

Winter in Raipur was like autumn in Delhi: mildly cold nights with pleasant days. We would move around in trousers and shirt, no woollens. We slowly became popular in the Bank as we mingled with people of all hierarchy and also for our dedication, vigour, energy and enthusiasm. Together we would promptly take the customers' requests: for posting of cheques or passbook entries; providing whatever information they desired about their accounts or balances. We would, without wasting our time, finish our work fast; and, then push off even before the normal time of 6:00 pm for that eagerly awaited game of cricket or for outings. During a short span of three weeks we had seen four movies, eaten at almost all the big restaurants in Raipur, savouring various types of food, and also visited the houses of many of the bank staff as well as some other people known to Hariharan, Jayaraman and Kishore. In a place like Raipur of those days, I was relishing life somehow.

The first pay cheque brought smiles on our faces and happiness in our hearts. Besides, the Branch Manager broke the wonderful news, 'You guys have to go for an Orientation Programme to SBI's Staff College at Hyderabad and later to some Staff Training Centre for Induction Programme in the second week of January. You can apply for advance for booking the tickets and for meeting the incidental expenditure.' It was party time; that day we had a delicious and sumptuous dinner in an upscale restaurant of one of the finest hotels of Raipur, Girnar.

In the silence of night, while in bed, melancholy would envelop me: I would miss my family and crave for being in Delhi with them. I would muse, 'I got the life of a Probationary Officer but at what cost? I am so far away from my people, with no contact and only letters.' Time was a major factor with letters. Each letter to and from my mother or sister would take at least three to four days. Similar exchange was with my father till one day …

31st December was the Bank's annual closing day, a holiday for customers. Bank staff was to settle only outstanding matters and reconciliation. In a relaxed mood, while we were at the Kutchery crossing, hotly debating some issue, I noticed a known face on the road in front of the bank. I was flabbergasted. Dressed in simple trousers and shirt, was my father, standing with an innocent face but eager eyes. For a moment I couldn't believe my eyes. I shouted, 'That's my father,' and ran and touched Papa's feet and embraced him. Papa's eyes were moist; he was exultant. But

I was a bit embarrassed, apprehensive that people might think, 'Rohit is still a child, his father has come all the way worrying about his welfare.'

'How come you are here Papa?' I asked.

'I had come up to Raigarh on tour and thought of meeting you; I didn't have any idea about your residence. So I just came straight to the bank. Your Accountant offered me tea. He too didn't know about your whereabouts, and suggested that I wait. I have kept my luggage in the bank itself.'

We went to the Accountant. He pulled me up, 'Rohit, you have not informed your papa about your local residence! You see, he was so much inconvenienced.'

'Oh, I am so sorry Sir. I never reckoned that Papa would be coming to Raipur. By the way Sir, is there work for us in the bank today?'

'No, today you people can take leave.'

I collected my father's small suitcase and a bag; but to lug that was a little awkward. From the corner of my eyes I saw Mitali busy in her work. As the main gate was closed, I had to move out from the back gate only and per force traverse the path which crossed Mitali's seat. I wondered how she would feel on seeing me thus. The best course in such a situation is to avoid eye contact. I lugged the bags moving much ahead of Papa so that she may not even know about his arrival.

We took a rickshaw, the ubiquitous vehicle of commute in Raipur. Papa got ready in an hour. We first proceeded to the Indian Coffee House for lunch. Papa enjoyed the food. He was constantly asking, 'How is everything here Rohit? Are you facing any difficulty? Are you happy in the bank?'

'It is only a temporary phase Papa; my main aim and passion remains Civil Services,' I replied.

I wanted Papa to have an enjoyable stay. So in the evening we took him to see a movie. Later we moved around in the market and then had dinner at *Girnar* hotel. In the night even the dirty and dull things look attractive and dazzling. Papa was glad to see me in such a fine position. In those times when government salaries were not very attractive, the banks were certainly paying enough for leading a good life or maybe for us bachelors, bank salary was a fortune.

At night father enquired about Raghavan's family and their lives at Chennai and also shared his own experiences at Bhubaneswar. As I had been missing my people for the last three weeks, Papa's arrival was a pleasant surprise and tonic to re-energise. Papa stayed for one more day. Next evening he also joined us for terrace cricket at Hariharan's place. It was wonderful and fun. 'I would be returning to Bhubaneswar tomorrow,' Papa said. I felt dejected but concealed my emotions.

Next day I went to see Papa off at the station. He was to go by Link Express. The weather suddenly changed and it started drizzling. 'I am very happy to see you having risen so much and so early in life. I am proud of you my son,' Papa's tone was emotional, 'I feel the bank's job is also good, and after having seen you in Raipur, I feel, I was wrong in discouraging you from joining this. Actually, now I feel that even if you are not selected for the Civil Services, you have a good status in society and I won't mind that.'

The train whistled. I touched Papa's feet, hugged him and alighted from the compartment. I stood in front of his window, putting up a brave face. When the train started moving, I also started walking along with it, waving to Papa. It gained speed. I waved one last moment, and gave in to the sentiments and emotions I had been holding back. Tears were profusely falling from my eyes. I sat down on a bench, and wept. After a few moments, when I regained my poise, I walked out.

New Cities, New Friends

Agog and apprehensive about our impending trip to Hyderabad, we kept on quizzing our seniors. 'In the Orientation programme sixty probationers from different circles are trained in one group for ten days. You are treated like a prince; you get fantastic food as in a five star hotel; you get newspaper in your room; a fellow polishes your shoes. It's like a dream. But later the three weeks' Induction programme at the Staff Training Centre is a shock as there is a steep decline in the quality of food and lodging facilities. Still, it's a life worth enjoying; later you would merely savour such moments and crave for such time,' the seniors advised.

'Hey guys, tonight you are accompanying me to a party,' Hariharan was emphatic when he visited us one late evening.

'Party! Where? Who is throwing that?' we were bewildered.

'At the residence of one of the esteemed customers of our bank,' Hariharan replied.

'Man, what we shall do there? We don't even know him. We will feel out of place.'

'If you guys are not going then I too won't, and the blame for spoiling my evening would rest squarely on you,' he expressed his annoyance …

We had to relent. I wore my light brown suede jacket, pink shirt and blue trousers. The party was in the courtyard. It was a small gathering where besides Hariharan, a few other staff from Andhra Bank had also come. They were very lively and cordial. The night was pleasant. It was a novel experience in a new place. The food was nice, but the event was not known. For us it was just another outing. And, for the first time I had the occasion to see many young ladies contrary to the notion of aridity that I had developed thus far for Raipur. I saw a few beautiful girls of my age, tastefully attired in colourful dresses, moving around to get noticed. Through my tenacious self-restraint, I ignored them. My nonchalance generated curiosity.

Every beautiful person has the inherent desire to get noticed. If one looks at him/her it is a confirmation of their looking good. It satisfies their ego. While relishing gajar ka halwa and gulab jamun, I discovered that two lovely girls, whose presence I had been ignoring, were now in my vicinity. From the corner of my eyes, I could see desperation in their faces as if they were imploring, 'spare us a glance please, at least one.' But I kept the same countenance of insouciance; though, deep in my heart, I was realising that my rigidity was too much, bordering on snobbery or haughtiness. That was not my true nature; I wished I had been introduced to those girls, and some brief conversation could have removed that uneasiness and curiosity. I, on my own, could not have taken the initiative as that would have been improper and against my self-imposed code of moral conduct.

I was wedded to the memories of Shama still, who would always remain an inseparable part of my life and psyche; howsoever I might have been away from her—in time and space … perhaps it was wrong to cling to those memories, especially now when I knew she rightfully belonged to someone else … but the heart has its own reasons and cannot always be controlled by the mind.

Just two days prior to leaving for Hyderabad, Balasubramaniam told us, 'Guys, a few officers of 1981 batch are put up in Hotel Girnar. They have completed their probation and are awaiting their permanent postings. They are very keen to meet you. They are on deputation to the main branch for balancing of ledgers. Main branch due its heavy work load has not been able to keep its ledgers balanced and has been running into arrears for almost six months.'

A day before leaving for Hyderabad we attended the dinner hosted by five such seniors at Hotel Girnar. After introductions they put us at ease completely. They encouraged us and also informed us about the prospects in the bank. They, in general, appeared to be quite happy in the Bank. After dinner we went to their rooms. The kind of rooms they were occupying amazed us. During deputation the Bank was bearing all their boarding and lodging expenses. I felt, perhaps, I had not committed any mistake by joining the Bank. They sang songs and cracked jokes; the conviviality was super; and on being coaxed to sing, I too shed my inhibitions and sang a mellifluous song. The time spent with the seniors was the harbinger of the nice time we would be having at Hyderabad.

The next day we bid goodbye to people in the Bank. After dinner we took a train for Nagpur at night and were to change to another one from there for Hyderabad. We were travelling by first class. Till that time I had travelled in first class only once, when my father had taken us to Ahmadabad and Mumbai while availing leave travel concession from his office. Thus it was thrilling. My elation at having become a PO in the SBI and earning a good salary coupled with the kind of perks the bank was offering was unbounded. Time and again when prompted I would broadcast this fact.

We reached Nagpur the next morning. The train for Hyderabad was in the evening at five thirty. That gave us an opportunity to have a feel of Nagpur. We moved around in the markets and had lunch in a good hotel–The Woodland. It was nice to see a big city after a long time since my departure from Delhi. Its high rise buildings, wide and well maintained roads, less crowd but calm and helpful people were appealing.

The train was just ten minutes late. South bound trains are generally in time as in India South is considered more disciplined and organised than North. It was my first trip down South. I had been to Bombay, Ahmadabad and Bhubaneswar earlier. At night I had South Indian food to which I had grown accustomed to since my arrival at Raipur. This time the food was tangier—portent of tangier things to come. I found people of South in the train, differently dressed; and with different habits and mannerisms. Most of them on their arrival in the train had changed to lungis and T shirts. They were loud like Punjabis and Haryanavis, totally casual and not at all bothered about lack of sophistication. Their language sounded as if a lot of stones were rattling in an empty vessel. It was a new experience altogether. Raghavan was perfectly at ease moving around in a lungi and T shirt, conversing with a few of them.

When the train reached Hyderabad quite early in the morning, it was amazing to see the station neat and clean; systematic and organised. It was easy to find an auto-rickshaw and reach the SBI Staff College. It was in a posh area—right on the main road. The entrance led us onto a sloping road inside the well-landscaped college complex, replete with trees and foliage interspersed with various residential and official blocks.

The auto took us right up to the reception. The office peons lifted our luggage. The receptionist greeted us with a warm smile, 'Welcome Sirs, room

No. 108,' and handed over the key to the peons, 'don't worry; the boys shall carry your luggage to the room, you kindly fill the details here in the register.' With the formalities completed, we strutted to the room, our heads held high and our bodies erect. The ambience and the treatment gave us an air of confidence. The boys opened the room and ushered us in. It was so nice! A well maintained room having two beds with well washed and ironed sheets and cushioned pillows, a dressing table, a study table with two chairs, and two wardrobes—well polished and made of teak. The floor was of white marble and the walls were newly painted in pastel yellow, in stark contrast to our poor room in Hotel Natraj. The bathroom had nicely tiled floor and shining steel and ceramic sanitary fittings. 'Breakfast closes at ten sirs,' the boys informed, 'we'll bring your morning tea/coffee in ten minutes.'

In ten minutes we were served hot tea in a tea pot brought in a tray along with the morning newspapers. A little later, a fellow came seeking our shoes for polishing. We got ready by nine fifteen and rushed to the dining hall for breakfast.

And, what a sumptuous breakfast it was! Lots of variety and nutritious too.

In the dining hall we got introduced to two probationers from Patna Circle. After finishing our lavish breakfast we retired to our rooms, and dozed off due to the exertions of the long journey.

At eleven thirty our bell rang. I opened the door and was greeted with a smile, 'Hi, I am Rajagopal; also from Bhopal circle; I am posted at Rajnandgaon.' He was of medium height, wheatish complexion, with good features and a very friendly disposition. He was from Kerala. We chatted for a while, and then he left saying, 'See you at lunch.' We had animated talks during lunch. Slowly the number of probationers in the Dining Hall was growing. There were young men from various states of India representing a kaleidoscope of its composite culture and diversity. They were different in appearance, complexion and regional accents as well as social and academic backgrounds.

Under the fading light of the evening the college complex with its verdure looked even more beautiful. A pleasant breeze laden with the sweet scent of flowers wafted in adding to the ambience.

At night, the Dining Hall seemed full. The television was on. It seemed almost all the participants had arrived. There were two girls too: Mohini Majumdar and Bhagyashree Aiyyar from Delhi circle. I figured out that they were sharing a table with one Sumit Mitra whom I had met in Law faculty while preparing for IAS. I wished them. At another table I found Satish Nagpal—my college mate in first year. Also I met one Randhawa who turned out to be the son of the Principal of Khalsa College where I had studied. Everyone was affable and enthusiastic while meeting new people in the arena of a prestigious institution.

Next morning in the huge lecture theatre where we reported at nine thirty, the Course Director introduced us to the Principal of the Staff College, the instructors, and other important dignitaries of the organisation. We too were asked to give our brief introductions; there was hesitation and apprehension because of the big stage and the enormous gathering. The Principal spoke, 'You have entered a prestigious organisation which has had an imperial past. SBI has a huge network of branches, in India as well as abroad. SBI has taken a lead role in the priority sector lending. Thus, as part of the bank you will be actively contributing to the nation's progress. The bank provides you excellent training, facilities and good service conditions; but you have to utilise the opportunities; as you work up the ladder, you would be suitably rewarded; your promotion channel is fixed; you have to compete amongst yourselves; no doubt there shall be cut throat competition, but the best reaches the top. So, each one of you can aspire to be the Chairman of the Bank.' *Those were powerful words articulating powerful thoughts, enough to enthuse young minds*.

In the evening, Dining Hall discussions amongst the probationers over the extravagant menu, centred on the future prospects in the SBI. At night, post dinner many of us would play badminton in the well lit open court, and would be joined by a few of the resident faculty members. Those not getting a chance would be enthusiastic spectators, clapping at good shots, long volleys and lovely drops. Others would form different groups and throng various rooms making friends and having animated discussions about their past and their future, about the places and branches they were posted and sharing their experiences of the last one month. I had never had the occasion to stay in a hostel, and now I was getting a feel of what it could have been.

In a span of five days, the camaraderie amongst the fellow probationers became exemplary irrespective of the region or state they belonged to. I was equally comfortable with boys from all states. The college became a melting pot of all cultures and regions. It was lovely!

In the evening we would visit the markets and the monuments like Char Minar, have snacks in the restaurants relishing Hyderabadi cuisine. On Sunday, there was an arranged tour by a chartered bus for the whole city including Golconda Fort, Birla Mandir and Salarjang Museum. We marvelled at the design and grandeur of the Golconda Fort especially its fantastic magical acoustic effects: one handclap at a certain point below the entrance dome could be heard at the highest point of the pavilion almost a kilometre away. Our guide told that in olden times, it was used for warning the royals in case of an attack.

In the bus a melodious song was being played from a new Hindi movie which I didn't know, but the song was very appealing:

'Tu mera jaanu hai tu mera dilbar hai,
Meri prem kahani ka, tu hero hai …'

I never knew that the song would become significant in my life in the coming days.

Days flew like birds …

Just three days before the culmination of our Orientation Programme, the Course Director announced about organising a cultural programme on the last evening. We were asked to prepare some items for the same. Bhagyashree, with whom I hardly used to talk said, 'I will present a dance number where I require a few boys; any volunteers?' I pondered for a minute. My love for music and dance made me cast aside my hesitation. 'I am willing,' I said, 'but I don't know any classical dance; I can only do free style disco.'

'Oh that would do,' she said nonchalantly, 'I only need people for company to fill the fringes, rest I will manage.' I didn't like her curt remark. But I agreed. Rajagopal too joined.

The planning started from that very night …

We were invited to the room shared by both the ladies. I found that Mohini was quiet; but Bhagyashree was ebullient and a live wire. She had a tape recorder, and one particular number in Tamil classical was being played. Bhagyashree gave us certain steps to practise and show in ten minutes. We did that; I gave enough evidence of the flexibility I possessed. In between there were two smart Punjabi boys Jatin Khanna and Inder Taneja who became little more friendly with Bhagyashree. The rehearsal took an altogether different colour. 'Oh the music is so dull and drab,' they said, 'Let us have some western number for dancing.' Now it was my moment to exhibit my forte. I danced in free steps moving my waist in smooth gyrations. Bhagyashree was bowled over and asked, 'How are you able to move your waist in such an effortless manner? Just show me again.' I blushed and danced again. Bhagyashree then told us the entire dancing plan, and Rajagopal and I felt that we would be just reduced to being side-kicks. Besides, Bhagyashree was also seeking approval of Sumit Mitra in between, 'Are my steps okay?' Sumit posed as if he was the director. We would have accepted his intrusions and his directions had they been meaningful; but his contribution was too little and his interruptions too many. Our egos were now hurt. After almost two hours of that melee, Rajagopal and I felt that it was just too much to tolerate. We decided to push off. On the way that night an idea germinated in our minds, 'Why not try a separate and independent item?' And that night we discussed its contours. We decided to dance to the popular number '*Koi yahaan aaha naache naache*' sung by the reigning Indipop queen Usha Uthup, from the movie '*Disco Dancer*'. Mithun Chakaraborty, the hero of the movie, was a rage in disco dancing in those times. We had not seen the movie. The very next evening we purchased the audio cassette from the market and played the song again and again on Rajagopal's tape recorder. For the next two hours we were deeply engrossed in the thing; our dinner that night was very fast and sparse. A call from Bhagyashree was responded with a polite no with the explanation that we were planning to have our own item. Together we first devised the dance steps on a piece of paper, and planned: how we would be covering the stage; how we would be synchronising our steps and the rhythm; the speed; the tempo; how we would start and give the finish. I wondered how the whole thing was coming out systematically. The planning was meticulous for each beat, and we animatedly discussed the actions of our hands, the movement of our feet, and the swaying of our waists.

We started rehearsals; with each take we were improving and evolving; the next day even during breakfast and lunch we were refining our steps; and by late evening a presentable version was ready. Only a few boys including Raghavan could see that. 'Amazing!' they said.

Another group was busy planning a skit; I also became a participant in a Tamil cum English song '*Surangani*' that had a Sinhalese tune. Meanwhile Bhagyashree too had prepared her item. Raghavan was to be the compere of the show.

On D day, in the evening, the show commenced before a gathering comprising all the resident Instructors, their families and all the Probationers. Raghavan was superb in compereing. The skit was very hilarious depicting the plight of a young probationer in the branch. It ended with the doleful song in the background –

'*I don't wanna any SBI. I don't wanna any SBI … Ooooooo man I wanna go … Noooooo man I wanna go … show me the way to go … home.*'

Bhagyashree looked absolutely stunning in her Bharat Natyam attire and performed with aplomb and vivacity; the twinkle of her lively eyes, the grace of her movements and her innocent face accentuated the performance.

The stage was grand and the occasion big. We were a bit nervous as our item was after Bhagyashree's performance. I was in blue jeans tucked in my half boots like a cowboy and suede light brown jacket over a sky blue shirt. Rajagopal too was similarly and smartly dressed. We reached the stage and with a slight bow wished the audience and stood erect waiting for the music to start. It started:

'*Koi yahan aha naache naache, koi yahan aha naache …*'

We covered the stage sashaying slowly, and returned to the starting point diagonally; then started the stamping of feet, pumping of arms, fluid movement of hands and simultaneous gyrations of waists to the rhythm that picked up slowly, then continued for almost five minutes and later reached a crescendo; it dipped and rose again. When the music stopped to a thunderous applause, we felt as if we had woken up from a trance. While coming down from the stage we were greeted by all the friends. Mohini even complimented me, 'You were looking very smart in your attire and you performed very well.' 'Oh thanks,' I said with a spontaneous blush. I had heard such comments from my relatives and family members earlier; but such compliments coming from a female colleague unnerved me. I was now in high spirits. A few of the instructors went to the extent of saying, 'You guys looked smart and handsome like soldiers.'

The programme ended on a very happy note. I congratulated Bhagyashree. She too was equally thrilled by our performance. Next day, a few of the instructors remarked jocularly, 'We wonder whether the bank has recruited officers or artists.'

We were split into two batches for our three weeks' Induction Programme at Staff Training Centres, Hyderabad and Calcutta. Luckily Raghavan, Rajagopal, Nagpal and I were assigned Calcutta. And, there was a magnificent surprise! Four of us belonging to Bhopal circle were permitted to fly as first class tickets were not available. Staff College straightway sanctioned the advance amount there and then! I wrote to Papa sharing my happiness.

The evening we were to board the flight was replete with excitement: all of us were to fly for the first time in our lives and that too at the bank's expenses. We had only heard of aircrafts, airhostess and the airport, and seen them only in the movies; now we would see their glamour.

We reached almost three hours in advance. After checking-in we loitered around to have a full view of the swanky airport: its large lobby, full of glass encased outlets, selling books, eatables and other wares; lovely elevators, conveyor belts, escalators and sparkling marble tiled floor; the high ceiling and elevation; the glass partitions providing the close view of the aircrafts taking off and descending at the tarmac. It was so spectacular. Smart flight pursers in chic outfits and air hostesses with shapely figures in elegant saris accentuated the ambience.

In the aircraft we were bowled over by the tastefully decorated interiors, cool air, carpeted floor, cushioned and adjustable seats. We were thrilled when the aircraft started running on the runaway, gained speed and in a few moments we were airborne. We savoured the delicious dinner served by glamorous airhostesses and pretended indifference as part of the decency drill. The aircraft reached Dum Dum Airport in two hours. A taxi brought us to STC at Alipore at 1:00 am. At the STC, we were in for a rude shock after the princely treatment at the Staff College as our room was only a few shades better than our hotel at Raipur. But there was no point in cribbing. We had to learn temperance. Raghavan kept on complaining and it took us at least fifteen minutes to be in the lap of sleep after hitting the bed. For me Shama's serene face was the best sedative and in no time I was lost in dreams …

The training session next day commenced with a lot of amusement. The instructor was a Bengali named Chatterjee with his cheeks apparently swollen. Later we learnt that they were natural. A few more days in Kolkata brought the revelation that most of the middle aged and old Bengalis had this trait giving the impression as if they had two rasogollas thrust into their mouths. So, when they would speak, it would lend them a peculiar accent. Five would be pronounced as *phive* and voucher would sound as *bhoucher*. When during the lecture the instructor said, 'The *phive* rupees *bhoucher* in the whole transaction is *bhery bhital*,' the whole class exchanged sly smiles, which after the lecture metamorphosed into huge laughter. The other instructors were Sarkar, Sen, Banerjee, Bose, etc. the surnames we would be seeing aplenty across the length and breadth of Kolkata.

Late night arrival had taken a heavy toll on our sensory systems. The casualty was our attention, resulting in loss of focus. Sleep deficit was constantly taking us to the realm of torpor and slumber, though we were trying our level best to maintain poise and keep our eyes open. But our eyes were becoming heavy making our vision bleary. 'Grogginess' would be the right word to describe our state which didn't escape the experienced and discerning eyes of Mr Chatterjee. Such a state is infectious, especially when the subject of instruction is drab and the personality and diction of the instructor vapid. The lecture sounded like a lullaby. Mr Chatterjee was not furious but amused as he also had a realistic estimate of his own potential and capability to bore. But the decorum of the class and the sanctity of the lecture and the lecturer deserved to be maintained.

Mr. Chatterjee was constrained to point out in a lighter vein, 'certain trainees in the class are succumbing to the temptation of sleep *bhich* is not desirable.'

To which we explained in all humility, 'Sir, the temptation is not because of the lecture, it is courtesy our late arrival last night.'

Mr. Chatterjee was a kind soul with innovative ideas for prescription. 'Those of you who are *pheeling* sleepy may make a small and thin roll of paper, and put it into your ears; just twirl that; *bhaaat* take care that you do not take it too deep inside lest you hurt your eardrum; you *bhould pheel* that the *pheeling* of sleepiness *bhould* disappear.'

We did try that; slowly but without any inhibition, and to our surprise did get some relief. We would be using that formula and tool quite often in future as many more lectures would be similarly dull and drab. To practise Banking under the scrutinising eyes of a bank customer is different from learning its theoretical aspects from such instructors as have lost enthusiasm in life.

The lecture was almost over, and then the trainees asked about the places of interest in Kolkata and the markets for shopping. The instructor's enthusiasm also was on full exhibition now: 'Oh yes, there are many places of interest here viz. Esplanade, Chowringhee, Garia Haat, Ras Behari Avenue, Victoria Memorial, Kali Ghat, Indian Museum, Birla Industrial and Technological Museum, Nehru Planetarium, Zoo, etc., etc.' The list was long and exciting.

The lecture was followed by lunch in the Dining Hall which compared to Hyderabad Staff College's Dining Hall looked like a roadside Dhaba with the caterers shabbily dressed and hardly observing any hygiene. The morning breakfast was okay but lunch was a torture as rotis appeared to be replicas of maps of different states of India having cooked plateaus and uncooked troughs; dal and vegetable dishes were not at all tasty though non-vegetarian food was just passable. The only saving grace was an item of sweet—some Bengali specialities like sandesh or rasogolla.

We ventured out the first evening itself and the mode of transport was the omnipresent tram. Kolkata tram was an amusing relic of the British raj. It would move at a leisurely pace almost always full; it could be stopped anywhere depending on the convenience of the passenger. It would move on the road along with other modes of transport, with mutual coordination and care. Even the people on foot were not at all intimidated by the movement of trams, and would cross the road right in front of one. There appeared to be full cordiality and camaraderie. Ballyganj, New Alipore, and Chowringhee ... In a few days we learnt about most of the stations and places.

One thing that pained me a lot was when I saw hand rickshaws that were being pulled by men instead of horses or bullocks. Men, women, and children whether of able bodies or incapacitated had no qualms about being carried in them. I always had a feeling of guilt while travelling in cycle rickshaws, but here the sight was nauseating. *Strange are the ways of mankind!*

The most striking aspect of Kolkata was the beauty, grace and elegance of its womenfolk. I had read about that in Nirad C. Choudhuri's *To live or not to live* where the prominence of sexual dimorphism prevailing in Kolkata had been emphasised; that the womenfolk were more elegant than men. We were awestruck by its stark manifestation. On the very first evening we got down at the *Ras Bihari Avenue*–and walked down the path; there were so many shops around all illuminated and shining at night; but more than the shops we were awestruck by the Bengali beauties. The ladies and girls were mostly in the traditional Indian attire i.e. sarees and very few in salwar-suits or other dresses. But the way they carried themselves with rare aplomb was remarkable; draped in sarees; dark black hair neatly tied in braids or puffs or simple ponytails; faces suave and resplendent with very little or no make-up and soft features. And, the most conspicuous were their sparkling eyes: nicely shaped, with arched brows enhancing their beauty. They would be reflecting life force and such a magnetic attraction that one could not avoid looking at them. But the norms of decorum had to be maintained; ergo, we would look at them with all casualness so as not to offend; we would pretend as if we were looking elsewhere, and that our eyes had just accidently met theirs; but in that one moment we would drink their beauties to savour later. The problem was of the abundance; but that was the solution too; as even if we missed one there would be another to behold. We marvelled at God being so benign in bestowing so much splendour on the Bengali womenfolk; compared to that God had been a little unjust with the menfolk; but perhaps that had been well compensated by the tremendous intellect God had showered on Bengali men.

Even otherwise it is said that generally women are appreciated for their good looks and modesty while men for their intellect and personality. Beauty is transient and ephemeral which vanishes with youth. Later in life men have to run the show with their intellect, wisdom, fortitude and toil; while women have to balance life with love, compassion, affection, modesty and resilience.

We were in Calcutta—the hub of art, culture and deep intellect and we were also face to face with Bengali beauty which was going to play an important role in my life too. This became a regular affair in our tenure at Calcutta: listen to the killing lectures on banking in the training centre, eat the torturing food in the dining hall and anxiously look forward to the adventurous evenings; the evenings that would carry us to important areas of tourist interest and those throbbing markets selling various wares. We would be primarily interested in clothing, we would eat the Bengali sweet delicacies like mohanbhog, rasogollas and sandesh at KC Das at Chowringhee to sate the cravings of our sweet tooth; but our eyes would imbibe the bounty of *eye tonic*. Our eyes would get tired but our hearts would ever be craving for more. It had profound impact on our psyche as that eye tonic would not generate lust but feelings of admiration for the fair sex. And, had we remained in Calcutta for a longer period, it could have led to close acquaintances, and in all probability to strong and permanent relations.

People in Calcutta also had a strange past time in Esplanade. At one place along the road there was a queer collection of interconnected rat mounds and holes covered by a huge steel mesh enclosure. There were thousands of rats–small and big–continuously moving around from one hole to another and a large gathering of people would be feeding them. Rats, I had heard were pests, and in Delhi I had seen people despising them, catching them in baits and killing them or throwing them out of their houses. But it was a peculiar sight … maybe the people were nurturing the mode of transport of Hindu God … Lord Ganesha. Strange are the ways of mankind … for which no explanation is possible.

We had the chance of watching one live show of Usha Uthup, the pop singer, who was a rage because of her fantastic ability to sing English and Hindi pop songs: it was a majestic evening where she played many hot numbers including that one of *Disco Dancer*. And, it was marvellous. We got the opportunity of seeing Kolkata audience appreciating the musical concert.

The tenure in Calcutta came to an end and one fine day we boarded the trains heading towards our respective destinations with fond memories of Calcutta, especially the beauty of its tender gender …

Raipur Again

We arrived in Raipur in the third week of February. On way to hotel Natraj, the city appeared to have become a bit warmer. And, we discovered another perceptible and obvious change: there was an increase in the number of ladies and girls all around, whether on the roads and streets or in the markets; amongst them a good percentage was appealing too. Had the onset of summer brought those beautiful creatures out of their hibernation? Perhaps, the mild winter of Raipur had kept the tender gender indoors. And now like the blooms of butterflies they were out presenting a lovely spectacle to behold and enjoy. The hangover of Calcutta instead of receding was now getting strengthened; anyway, it was good for keeping our spirits elevated, and providing an escape from an otherwise boring existence if one contrasted Raipur with our recent visits to big cities like Hyderabad and Calcutta.

We didn't find any difficulty in getting accommodation in our earlier den–Hotel Natraj. After getting ready and attired in our new apparel we arrived at the Bank to a rousing welcome. Everyone, right from the Branch Manager to the messengers, was enquiring about our training and stay. And to our surprise, the manager called us later in the afternoon to announce that we were to go again for training.

'Training!' I wondered, bemused, before the Branch Manager, in Raghavan's presence, 'We just returned from training.'

'It is an Interface session with the Manager (HRD) of the Bhopal Circle, at Bhopal Staff Training Centre; maybe they wish to meet all the probationary officers of your batch,' remarked Mr Ganeshan calmly. We had to immediately apply for advance and book the tickets as the said session at Bhopal was hardly ten days away.

The advance was applied for, and while planning bookings for Bhopal we got an idea, 'Why not take a break in between and meet our near and dear ones?' It was a godsend opportunity for us. Both of us decided to go by Chhattisgarh Express. I would be going up to Delhi while Raghavan would get down at Bhopal to go to Dewas and meet his cousin. Dewas was just four hours journey from Bhopal by bus. We planned to return after three days to Bhopal. The tickets were frantically and enthusiastically booked. We had to collect our relieving-cum-introductory letters from the branch for attending the training. But as the young clerk in the establishment section was not conversant with the work, I had to make many anxious visits. In the process, my eyes on a number of occasions met Mitali's; since my return I had not established smiling frequency with her; partly due to circumstances and partly due to my own hesitant nature. Somehow, I had not become natural with her.

Sitting in the first class compartment of the train, we were having animated discussions about our people. Raghavan said, 'My cousin and her husband like me very much, and they would be surprised to see me.' Raghavan had developed homesickness; he badly wanted to leave for Chennai. He was not enjoying the bank job and missed the company of his friends with whom he used to have regular discussions on cricket, politics and English language. On many occasions he had said, 'I wish to quit.' But I found it so disparaging and irritating. I too was not sure of remaining in the bank and considered it only as a stopover before entering the Civil Services. But I was not that resentful; I felt indebted to the bank for a well-paid job. Though I too was haunted by homesickness off and on, I was aware of the stark reality that I needed that job for a steady income, to alleviate my family's economic condition as it was difficult for my family to run two establishments.

In life very few people have the liberty of making choices; in fact the first instinct is survival; in order to fulfil the basic necessities of life one requires money, and for that a job or an occupation. Once you get a job, you start evaluating its merits and demerits; but even if one finds the job is not fulfilling one's aspirations one doesn't leave it straightaway; one waits for the opportunity to find a better and comparatively secure one.

Next day, early morning Raghavan got down at Bhopal. I had to traverse the rest of the journey of more than eleven hours alone. I killed time by reading newspapers, magazines, and in discussions with one co-passenger. One after another stations were passing: Vidisha, Gwalior, Agra, Meerut and Mathura. By the time the train approached Hazrat

Nizamuddin Station, it had grown dark. While standing at the door of my compartment, I watched the lights twinkling all along. All of a sudden an old song from the movie *Jis desh me Ganga behti hai* started echoing in my mind:

'Aaa abb laut chale ...
nain bicchhaye, bahey pasaare,
tujhko pukaare des teraa ...
aaa abb laut chale ...'

My eyes welled up. Two and a half months back I had gone from this very station, away from my family members, in search of greener pastures ... for a prestigious job!

I was dying to leave the station without waiting for a coolie. I didn't have much luggage. Swiftly, I proceeded to the exit, and in no time found an auto-rickshaw. In the waning winter, the journey back home was pleasant. I breathed in the familiar scent of Delhi!

The train of thoughts made the journey shorter as in no time I found myself guiding the driver towards my house through the lanes of my locality. The auto slowed down in front of our gate; the lights of our courtyard were on. I got down. After paying the fare, I slowly opened the gate ... I wanted to surprise them. 'Someone has come.' I heard Mummy's voice. Through the window I could see faintly a figure coming to open the door. I was dumbstruck and felt my knees becoming weak with expectation ... And, I saw Papa with his spectacles on, coming out and lifting his eyes in the dim light; his eyes gleamed and his face brightened into a wide smile.

'Rohit!' he beamed, 'you never wrote that you had any plans; what a pleasant surprise!' I hugged Papa tightly and our eyes were moist with overflowing emotions which increased when Mummy and Nalini too joined. *It was a scene every Indian family loves. It manifests deep bonds of affection; in fact the strength of these cords helps people counter and face all adversity in locales away from home as they know that they have their near ones in the world who love them so selflessly and intensely. The profoundness of such emotions cannot be matched by any material possessions ... these bonds of eternal love are worth cherishing lifelong.*

Next few hours, followed by dinner were of non-stop conversation … we had so much to share. The main focus was my welfare. Even though I had kept them posted all along through my love-laden epistles, the face to face chat had to be profound. They updated me about developments at Delhi. Papa was likely to be transferred shortly to Ludhiana, in Punjab; just six hours' journey from Delhi. He would be able to come home every week.

So engrossed were we in our conversation that only the watchman's nightly laathi knock made us realise that it was time to sleep. It was an unending spell of fun, unbounded flow of love and sharing. After a long time I slept beside my parents and woke with that warm and cosy feeling fresh in the morning. After my daily morning routine and bath, I was served sumptuous breakfast of *alu paratha* with butter and pickles—all deliciously made by Mummy and Nalini; garnished with deep affection of my parents who looked at me dotingly while I ate. I had missed that for a long time despite having feasted on rich food of many good hotels.

I proceeded to Om Mamaji's house to meet my cousins, especially Neelima. I found them basking in the sunshine on their terrace. I touched my mamaji's and mamiji's feet; they embraced me and kissed my forehead. My cousins Neelima, Neerja and Shailja were ecstatic and hugged me. It was a beautiful moment. Neelima recounted and praised my elaborate missive that I had crafted while attending one of the boring lectures at Calcutta. I had described therein my experiences at Raipur, Hyderabad and Calcutta; my emotional and mental state, including the blissful experience of my maiden flight … We had unending animated conversation; going down the memory lane and recollecting the irony of fate–aspiring to become doctors and ending up as bankers. Neelima although having a Master's degree in Zoology was working as a clerk in a nearby branch of SBI at Model town.

'I am on a paid Leave Travel Concession in my probation period,' I chuckled, 'let us hope that I get selected this year in the Civil Services; then I can say goodbye to the bank' my tone was expectant and jubilant. I could see mixed expressions on Neelima's visage.

Then they took me inside and asked, 'Have you heard of this new song?' And, in no time, the cassette player started playing the mellifluous song from the movie Hero:

'Tu mera jaanu hai, tu mera dilbar hai,
meri prem kahani ka tu hero hai;
par prem granth ke panno par,
apni takdir to zero hai ...'

'I have heard the song and seen the movie too, in Calcutta' I said. The song somehow filled me with strange vibrations and feelings!

'This is not fair Rohit; despite having succeeded in so many exams and now a PO in SBI, still you have not given us any treat. Why are you such a miser,' Neelima remarked.

'Oh, when have I refused? Tell me when. I am always ready,' I said defensively.

'Okay, tomorrow. Let's all go to Connaught Place and have fun.'

Next day we took a bus as planned. We first visited Hanuman temple to pay obeisance to God for the fortune bestowed on us. We moved around in Palika Bazaar where I purchased a nice dress for Nalini. Sona Rupa–a South Indian eating joint was our choice for lunch. We ordered dosas and idlis, a staple breakfast diet for South Indians but a fad for North Indians. It was sumptuous and the chefs had a nice and innovative way of cooking it. The chefs would toss it from the griddle to another work station, where other workers would put it in the plate with all the accompaniments. The bearers would then serve it with all refinement. After relishing those dosas and idlis, we hung around at Janpath, surfing for cheap ready-made materials and even to the Tibetan market. Twilight was approaching slowly and the dwindling natural light was gradually being replaced by beautiful artificial lights spread all over, even showering glints and resplendence on the trees and vegetation around. In the Central Park there was the soothing sound of fountains with jet-streams of water falling on the waterproof lights at the base that imparted multiple bright hues to rising and falling streams. It was a sight worth beholding. Having walked around for an hour we thought of having ice-creams at the Standard's Kwality restaurant. Our joy and conviviality was tremendous and our spirits high. It was real celebration with my kin and kith.

I reminisced those tough times when I used to roam about in Connaught Place scouting various offices and confronting perfect strangers for selling those duplicating machines, sometimes with enthusiasm and sometimes with deep depression; those were the hard times when I would go on foot in the scorching and perspiring summer but with a firm resolve to get a good job. Now, I had come a long way; just in the span of two and a half years! Although not too rich but now I could open my wallet with confidence and didn't have to think too much for satisfying my palate or for sartorial indulgence or for splurging on movies or local jaunts.

While returning by bus, seated beside Neelima I expressed, 'Neelima, I have such a good job; hopefully things will improve in future. But, so far away, really I miss you all.'

'Rohit, we miss you too. Our childhood was so enjoyable. We attain so much in life but we lose our childhood. We wish your early return.'

My parent's marriage anniversary was on 1st March, the day I had to depart. We didn't celebrate much except that we cut a cake late afternoon. I left home at 5:30 pm. My parting turned out to be very emotional as I had returned after a long time and was leaving too soon. I left with a heavy heart. While moving in the auto-rickshaw I could not control my tears; but sensing that the driver might see my burst of emotions in the rear view mirror, I hid my face in the handkerchief, wiping my cheeks and eyes, pretending that I was avoiding the onslaught of wind.

In the train I was again smitten by the same sense of homesickness and the pangs of parting; but there was no choice, and I had to move ahead. I had to become realistic and practical. The night's spell enveloped me in cosy slumber bringing the ever sweet memories of Shama, and I woke up next morning at 5:30 to the din and bustle that announced the arrival of Bhopal.

It was a fresh morning, and in no time I was at the Capitol Lodge–a cheap and convenient hotel near the station, not very far from SBI's Staff Training Centre, Jehangirabad. Having reached so early gave me ample time to get ready, have a good breakfast, and reach the STC well in time. It was an opportunity for new probationers of Bhopal circle to get acquainted with their batchmates. It was an 'Interface Session' where the stage was stolen by one smart and articulate batchmate of ours–Sreenivasan Narasiah. He highlighted the apprehensions regarding postings, perks, job security and the powers of the probationers.

The Manager HRD boosted our morale, 'Be optimistic friends; and brace up for the challenges ahead. The bank infuses fresh blood so that youngsters with their innovative and fresh ideas give a new direction to the policy and implementation strategy of the bank.'

The session was over and we dispersed for lunch.

It was my first exposure to Bhopal. It was far advanced than Raipur; very green and with a lake right in the heart of the city. There were bustling markets, good hotels and eating joints. Most of us started harbouring wishes of getting a posting there. It became a place to be coveted and competed as the city had glamour which other places lacked; besides being the capital it was also the best connected by superfast trains between Delhi and the South.

We left for Raipur in the evening. Our train reached Raipur at 10:00 am the next day. We got ready, gulped our breakfast and reached the bank almost an hour and a half later than the scheduled time. Our colleagues were happy to see us return.

Life now followed the same old routine: hotel to branch, branch to hotel, meet Hariharan, have dinner, stroll at night and then retire to bed. In between we would occasionally see a movie. The weather started getting hotter, and the month of March compared to Delhi, was scorching. Since our return to Raipur, we found our expenses getting escalated as the hotel room rent, despite the twin-sharing basis, was costly.

'Why don't you take that house offered by Mr Bakshi,' advised Hariharan, 'Bala and Ram Mohan have vacated it.'

We had seen that earlier, and now with full four months of stay remaining at Raipur, the rented accommodation appeared to be an economical option.

We shifted in the middle of March. Though our privacy was restricted a bit, the place was better and neater. Mr Bakshi had two young daughters, and one son. His daughters and son would be mostly out in their huge courtyard along with their mother, while Mr Bakshi when at home would be sitting on a swing settled right in front of their drawing room. The courtyard spanned almost 100 feet from the main gate to the entry point of our respective portions. We had been provided a double bed, a table and chair. Water was a bit of a problem as we had to fetch two to three buckets from the hand-pump installed in the backyard. Being a residential locality, the surroundings had an environment suited for families.

I used to take the morning tea served in the bank. One day while working, I felt something flowing from my nose, and when it trickled down, I discovered a few drops of blood. During the hot summer of Delhi, mid April onwards, I used to have the problem of epistaxis i.e. nasal bleeding. But, in the extreme heat of March in Raipur, the problem manifested earlier. I gave up tea. It became a butt of jokes for the people around.

The routine life and the absence of family members started affecting us after a few days. Raghavan was more vocal about it. Raghavan started visiting Bhilai to be with one of his friends who had joined as a management trainee in Bhilai Steel Plant. Bhilai was hardly an hour's journey by bus. He also got the company of a clerk of our branch who used to commute regularly from Bhilai. I felt lonely, and the problem accentuated when I saw the results of Civil Services Exam, 1983 in the newspaper. I didn't qualify. It was totally unexpected.

What had life in store for me? Would I have to stay in SBI only? I was not sure whether I would be joining the Group B post that I would be getting on the basis of my first attempt in Civil Services as my fellow probationers and few seniors had inculcated the notion that a Bank PO's job was better than a Group B post. I had filled up the application form for the third attempt before leaving for Hyderabad and now I would have to give it my best shot. '*How life changes in a matter of days and months!*' I wondered. The preliminary exam was almost three months away, and I didn't foresee any problem in clearing the same.

Strange Stirrings

Something was changing subtly. I would move around in the branch in apparent abandon but was always conscious of Mitali. The moment I would enter, till the time I would reach my counter or when I would go to the washroom or move to any place in the branch, I would be haunted by this unmistakable feeling that she was watching me. I dismissed that feeling as a product of youth. But coming to love, I loved only Shama; even if she couldn't be mine in this life. My subconscious mind was deeply under Shama's influence; her strong charm was profoundly ingrained in my psyche, and everything else was just illusion … and to some extent entertainment for the bored and tired mind … seeking some relief from the mundane life.

My loneliness was causing problems now. I tried to find solace by immersing myself in reading newspapers and magazines. In the evenings Hariharan started giving me regular company. He liked me. The Manager of Sharda Cinema hall was a customer of Andhra Bank. So, Hariharan would take me almost every third day to Sharda Cinema to watch whatever movies were being screened: new or old; romantic or social; action or those with bhakti flavour. Somehow, my boredom reduced. But in the office, I felt like getting introduced to Mitali. I didn't want any friendship or regular talks with her; but I wanted at least a 'smiling relationship' so that in the bank I may not have that unnecessary tension of keeping my head down and moving around with that load of becoming conscious about her. *Why had I become so conscious?* I just didn't know. I didn't have anything to do with her, I was sure in my mind; but as a matter of youthful gossip I would discuss a bit about her in a jovial manner in the company of my other friends.

A few days elapsed. One fine morning while I was seriously working in the savings bank—picking up cheques of customers, finding the account pages in the respective big ledgers, posting the entries, issuing tokens and making entries in the passbook—I heard a sweet and firm voice. I lifted my head. Mitali was standing before me. 'My father has a pension account; his pension must have been posted; please update the passbook and return it to me.' It was a Godsend opportunity to strike a smiling relationship. But I didn't like the tone and the wordings, '... *and return it to me*', as they conveyed a command. I just smiled and nodded. On finding time, I opened the relevant ledger and the account page. I read the address out of curiosity: '43, Ballar Bhai Nagar, Raipur'. It was in the slightly unclear handwriting of one officer, Mr Singh. I updated the passbook and put it in the small aluminium box where many other passbooks were kept. I had the choice of going to Mitali, and like young men or indulgent middle age men, could have delivered it politely or fawningly; and would have felt nice about bestowing a favour on a beautiful girl. But my persistent training on self-restraint made me skip that choice. With a naughty feeling I safely latched the box!

Days passed; on a number of occasions I passed across Mitali in the same style: my head slightly bowed or if upright I would look elsewhere; if at all our eyes would meet, I would give a nonchalant look. And, why I shouldn't have behaved in that manner? *I was not interested in her*. Almost ten days passed thus. She came one day and asked, 'I had given you a passbook; have you updated that? You didn't return it to me?'

'Oh! That passbook; you never came to collect it; I too forgot about it; let me check-up; it must be there in that box,' I casually opened the box and despite knowing the exact location, feigned as if I was laboriously searching for the same. 'Ah, here it is; you see with the lapse of time it too had receded into oblivion,' I said, and with a casual smile handed that over to her. She thanked me while I deliberately didn't look at her, and left.

That was the second time when I heard her sweet voice, and I had furtively looked at her while she didn't notice. After that I felt like looking at her whenever I got a chance while she was not looking at me. I found the venture interesting and entertaining. *Who in his senses would miss a moment of looking at a beautiful girl?* That instance removed my discomfort—which had largely been of my own making—of not making an eye contact, and not wishing her. The smiling relationship had begun. I would, thenceforth, after entering the branch look at her once, and if our eyes would meet, wish her in a decent and innocent manner. Like a good office colleague.

But I was a bit perturbed; I started harbouring a wish if I could stand beside her, introduce myself and if we could chat for a moment or two. That didn't happen. Things continued in the same manner. The festival of *Holi* arrived. An evening before *Holi* a list was circulated amongst the staff, detailing the names of the officers and some slogans beside each name in Hindi. I had been given:

'Chai nahi lagti acchhi, doodh pilao yaro,
Gai bhains ka nahin to bhed bakri ka hi lao yaro'
('Tea, I don't relish, get me milk instead my friends;
if not of cow or buffalo, at least of sheep or goat.')

I marvelled at their keen observation of my not taking tea and the apt slogan. Out of curiosity I checked up the list and found that Mitali had been assigned:

'Miss Mita looks Smita,
Bank me milaa kaam ghisa pita'
('Miss Mita, resembles Smita,
but got drudgery in the bank').

I too realised that with her penchant for sarees, her shimmering black hair, her round moonlike face and the bindi on her forehead, Mitali did resemble Smita Patil, the popular heroine of that period. I noticed that her movements had grace and elegance and her overall composure, visage and torso looked decent.

Now, irrespective of my location, I could always track down her position, and just one glance of hers was enough to give me fillip for my day's work. I could see her from a distance talking to various male colleagues and wished I too could be so free and comfortable with her. But I wanted the opportunity to come naturally and not through any deliberate act on my part.

Time passed. On 31st of March, the bank was geared up for government closing. The bank was to remain open even during night to honour all government cheques issued by the Treasury. The work was in full swing. Besides, staff was allotted ledgers for jotting down the balances of individual current accounts for final balancing. I too had been assigned two. While I was busy jotting, my eyes caught sight of Mitali sitting on the arm of her chair in the hall and jotting down balances. It was almost six in the evening; I had never seen her sitting so late in the office. She got up and proceeded to the back door. I saw her, and admired her gait. Then after almost five minutes she returned; the movements at a distance made me lift my face; our eyes met, and at that particular moment the eye contact was a trifle longer. I wondered at my audacity; but realising my lapse, I immediately lowered my eyes. *What had happened to me?* I pondered over but did not get any answer; but I was thrilled at the event!

An evening in the month of April …
I was watching the movie, 'Hero' in a cinema hall along with Hariharan, Jayesh and Raghavan. I had seen the movie earlier at Calcutta and had thoroughly enjoyed it. We used to see movies mostly for pastime but that day 'Hero' was chosen as it had become a rage. As usual I saw Shama everywhere in the movie: in each expression, movement, dialogue and dancing poses of Meenakshi Sheshadari; her face would mask the face of Meenakshi, filling me with the familiar sensations of love and passion. Immersed in Shama's thoughts and the beautiful plot of the movie, I became more excited when the scene shifted to the lilting title song where Meenakshi and Jackie Shroff passionately sing:

'Tu mera jaanu hai…. Tu mera dilbar hai …,
Meri prem kahani ka, tu hero hai …'

Suddenly, I was startled by an awesome hallucination: the face of Meenakshi Sheshadari was getting superimposed by some other face … Who was it? I tried to figure out, but could discern after a few attempts … the bindi adorned forehead, kohl eyed; with glistening black hair … it was the round, luminous and chubby face of Mitali … a vagrant wisp of her smooth and lustrous black hair on her brow. Time and again in the song the torso and face of Meenakshi were replaced by Mitali's graceful and elegant figure. *But why Mitali?* I couldn't find an answer for a long time.

Even at night while going to sleep, I mulled over what I had experienced; but answers were hard to come by as Shama was still beside me, and I didn't have any doubts about my love.

But something was pulling me in the office. I felt the powerful presence of Mitali. Was it to get some recognition from the tender gender to satisfy my ego? Or was it something more?

The working area of the branch comprised of a huge hall. The savings bank counter where we were posted was near the main entrance of the branch, and it was in the front row. Mitali sat in the inner flank of the hall with her back towards me. The distance between us was at least twenty feet and in between there were four pillars in a row; and there were three huge tables behind which sat three officers with their midget almirahs and small side racks. The whole arrangement while being seated resembled a partition, blocking the view; only on getting up, one could get a glimpse of the people on the other side of the flank. Slowly, I was being possessed by a strong craving for being around her so that ultimately I may get an opportunity to talk to her one day! I wished it to happen naturally; but I also wanted to create an opening for that.

As per the training schedule, we were supposed to be rotated at all the counters for exposure to all areas in banking. But we were being utilised only in the savings bank and current account, and hardly three months remained of our first branch training. I discussed with Raghavan. 'I am least interested in banking and am likely to quit; I am least bothered where I am placed,' was his refrain, 'You can go ahead and do whatever you want.'

'Man, I too am not sure of remaining in the bank; but I don't want us to be simply used as savings bank or current accounts clerks,' I retorted, 'after all we are officers. I will speak to the people concerned.'

With such a rational and patent objective, but with a hidden intent of being around Mitali, I approached the Accountant and the Head Clerk. 'Sir, we have been here for almost four months and our training would be over in another two months; we have hardly worked anywhere except current account and savings; I wish you could give us exposure of other sections,' I entreated with earnestness and humility. My face exuded innocence. There was hardly any betrayal of my inner emotions and my true intent. The Accountant, a portly man of medium height was always busy; he was very sincere but his face evoked pity, which would intensify if one, saw his sagging trousers; it conveyed the amount of load he was carrying on his shoulders. He would twitch his eyes after speaking two sentences, and move his eyebrows upwards whenever anyone spoke as if he was already getting overawed by the impending load, even if nothing more was being thrust on him. The Head Clerk was slightly dark complexioned, with his hair dyed black and combed back, displaying his dark forehead; his face was a bit rough, manifesting an element of crookedness, which perhaps, was his inbuilt nature. Despite his well-oiled hair, he gave an untidy appearance, accentuated by his choice of dull clothes. They had their desks facing Mitali's. And, while putting forth my point, I hardly looked at Mitali, who out of curiosity, glanced in our direction many times. But I had trained myself to curb my instincts to look towards females unlike the normal ways of most of the males. The conversation moved on well, and in a manner I had desired. I could convince them with the sweetener, 'Sir, as and when necessary I would be available for the savings counter.' Since Raghavan had not shown any interest in his deployment, the Accountant said, 'Due to administrative constraints it is not possible to give comprehensive training to both of you at all the counters simultaneously. Both of you can mutually work out.'

So, the very next day I was attached for one week to an officer, Mr Aggarwal, who was handling 'Fixed Deposits'. He was a stocky fellow with a casual and affable manner. His desk was diagonally opposite to Mitali's but they had their backs to each other; in between there was a pillar as well. But that place was much nearer to her compared to the savings counter. Of course, it gave me a better view. As and when I would get up, I could steal a glance at Mitali, with the high probability of seeing her face and the meeting of our eyes. The plan was working a bit although to everyone around it would look like an accidental meeting of eyes. I learnt about the intricacies of 'Fixed Deposits' with the limited capability at the disposal of Aggarwal to explain the things. A week passed; I got ample opportunities of seeing her and the occasions of meeting of our eyes increased. At that desk, I was witness to the unfolding of an interesting episode:

One day, a less educated man came to our counter; after understanding the mechanics and benefits of fixed deposit, he went to deposit five thousand rupees; in no time he was back, and asked for the fixed deposit receipt. The officer said, 'Let the voucher come and I shall issue you the receipt.' The man kept coming after every five minutes, and repeated his request, to which he heard the same stock reply. When the issuance did not materialise, the customer growing impatient asked, 'How far has that Voucher gone? I don't know how in the bank they allow the people to have such long breaks for tea, snacks and breakfast?' I burst into hearty laughter. The customer felt insulted. 'I am so serious, and see this young man,' the man said with exasperation, 'he is laughing.'

'What to do Sir? You are thinking that a voucher is an employee of the bank; it actually means a piece of paper, a receipt of having deposited the money; it is a challan kind of thing,' I explained. The customer was no longer indignant; he too burst into a paroxysm of laughter. With such spice, I completed my 'Fixed Deposits' training.

The next work station was Transfer Scroll, handled by one Ms Dongre. She had a wheatish complexion with pockmarked face; no aspect of hers was attractive except that she was young, apparently in early thirties. Her desk was just outside the Branch Manager's chamber, and it was at right angle to Mitali's. I was now in Mitali's vicinity, within a distance of less than ten feet. I would sit with Ms Dongre, deeply engrossed in whatever she taught about the Transfer Scroll. She was very diligent, dedicated and competent in her work. There were some government vouchers that were tricky. I paid full attention, but surreptitiously I could capture and enjoy the vivid image of Mitali. At the approach of lunch hour, Mitali would come to her for proceeding for lunch. The three ladies of the branch including Mitali would have lunch together in the ladies' common room whose approach was from the back entrance. Near the common room, there was a water cooler where the staff could take water and also after returning from the toilet wash their hands. Many times I had bumped into Mitali there, and as usual would pass across with my head bent down; with that strange tension that grips young men—who have come of age—on seeing a beautiful young female.

At the end of another week, I moved on to the 'Cash Book desk', manned by two competent gentlemen, one of whom was an engineer. In our Orientation and Induction trainings we had been told that 'Cash Book' was the most important desk where transactions of the whole branch were reconciled. 'Cash Book desk' was just opposite to the 'Transfer Scroll desk' and again at right angle to Mitali's desk. Now I came to know that she used to handle only government challans.

Just beside her there was another desk designated as 'Cash Scroll' for entering vouchers involving cash transactions. 'Cash Scroll' was initially handled by one Sahu when I had joined the branch. Later one young Sindhi boy, Kumar Bhatia, was managing the show. I used to watch Mitali and Kumar in confabulations whenever free. It would send pangs of jealousy down my heart. Though I had nothing to do with Mitali; but I just could not withstand that. I would desire if I too could talk to her one day. That at least would settle my uncomfortable situation with bottled up feelings. *How very piquant it is when one likes a person but is unable to speak to him/her?*

I now had the opportunity to be near her for one more week. I displayed all sincerity and devotion in learning 'Cash Book'. The officers had enough time to complete their task. Ideally, the Cash Book was to be balanced on the very day of the transactions. But the size and scale of the branch and the enormity of the transactions provided enough leverage and exemption to complete it by the evening of the following day. Cash Book staff could seek clarifications and explanations from all officers and staff of the branch whenever any tedious or complex transactions and their calculations were to be checked up or their genesis became imperative for thorough scrutiny.

On a few instances, I was told to seek information from Mitali. 'Madam, sorry for disturbing you; would you please explain how this amount was transferred to the government account? Madam this transaction is little complex, will you please throw some light on this?' I would approach her in my soft, polite and genial voice, with my eyes firmly on the point on the vouchers where I would put my finger. I would evince no inner rumblings, no emotions and no nervousness. My face would betray nonchalance and innocence; but my heart would beat faster and even miss a beat; I would be losing my breath but would breathe deeply as if I was in full control. My simplicity and innocence had accorded me a serene visage and a winning smile. I was, perhaps, the embodiment of the saying, 'Face is the index of a person's mind.' Thus, my honest histrionics always appeared credible as I had mastered that art of making people believe in my simplicity!

Rendezvous with the Mentor

In the third week of April, I got a wonderful news from my father, '*Rohit, by God's grace, I have been transferred from Bhubaneswar to Ludhiana. Your Mummy and Nalini have already arrived here. I wished all of you to enjoy the city before I leave. So, you can also plan a visit here.*' I always felt homesick in Raipur. The news came like the discovery of a pond in an arid desert.

But, there was no direct train and tickets could not be booked at such short notice. Yet the overwhelming desire to visit my family made me chalk out a plan with Jayesh whose father was in Railways in Bilaspur. I would accompany Jayesh to Bilaspur and his father would arrange something. I was young, and presumably could face the inclemency of unreserved travel too.

We moved to Bilaspur by the evening train. Jayesh's family had a small flat in the railway colony. While having the South Indian dinner which his mother had affectionately prepared, his father said, 'You see, night journey to the station from our house is a bit dangerous as the path is infested by stray dogs. I feel it would be better if Jayesh drops you at the station by ten. You can board the Bombay Howrah Express which arrives at around twelve. You can reach Tata Nagar in the morning and safely take a connecting train for Bhubaneswar that arrives in the afternoon.'

Jayesh dropped me at the railway station and gave me suitable directions. The train actually arrived at one in the night. Though without any reservation, I got into a second class reserved compartment. People were sleeping on the berths, and there was no place to sit. I managed to squeeze my suitcase under a berth, and remained standing, praying. After half an hour, one of the passengers occupying a lower berth woke up for toilet; while going he appraised me. After retuning, he asked, 'Where are you going young man? Don't you have a reserved seat?' The man was wearing a lungi and banyan and didn't appear to be too well off; he was travelling with his wife and two sons. 'Tatanagar; thereafter, I would be taking a train for Bhubaneswar,' I replied innocently. 'Tatanagar; then Bhubaneswar!

Will you go standing all the way? Come on; just squeeze in and sit down at the corner of my berth,' he said in a kind voice.

'Thank you so much Sir,' I said gratefully, 'but it may cause you unnecessary discomfort.'

'Don't be so hesitant son. Just sit down and ensure that you repay this debt by helping others similarly in future.' I sat down. But it was difficult in a three tier compartment when all the berths are spread out; more so if one has good height. Gradually when my conscious self was overcome by languor, I started spreading my legs, and ultimately he allowed me to sleep beside one his sons on the lower berth. I had a slightly disturbed sleep. In the morning at around nine thirty, I got down at Tatanagar after profusely thanking the gentleman.

I deposited my luggage in the cloak room. I devoured whatever I could lay my hands upon to satiate my hunger. The train came at three thirty. But nothing mattered. The enthusiasm of meeting my parents and sister helped me in surmounting all boredom and exertions.

I wondered how three years back I had travelled in the same train with my people to Bhubaneswar as a teenager who had just finished his first year of law course. The Bhubaneswar trip, at that time, had turned the course of my life. My mentor Darshan had guided me to a different path; he had instilled confidence during our financial distress and my uncertain future.

Really nothing lasts forever. God, our creator and producer-cum-director of the drama, enacts various scenes and makes us act out our roles in our lives. Life is on a predestined course.

I looked out from the window: green trees lined on both sides of the tract were running parallel to the moving train with the chain of mountains, the Eastern Ghats in the background. There were verdant meadows with grazing cattle; farmers toiling in the fields, rearing crops in the bright sunshine for filling the nation's granaries. There were thatched houses. People were moving around in ordinary clothes, reflecting want and penury; ogling at the moving train in awe and curiosity. Far in the horizon the sun was receding; a red fireball, its glint gradually dimming, leaving a golden orange trail; the fluffy and shining cumulus clouds acquiring azure and crimson hues. Birds were returning to their nests after the day's grind.

My journey too was similar, anxious to meet my people at Bhubaneswar. Afternoon melted into evening; a few minutes later the evening twilight gave way to the beauty of night, with only artificial lights guiding the path and the surroundings. I was counting moments. *The last lap of journey is the most tedious as even seconds seem to crawl.*

The train touched Bhubaneswar at one forty-five in the night. Bhubaneswar is a safe place. I hailed a rickshaw for Shaheed Nagar. It was pitch dark at certain stretches but I had God on my side. In almost thirty minutes, I was at the doorstep of my father's office-cum-residence. I paid the rickshaw puller and patted his back with gratitude.

I pressed the bell. In a few moments the lights were on, and I was hugging my family.

'Did you have something on the way?' my parents asked.

'Yes I did, though it was not sumptuous or tasty.'

'Then, you must take some milk and fruits,' mother said.

'No, it is okay; I will manage,' I said feebly, 'we can wait till tomorrow morning.'

'What morning? I will get you some milk,' my papa proceeded to boil some milk.

'Come on freshen up and have these,' my mother brought some sweets and fruits.

My eyes welled up. In no time Papa arrived with a glassful of milk, which I devoured with sweets and fruits before their doting eyes. *No amount of riches can match that care and affection which a loving family provides*. We prepared to sleep. But there was so much to talk, and we could not wait for the morning. The conversation slowly started sounding like a lullaby till we segued into languor and slumber.

The morning was hectic as the office staff were expected by 10:30 We got ready early, and had our breakfast. Papa introduced me to some of the office staff; I had met some of them earlier too. But now the introductions had the tinge of elation and pride at my achievements. I desperately wanted to meet my mentor Darshan. Papa contacted his office 'Save Grain Campaign' and learnt that he was there.

I proceeded to meet him on a bicycle. I had been to that office earlier. It was at a short distance in the same locality. On the way, earlier episodes and events flashed across my mind. I was filled with gratitude for the man who despite his humble beginnings and background, possessed sagacity, confidence and fortitude worth emulating. He had proved to be a messiah during my trying times of diffidence, and was instrumental in facilitating my ascendance. I parked the bicycle in the office complex.

Bicycle, in those days of less mechanisation, was a prized possession which normal middle class youth could ride on without inviting any disparaging looks. It was in total contrast to the present day mania for sassy motorbikes and swanky cars which youths consider imperative for acquiring minimum respectability in society. Cycles, nowadays are identified with the lower strata; only flashy geared ones are considered okay for sports purposes. Thus, a probationary officer working in a bank but riding a bicycle was not incongruous. I didn't have to worry about that.

Only a minor enquiry guided me to Darshan's room which he shared with another colleague. He was sitting alone behind his table, grappling with the contents of one file.

I entered quietly and wished, 'Good morning.'

Darshan smiled widely, 'Oh Rohit! Your father had told me about your possible visit; but he was not very sure; it's a pleasant surprise to see you.'

Before, he could say anything further; I bent and touched his feet. 'What man? Please don't embarrass me; I do not deserve this,' while saying so his eyes became moist.

'Oh, I know how much you matter in my life. But for you, I would have been rotting like an urchin; you boosted my morale when the chips were down; you guided me when I was floundering in labyrinthine circles, unsure of myself, my potential and my capabilities; when everything appeared dark and gloomy. But for you, I would have still been a salesman in that duplicating machine company or at the most could have become a medical representative; you illuminated my path; how can I forget that? You are my guru,' I said it all in one go.

Darshan hugged me and said, 'May God bless you! You are destined for much more, and above all like your father you are a good human being. Humility is an asset to be nurtured and cherished. It helps you in cultivating long lasting and enduring relationships. I am deeply touched by your gesture ... I am proud of you.'

Darshan had to go for field duty. 'I will come to your place in the evening,' he said with an affectionate smile. I returned home full of energy and enthusiasm.

The procession of people—who were learning about the impending departure of my father on transfer to Delhi—continued. They were from different Government offices, Public Sector Undertakings and banks. I knew, through my limited knowledge, that my father's job did not endow him with much power or prestige. He used to merely collect data regarding the implementation and efficacy of various government schemes and submit reports to Planning Commission. But his simplicity, affectionate nature and graceful mannerisms had endeared him to people of all castes, communities, religions and regions.

The day swiftly passed. Darshan came in the evening and after a brief interaction insisted that I accompany him to his house for dinner and night stay. I took my clothes and toiletries and moved along. His house was almost fifteen minutes' walk.

A little ahead we saw a congregation of two dogs, a cat, and a cow around a large community dustbin. Each of them would bark, mew or moo according to their voice culture, expressing some anger or resentment at the other encroaching on their territory. Beside them were standing two pensive men with long hair, smoking cigarettes; observing the congregation, and speaking to each other in monosyllables and occasionally nodding their heads.

Darshan commented in Punjabi, 'Look at Mr Lamarck and Mr Darwin in the animal farm and brooding over whether the data would be useful for validation of their theories of Genetics and Evolution.' Darshan's spontaneity and wit were remarkable. I found it difficult to rein in my laughter. A snigger was natural; but I ensured that I didn't look in that direction so as not to disturb their discourse and obviate the possibility of their taking any offence at my misdemeanour.

'You will get us into trouble by your unrestrained nature,' observed Darshan.

'I just can't control my laughter,' I said.

'Don't worry. People don't understand Punjabi, and they cannot make out the true import of our wordings,' Darshan said reassuringly.

His wife and their two-year-old son welcomed us in their modest but nicely decorated home. He had a fine collection of books, orderly arranged on the bookshelves along with another wonderful selection on books of Hindi literature, his wife's passion.

A tape recorder placed nearby played beautiful Ghazals by Jagjit Singh and Chitra Singh. The pervading serene ambience was mesmerising. His wife served simple but delicious dinner that she could manage at very short notice. I fondly saw their son playing nearby, lost in his own world, with small replicas of animals, birds and dolls.

At night Darshan chose to sleep in the guest room to give me company.

He said, 'I know what must be going on in your mind; you are young and have attained a fair bit of maturity; I must tell you, love is the greatest thing in life. You may have everything; but without love, they are cipher; it is love that gives you a sense of emotional security, zest and enthusiasm in life; it is a catalyst for fulfilling your ambitions with zeal and passion. You remember, during your last visit, I had told you about the girl with whom I was in love. My father was against our match and wanted me to marry elsewhere. Though dejected, I bided my time. I had intense love for her and wanted to marry her only; my parents could not understand; but I waited taking a firm stance and also trying to convince that otherwise I will never marry. My perseverance paid off; finally I could convince them that ultimately it was my life, which I wished to spend with the partner of my choice. They relented, and look now I am married to Urmila, whom I have known since my college days. With my humble social and economic background I could get a respectable job and some status in society; I had an ambition of becoming an IAS but that was not my destiny. But, I must say that God has been kind to me as I got my beloved as my life partner. We are in bliss! Rohit, please understand that true love in life is hard to get, and if you do get it, then ensure that you do not sacrifice it at the altar of your ambition; you must cherish, nurture and preserve it.' He went on, 'Of course, your first aim in life should be to make your career, and you must go headlong for that; but it is quite natural that you may get true love in your life during the same time; then you may wait, and mind you true love teaches us patience and sacrifice too; it withstands the testing times. A life with a life partner whom you love is worthwhile and meaningful. I had given you lessons in career counselling; but now I feel that the kind of emotional and sensitive person you are, you deserve lessons in love. I hope when you find true love you would value it. By the way, have you not come across anyone in your life thus far?'

I tried to remain quiet. But Darshan's nudging unfettered my hesitation. 'Yes, I did come across a girl when I was just sixteen. She was and has been my love: pious and pristine.'

'Oh wonderful! You never told me last time,' Darshan was exultant.

'But, I have not been lucky like you,' I told in a sombre tone.

'Why? What happened?' his voice had concern.

Then I told him about Shama, my love; that how I worshipped her but lacked any guts and planning; that how my overriding desire to excel in my career made me lose track of her; that how I had built up an imaginary pact and got far removed from the reality; that finally, when I did have the calibre and the social status after getting the bank job, it became too late; that when I did discover her coincidentally, it was in a marriage hall while she was getting married to someone else; that I lost my love yet my heart was the abode of my beloved Shama.

'Rohit, I am so sorry to learn. My God! You have been carrying this load alone for so many years. I am happy for one thing that you felt intense love for someone. And, you still are in ardent love with her despite knowing that she can't be yours. It is good on your part that you have reconciled to the situation and never tried to give her any problem. I would say that this is also maturity and manifestation of your poise. But, yes as you have done so far, accept the whole fault as yours and partly of destiny. Shama hardly knew about your love. You only had woven your own set of norms and rules. But Rohit, now you have to become a realist. It is difficult to lead a life just by clinging to memories of the one whom you can't attain. You have to learn to let go. You have to think about yourself and your family. An eligible bachelor should not remain a bachelor. You are young and sensitive. There is every possibility that you may come across someone in your life whose love could be true. Just listen to your heart, and don't ignore the signs if your heart truly starts throbbing for someone. That time you must cast aside the mist of your first and unrequited love. If you don't listen to your heart and ignore that person, you would be causing great pain to yourself and that someone. You must face reality and not live in the imaginary world. God has his designs and he has created someone for each of us. I hope you will heed my words.'

Darshan's wordings coupled with Shama's memories were like lullabies; they carried me into the dream world. When did I slip into deep sleep, I didn't know. I woke with the sweet cooing of a cuckoo, sitting on a tree in his courtyard; the cool and refreshing morning breeze wafted in.

I got ready in no time. Darshan's wife served us delectable alu parathas with sweet curd. I bade them goodbye in all humility and affection. I gently pulled the baby's cheeks. And, with dreams of the future in my mind, just like Darshan's happy domestic state, I came out with him. It was a wonderful experience with my mentor ... absolutely unforgettable!

Father had planned a visit to Cuttack and Puri. The bus took us to Cuttack in hardly forty-five minutes. Cuttack being a good marketing place we could go around for shopping. The market was throbbing and the people nice and simple. Mummy purchased a beautiful cotton saree, a speciality of Odisha. We took lunch in a good hotel; and then proceeded to Puri by another bus. We had been to Puri on our earlier visit too. The grand temple of Lord Jagannath situated beside the Puri beach looked majestic and serene. There was a huge rush of devotees and tourists who had thronged to the place which in the Hindu tradition is considered as one of the four important holy dhams or tirtha yatra places in India; others being Badrinath in Northern India in Uttarakhand, Dwarka in Western India in Gujarat and Rameshwaram in the Southern state of Tamil Nadu.

We paid obeisance to the deity, expressing gratitude for culmination of my father's transfer after four years and also for the success I had attained in life. I prayed for the overall well-being and happiness of my family members and for illuminating my path in future. We spent some time on the beach. People were enjoying nature's dance and drama. The thrill of the waves and vibrancy of the atmosphere, despite the cacophony all around, were idyllic to the heart and mind.

The return journey was tiring but enjoyable and we reached Bhubaneswar by 5:30. Father reminded us of the invite for dinner at the house of Mr Srivastava. Mr Srivastava worked in the Department of Malaria Control. He had a daughter and a son. I had learnt in my previous visit that his son was studying Electronics Engineering at Pilani. I had not met him last time, but then his studying at Pilani had smitten me with nostalgia, a tinge of jealousy coupled with a feeling of inadequacy. But that was a bygone memory. My prestigious job in the bank and my success in the Civil Services' exam had accorded me elation and self-esteem. I was eager to meet him.

We reached their place sharp at seven. Mr Srivastava and his wife were of similar attributes: portly, of medium height and with lively and pleasing visages. They welcomed us with all humility and camaraderie. They were a cultured family who loved art and music. Mrs Srivastava was a good painter and short story writer. Their daughter was cute, studying in eighth standard, and son was good looking though a little plump.

Before dinner as usual the singing session started. My father sang a beautiful *ghazal* from an old Hindi movie; Mr Srivastava sang an old Hindi film song. Mrs Srivastava recited a few of her poems. Then their son in his deep baritone voice sang a lovely *ghazal*:

'Kaise sukoon paoon, tujhe dekhane ke baad,
Ab kya ghazal sunaoon tujhe dekhane ke baad,
Kabe ka ahetram bhee meri nazar me,
Sar kis taraf jhukaoon, tujhe dekhne ke baad.
Kaise sukoon paoon tujhe dekhane ke baad'

It was from *Talat Aziz's* album. Its lyrics and notes were quite appealing and they kept on ringing in my ears for a long time. I didn't know then that they would become integral to my psyche, and an important ingredient of my life's story.

When coaxed, I sang a famous Jagjit Singh's song from the movie *Arth*, which I had started liking very much:

'Tumko dekha to yeh khayal aaya,
Zindagi dhoop,tum ghanaa sayaa',
This song too was to play a major part in my life.

When the session was over, the chit chat started. Their son had completed his engineering and was waiting for a job; he had applied in various public and private sector companies. When they asked about my bank job and my salary, I informed with a glint in my eyes, 'I am in the scale of ₹700-1600 and have started my career at the basic salary of ₹840 plus dearness allowance.' Their jaws dropped. For once, I saw my parents' heads high and my voice carrying pride. It gave me solace after having undergone depression and heartburning for almost three years.

I boosted the morale of that young engineer, 'Don't lose heart; Pilani is a wonderful and well-respected institution whose alumnus are picked up like hot cakes in the job market; Your time too will come, and you will succeed.' We left their home in a cheerful mood.

In the remaining period in Bhubaneswar, we had many visitors. Everyone had his own views on my bank job. Many suggested that I should remain in the bank. Others felt that a gazetted officer's post in government was far more rewarding even though the pay may be slightly less. They advised me to concentrate on my last attempt for Civil Services as nothing could match IAS.

I gave a list of my books to Nalini with a request to have them parcelled at the SBI's address at Raipur at the earliest. Papa, however, was a little ambivalent after having seen the comfortable life I had been leading in Raipur, with enough financial stability.

Time evaporated like 'dew drops' in the bright summer sunshine and our last day of stay at Bhubaneswar arrived. The night before was hectic; the last visitor left our place at twelve at night. I envied the love, affection and appreciation my father got. It was a highly emotional moment. We might or might not return to Bhubaneswar, but fond memories were our treasure to be cherished.

On the last day we took the train in the afternoon, with a few friends and acquaintances even coming to see us off at the station including my mentor Darshan. The parting was unforgettable!

On the way, I was to get down at Tatanagar to catch a train for Raipur. We would be having eight hours together. Thereafter, we had to part. On the way, Papa tried to persuade me to remain in the Bank instead of trying for Civil Services. May be his experience in the government job had set in some sort of disillusionment or may be the grass on the other side always looks greener.

Time passed. The train reached Tatanagar in the evening. I got down touching my parents' feet, embracing them and my loving sister. Their eyes were moist. After almost ten minutes later the train started. I stood at the platform, waving to them while keeping an eye on my luggage. I wished the train would not proceed; I wished I could also go along with them; but the reality of the moment dawned on me; I was overwhelmed by that one moment of separation from them; the train slowly gathered momentum and so did my tear ducts; with the increasing speed of the train, the flow of the tears from my eyes also increased. I stood there … tearful, with a sense of deep loss and melancholy, till the train disappeared.

Composing myself, I realised that full four hours remained for arrival of the Bombay Howrah Express for Raipur. I got up and had a cup of tea and some snacks that mother had given, dipped in her love and affection. Then, I sat on a bench pondering over my future and the past. The memories of my childhood, the happier time spent with my family started haunting me. 'When would this separation end?' I asked myself, and looked up at the sky to find answers. But everything was quiet. Time, perhaps, was not ripe for any answers.

Boredom increased my hunger, and at eight I proceeded to the canteen for dinner. It was not very tasty but my hunger made it tastier. *It is true that only a full stomach makes you to raise tantrums of food being not tasty; if you are hungry, the stomach makes you hear only the rumbles and growls of hunger and everything else is forgotten. The body needs energy to survive, and that remains the foremost priority; after all the instinct to survive is dear to all living beings.*

The train arrived at twelve at night. I managed to enter into one of the unreserved compartments as getting into a reserved compartment at that hour would have created problems. The torture I had faced while going to Bhubaneswar was nothing in comparison to this. The compartment was jam packed. I waded through the crowd, and managed some space on the side upper shelf to only keep my suitcase. But, I had to remain standing till 3:30 am, when a gentleman who was seated and had been watching me in between the breaks of his own nap took pity, and allowed me to share the limited place beside him. But, sound sleep was not my privilege as I had to continuously keep an eye on my suitcase too. It must have been six in the morning when I could get a comfortable seat to spread myself and ease my fatigue further. Still the impact of such journey was enormous.

The train reached Raipur at nine in the morning. On reaching home, I rushed through my morning routine. Soon, I was at the Indian Coffee House for breakfast. I feasted on the idlis, dosas and coffee to replenish energy for my depleted body, and filled myself well for grappling with the tasks of the day. Then I proceeded to the bank. Dressed in a sky blue full sleeved shirt, blue trousers and my shining patent black leather shoes, with my head heavy due to lack of sleep, I entered the branch, lost in my own thoughts. I was late by almost half an hour and it was a Saturday. All of sudden, I encountered Mitali who had, per chance, turned her face towards the entrance; our eyes met, and in my insouciance I wished her with the gentle bow of my head. She too responded in a pleasant and innocent manner. It was a good beginning to the day and also a resumption of a smiling relationship which I always wanted. *Why there should be so much of ice and why should it not be broken at least on the surface?*

I met Mr Ganeshan, the genial Branch Manager, to inform that I had returned. Later, I somehow concentrated on the work allotted to me. As it was a Saturday, the public dealing was over by one thirty. I could afford to leave by two thirty and reach the Punjabi Hotel, Ambassador, for lunch. The effect of a long journey coupled with loneliness had reduced my hunger; I only had vegetable biryani and curd. While returning home, I was feeling giddy, barely able to keep my eyes open; desiring some well-deserved rest.

As the weather was hot, sleep was not so easy; I picked up a magazine and lay down on the bed. In no time I dozed off. Soon, I was lost in dreams: dreams of my arduous journey; the time spent with my parents and sister and the plans of my future. Slowly I slipped into deep slumber. In a short while I was woken up by a strange mixture of the mellifluous sound of a cuckoo and the cacophony of utensils employed for filling water at the hand pump behind my room.

'*What must be the time now?*' I wondered.

It appeared to be twilight and the wrist watch indicated five fifteen. I got up for a bath. There wasn't much water in the bathroom; so I picked up the bucket to fetch some water from the hand pump. But, the outside world presented a strange surprise! The sun was a bit bright, and the way utensils were lined up outside, it could be morning only. Mr Bakshi's son and daughters present there looked at me with sly smiles. It was not dusk but dawn! '*Oh my God, what is this? I have slept for full thirteen hours!*' I wondered. I was amused. Never ever in my life had I slept for so long. I laughed at myself. I got ready. When I stood outside in the small veranda—while the maid servant was cleaning—I happened to see Mr Bakshi.

With a smiling face he asked, 'Hey man, what happened to you yesterday? You slept for so long. Are you alright? You know I came to your room at around ten and found that you were deep asleep. I switched off the lights.'

I was embarrassed; I somehow managed to say, 'I am sorry for the inconvenience; actually I had gone to Bhubaneswar and could not have proper sleep for a pretty long time; I am perfectly all right otherwise.'

Mr. Bakshi's smile broadened at my innocence.

In no time I settled into my daily routine, and eagerly waited for the parcel of books from Delhi. Just two months were remaining for the Prelims. I was a bit lonely after Raghavan had left for Bhilai. Hariharan would come in the evening as usual, and accompany me for dinner and walk. It had hardly been a week when one fine morning, I was introduced to a nice young man by Mr Shukla, 'This is Pradeep Kulkarni, a Trainee officer; he is joining today for his first branch training.' Pradeep had very common looks and slightly grey hair which was too much for his age of twenty-eight that I learnt a little later. But he had a very amiable disposition, and I didn't know that in two days he would become my best friend.

State Bank had a unique system of sifting the best and the brightest from amongst the clerical staff; a clerk after five years of service and after succeeding in part one of CAIIB (Certified Associate of Indian Institute of Bankers) exam could compete for Trainee Officer's exam comprising written test and interview. Once selected, TOs were treated at par with POs as regards their training and promotions.

I took him out for lunch during the lunch hours. I found him very affable and cultivated. I felt totally at ease with him. I checked up with Raghavan whether he intended to return to Raipur.

'Oh, no way man; I am perfectly fine at Bhilai with my friends plus I am getting the food of my liking there; we have a cook who cooks South Indian food for us,' Raghavan replied.

At that very moment I decided that Pradeep would be my roommate, if he agreed. That besides giving me company would also reduce my rent liability as we could share that. Pradeep agreed readily. So it was done. In the evening we went straight from the office to his hotel; after settling his account we put his luggage on the rickshaw and headed for Tatyapara. In just two days time we developed a fantastic equation. Rhonda Byrne in *The Secret* has postulated that as is our thought process so we attract similar individuals, circumstances and situations around ourselves. I didn't know that Pradeep was to play an important role in my life in the days to come.

I was washing my hands and face at the water cooler that was near the ladies common room. While wiping my face with a handkerchief, I heard a voice from behind.

'You walk with that key ring dangling from your pocket; what will you do if I steal it?'

I was startled to see Mitali standing just next to me and posing that question. I used to hang my key ring having a blue coloured oval plate of plastic, with my name 'Rohit' inscribed in silver white.

It used to sway according to my movements. I never knew it would invite such comments.

'No, it cannot be taken out,' I replied with a perfectly innocent air and a half smile. I maintained my poise although the question unnerved me.

'Be careful, it can be taken out; then how will you open your house lock?' came her prompt reply.

I said feebly, 'I'll be careful.' She had a naughty smile on her face.

'So, she wants me to be naughty too; okay no harm; I too can have fun,' I thought.

Those thoughts kept passing through my mind during the rest of the day and Sunday too. At last I thought that I could have a comfortable time in the branch as otherwise the non-communication with her had been causing needless tension. Finally, I had the occasion to talk to her, and like other persons in the bank would be able to interact with her in a normal manner.

On Monday, I maintained my usual calm and indifference. But I thought that as and when I would come face to face with her I would raise my eyebrows conveying, '*What is the matter?*' I met her again while she was moving towards the ladies' room from the main hall and I was returning from the water cooler side. I looked at her and she smiled. In return I smiled too; I tried to raise my eyebrow but found myself restrained in the track by my nature. Maybe I was not like a road-side Romeo, and it was not natural for me to behave in a manner that did not gel with my nature. '*Why should I try any nonsense when this is what I wanted and I got?' I wondered.* My aim in life was different, and my parcel of books that arrived in the evening from Delhi reinforced my resolve. Only a couple of months remained, and I had to seriously prepare for my exams. The 'exchange of smiles' had however begun; and with that my tension too had eased.

At home, I had made my resolve known to Pradeep that I had to seriously study for my exam as hardly two months were left. So, I tightened my belt and started getting up in the morning at five. As I had no craving for tea in the morning, I would get ready in forty-five minutes or so and settle down for an arduous regimen of studying at a stretch for almost four hours. At around nine forty-five we would prepare to move out and leave by ten for Indian Coffee House for breakfast. By eleven we would be at the branch. In the evening too I was able to spare at least two hours for my focussed study. In a span of three days only, I was certain that with Saturdays and Sundays at my disposal, I would be able to prepare well. Pradeep was of tremendous support as he did not disturb me at all. He, in fact, had planned to avail one week's joining time to visit his native place Ujjain in the middle of May.

The week just passed.

Cupid Strikes Again

A strange thing happened that I hadn't even remotely dreamt of. I was busy in my savings bank counter. At around eleven thirty, the Accountant came to me, and said, 'Today you may have to work on the "cash scroll desk" as that boy Kumar is absent.' For a moment I was befuddled, and the Accountant's voice seemed to be coming with echoes from a valley. My mind and heart were overwhelmed with queer feelings, but I did not allow my face to betray them. With complete nonchalance I said, 'But I hardly have any experience of that desk,' and added a further punch, 'can't you look for someone else; there is so much of work here and Raghavan is alone.' *I didn't want to show that I was ready to lap up the offer, and feigned reluctance; though deep in my heart I was on seventh heaven for getting such opportunity of sitting beside Mitali.* 'You see, we have tried and are finding it difficult to have any other person; moreover you are dynamic and fast ... that seat requires someone like you,' he pleaded in his typical sympathy seeking manner. I looked at his pitiful visage, and after showing a bit of reluctance condescended, 'Oh that being the case, I must follow your orders in the overall interest of the branch.'

I took five minutes in winding up the things and slowly moved with the Accountant to the 'cash scroll' desk. My heart wanted me to fly and reach there at once, but I deliberately took my time.

I distinctly remember I was wearing a light pink shirt and blue jeans that day—my favourite dress in those times. The same I had worn the day I had joined the bank except that then I had also worn a jacket on top. My hair bouffant with undulating waves, gave me added confidence ... yes the confidence that had increased after having worked in the bank for almost five months. I was certainly not that raw PO of December. Training at Hyderabad and Kolkata as well as my interactions with Raghavan had transformed me. But Mitali was a lady, and before ladies even the most confident of decent individuals lose their composure.

'Hullo, Good morning,' I suppressed my inhibitions and apprehensions and wished her on reaching that desk. Only I know how much those five minutes meant to me when I reached there. 'Good morning,' she responded cheerfully that helped in boosting my morale. I barely glanced at her while wishing. Draped in an off-white saree, a simple artificial pearl necklace adorning her neck, a small light red bindi on her forehead, her dark black shimmering hair nicely tied in a single braid, a smile lighting up her face, she looked very sweet and appealing.

'How come you are here?' she posed a natural question.

'Oh, your colleague has not turned up and I have been drafted for this musical chair,' I tried to sound natural, 'wherever there is vacancy, I am chosen to fill it up; what to do? I have to work wherever they post me.'

'So you are unhappy having come here.'

'No, not exactly; you see at other places at least I have worked; but I just do not know the *ABC* of this desk. I hope I can look forward to you for help.'

'What is there to understand here? It is the simplest of all; you have to just keep on entering all the cash vouchers in this long book, and assign them a running number.'

'Uh, it sounds simple; anyway, I will seek your help in case I face difficulty or have any doubts.'

The first interaction itself was quite encouraging and friendly and it made me lose my inhibitions to a great degree. We had tea in between when it was served by the office peon. All of a sudden while picking up some vouchers, the tea from my cup spilled on my table. To my amazement she immediately took out her beautiful napkin and wiped the table in one swift motion. It immediately made me revise my opinion of her having any kind of haughtiness. She appeared to be a very fine individual, totally contrary to the rumours that a few of the young clerks had spread about her. In that split second I noticed that her eyes were large, shapely and expressive and their shape was accentuated by kohl lining at their corners.

It took me just fifteen minutes to understand the working of the desk, and in no time I was able to enter 'the lot' of vouchers that were brought to me. I found the job very easy and in fact the quick disposal of 'the lot' gave me ample opportunity to move around. I didn't want to show that I was enjoying the desk and her company. To demonstrate my indifference I went to Raghavan who was grappling with the savings counter. I had a little chat with him.

'So, how do you find your new counter and new companion?' he asked with a sly smile.

'Oh nothing in particular, it is just like any other counter; and I am not interested in her,' I said hiding my inner thrill. 'I have to just jot down the cash vouchers and number them; the job is much easier than savings bank, and you don't have to face the customers,' I replied. 'Oh, lot of vouchers have again piled up on my desk; I will make a move,' I showed urgency and excuse to come back to that desk. In the process, I also played two tricks: one, I showed Raghavan that the calling of work required my return to the desk; two I portrayed absolute insouciance to Mitali that I was not perturbed by her presence and did not crave for her company unlike other young or even older men who were always running after or looking for an opportunity to converse with or to be in the company of females.

Mitali felt at ease and asked, 'Where do you hail from? Are you happy in the bank?'

Her questions sounded like music to my ears. I was raring to answer but I didn't show any excitement; and quite coolly, I replied, 'I am a Delhite; this is the first time that I have come out of Delhi; since I am in the bank, I have to per force enjoy it; though I am trying other avenues too.'

'Where else?'

'I had appeared for Civil Services in 1982 and qualified for a Group B post; I don't know which service I shall be allocated to; I am likely to get the call shortly. I appeared again in 1983, but didn't clear the Mains; I am appearing this year too,' I disclosed honestly. I thought that living in a small place like Raipur, she might not be aware of Civil Services.

But in the next few minutes I had to change my perception. 'You know, my father was also in the Central Government; he was in-charge of Dandakaranya project, meant for rehabilitation of refugees from East Bengal after Partition of India. We had also stayed in the tribal dominated Bastar District.' I was startled at her fluency in English. It appeared as if I was talking to a Delhi University student with a public school background. It was totally unlike the notions I had harboured about her.

'You have any brothers and sisters? Where is your father employed?' she asked with interest.

'Oh, he is a Group A officer in the Central Government in the Planning Commission; He was in Bhubaneswar for almost four years; only last month he got transferred to Ludhiana. He comes down to Delhi during weekends. My sister is in 12th standard; she is four years younger to me.' *I wondered how I divulged all our family details as if she had been a long-time friend.*

'What about you?'

'My father retired six years back. Presently he is employed with Kay Oils limited; he prepares their project reports. My eldest sister too is in SBI; currently in the Regional Office at Shankar Nagar. Another sister elder to me did her Masters in Music, and my younger brother is still studying.'

'You know one of my paternal aunts also did Masters in Music; she is older to me by three years.' I said innocently. *I just did not know why I was discussing all those minute details.*

'What does your sister aspire for?' she asked with interest.

'She has just appeared in her senior secondary exams; but she is not all that diligent; though I keep cajoling her to work hard; I will exhort her to appear in the Competitive Exams.' I explained more than what I should have. It appeared that restraint had eluded me and I was laying bare my family's history to her; I don't know why it did not appear odd to me at all discussing personal details with a person who was a perfect stranger to me till the other day.

'My brother has been promoted to 10th standard. He wishes to become an engineer.' She spoke without my prompting. We discussed many more things about Delhi and Raipur; about my boarding and lodging; about my routine. How the day passed, I just couldn't keep track. Luncheon discussion with Raghavan moved around many issues, and he casually remarked, 'Enjoying your new company!'

'Oh nothing like that man; it is just another desk,' I stalled further discussion with my terse reply. But in reality, I certainly liked her company. It was so refreshing. In my life I was able to hold conversation and interaction with a person of the other gender, other than my mother, sister, and cousins. Otherwise, I had always been stung by this strange inhibition while talking to members of the fair sex.

At four in the afternoon, I was assigned a day-book where I had to enter all the cash and transfer vouchers of some specific ledgers. By the time I finished it was four forty-five; she too was busy writing a day-book; at around five she packed her things and picked up her purse and proceeded to move out.

'Okay, Good night, see you tomorrow,' she said in a very simple and affectionate way. 'Oh, Good night,' I said but somewhere I felt I had lost something. *What was it? I did not know.*

I too picked up my things a little later and along with Pradeep proceeded to our place. On the way, while having some snacks at the Indian Coffee House, Pradeep was observing me closely though he did not say anything. I was a little quiet unlike my usual ebullient self. We discussed the day's affairs, and Pradeep excluded any reference to my new company in the bank. 'Cash scroll is an easy desk, and there isn't much application of mind involved; but it is good to have a break in between our regular strenuous desk; I hope you must be enjoying the break,' he said casually.

'Oh, yes; I found it very light, though the work appeared monotonous; anyway I did not ask for it, it was thrust on me as you know that Kumar was absent today,' I reacted philosophically. I knew I was feeling very good and excited; but somewhere deep some heaviness was developing. *What was that? I could not make out.*

After reaching home as usual, I had a bath as summer in Raipur was at its peak. Then I picked up my books as time was fleeting and I wanted to use it to the maximum possible extent. I had told Hariharan not to come in the evenings; that we would be moving out only at around eight for our dinner and he could come around that time unlike on earlier occasions when he would show up at six or six thirty as I wanted to pack in two hours of focussed study.

The next few days just passed like a dream. I was now having colourful company as Mitali would come attired in lovely suits or sarees, each day a different colour: on Monday it was a white saree; an orange suit on Tuesday; on Wednesday I saw her in a light green cotton saree; it was a pastel yellow cotton suit on Thursday; a red kameez and black salwar on Friday and on Saturday she came draped in a beautiful sky blue cotton saree. Perhaps she was following the colour codes that are worn according to the various Hindu gods associated with different days of the week. *Chandra* or Moon for Monday; *Mangal* or Mars for Tuesday; *Budh* or Mercury for Wednesday; *Brihaspati* or Jupiter for Thursday; *Shukra* or Venus for Friday; *Shani* or Saturn for Saturday; and *Ravi* or Sun for Sunday. She would wear a matching bindi on the forehead and matching glass bangles on her wrists. Her luxuriant ebony hair, sometimes in a single ponytail, sometimes, in two braids like young school or college going girls or some film heroines in old Hindi movies; twice she came with her two braids further rolled and tied as two small buns; she looked like Mickey Mouse, cute and lovely. Her lunar face had the effulgence of the sun and the soothing serenity of the moon.

It was not that I had made any specific efforts for having her sight; instead her visage and attire would be visible through a quick look from the corner of my eye while I would be shifting my stance to collect the vouchers on my table, while I would be entering them in the registers, and while I would take a glass of water or occasionally a cup of tea. I could not have looked at her directly as firstly I would have been easily noticed by the staff, secondly it would have also made me nervous and made her conscious. I was just enjoying the way things were shaping up; at least that unnecessary tension of mine of not talking to her had evaporated and it was a very pleasing and healthy interaction that made me feel very good. Moreover, for me she was any other person of a different gender, and she was not my interest … I was still wedded to the memories of Shama. I was only a traveller and Raipur—my temporary station. I would be moving out from there in another two to three months. My training schedule had arrived and my stay at Raipur would be over by mid-July. Thereafter, my next branch training would be in Dewas, a place near Indore.

Despite the excitement of her company in the branch, my family's absence pricked me. I had still not overcome my homesickness. May be that sensitivity was an integral part of my personality, and that was to play an important role in my life. Every day, after returning home and freshening up, I would immerse myself in my books. It was perhaps Wednesday evening, and Pradeep had gone to meet one of his friends. No letter had come from my family for almost a week.

While at the branch, the next day, Mitali casually asked, 'Do you get letters from your people regularly? What do you do when it doesn't come? You know when I was in a hostel and my parents were staying far away, I would cry if I didn't get one from them,' she continued.

I was already very depressed, and her question reminded me of my family and home. 'I do miss them,' I said, 'and I too sometimes cry.' I do not know how I could tell this to her as normally a man is not supposed to cry; and if at all one does, it is not disclosed. That day while returning home I felt desperation … desperation of running away from Raipur; I was terribly homesick and wanted to be with my people. I started cursing myself, 'Why did I leave my place and come to join at Raipur? Why? Just for the sake of money and status? And, sacrificing the love and affection of my people?' I craved for them but I was not in their vicinity.

Life is strange and imparts us lessons at various junctures: when we are with our near and dear ones, seldom do we realise the true worth of their affection and emotions; then we take it for granted and also sometimes feel that that is excess; it is when we are far away do we realise their true value, and we crave to reach out to them; to drink from the fountain of their love and affection.

By the time I reached home, I was choking, with my heart becoming heavy. I moved to the bathroom for ablution, and started singing as was my wont. Just one mug of water was enough to make me sing. But that day I was brimming with emotions and submerged in pain and melancholy. I started singing a song full of anguish from the movie *Masoom* that highlighted the dilemmas and stark realities of life:

'Tujse naaraaz nahin Zindagi,
Hairaan hoon main,
Tere masoom sawalon se,
Pareshaan hoon main…'

The pathos inherent in the song, coupled with my emotional state made me lose control over myself; by the time I had finished the first paragraph I was in tears. I continued singing with tears flowing down my cheeks; my throat clogged in between; the last few words hardly coming out from my mouth and remained stuck in my larynx stressing it with too much of pressure. I slumped on the bathroom floor, devastated by depression. After almost ten minutes I regained my composure and proceeded to have a bath. Cold water soothed my nerves, and I felt better; I appraised my situation, and then my mental tenacity took over; my determination was back.

After getting ready, I controlled my emotions and sat down to write one more letter to my mother … telling her not to worry about anything as … everything was under control.

It was Friday. Our friendship had grown well and on pious lines. In a few days she had become so friendly that she even asked me, 'When do you get up in the morning? Do you find enough time to study after the tiring schedule of this bank? Where do you have your meals? What do you prefer to eat?' I too without thinking much revealed everything.

It appeared that I knew her for a long time. I wondered how I had spent five months in the branch without ever talking to her! Now I even revealed to her, 'You know I have a friend named Hariharan; he is in Andhra Bank. The manager of Sharda talkies is his customer. And, till a month back we had been watching all kinds of movies whether kosher or kitsch, courtesy that manager.' When I recounted the names of those movies she laughed heartily.

I could make out that our interaction was now viewed by some staff, especially young ones, with some jealousy and even mystery. A few of them even made oblique references to her during their occasional conversation with me. I just told them curtly, 'Please, do not take it in any other manner; it is just a healthy interaction; you should not, always, interpret an interaction between the opposite genders with a jaundiced eye.' In fact, I became sour with a few who had passed acerbic comments imbued with cheap connotations. I stopped responding to their calls and even regular wishing of 'good morning'. Since I was quite affable, they too realised their follies soon and begged pardon. In no time, with the air cleared, the relations became normal.

That day she had come attired in a beautiful red kameez and black salwar. The shirt had some floral pattern of yellow. I had now become free with her. And, as was my wont, while working I started humming a song under my breath. I didn't know when she noticed that. While discussing certain things she just remarked, 'It seems you sing well.'

'Oh! No, I am not a trained singer. Though, I like singing very much.'

'Do you like singing?' I asked in return.

'I like it but I do not sing. My brother and sister sing well. They also sing ghazals which is the latest fad.' I had marvelled at the level of our interactions.

At four in the afternoon I saw her munching Cadbury's Five Star chocolate. I happened to notice that while moving in her direction to pick up a voucher that had flown by the air current of a pedestal fan. When she saw me she too felt amused. She immediately took out one more bar and offered it to me. I was wonderstruck at her simplicity and affection ... A *young female offering a chocolate to a young man*! I had seen such things only in television advertisements and not in real life. But, then I was now the recipient of one! I took it innocently with a natural smile and said, 'Oh! Thanks. Are you fond of chocolates?'

'Yes, very much,' she replied readily. While accepting the chocolate; I admired her simplicity and childlike nature. Before leaving for her house she asked me, 'Do you have that General knowledge Book by O.P. Khanna?'

'Yes; why?'

'My eldest sister is also appearing in the Civil Services Exam this year; she wanted that for a few days. Will you lend it to me? I will return it on Monday.'

I took a minute to decide and said, 'Well, I can do that; but you must return it positively on Monday; you know, there isn't much time left for the exam and I need it. For the time being I would make some changes in my study schedule. I will bring it tomorrow.'

I was happy. She had asked me for a favour. It was not a bad bargain for a chocolate!

The next day I gave her the book. I too made a request, 'You told me that your brother and sister are fond of Hindi ghazals. Do you have that ghazal album of Talat Aziz with the song, "*Kaise sukoon paoon, tujhe dekhane ke baad, Ab kya Ghazal sunaoon tujhe dekhane ke baad...?*" If so, then kindly get me the lyrics, I like that ghazal very much.'

'Oh, I'll try,' she replied.

After the evening routine, and finishing my studies, I came out for dinner with Pradeep and Hariharan. During dinner Pradeep commented jovially, 'Nowadays he is enjoying the good company of Mitali in the bank; today she even gave him chocolate.'

Hariharan chuckled, 'Oh is it so? That's great news. So finally you could make friends with that lady. You were very curious about her; weren't you?'

Like normal conversations of young men, Mitali used to figure in our talks earlier. Young girls are always the topic of curiosity for young boys though not necessarily in a vulgar or malicious manner. It is just healthy interest in the opposite sex, a law of nature.

'Oh nothing special about that; I was assigned the cash scroll desk next to her as the regular clerk had gone on leave. It's just a healthy interaction,' I clarified with a lot of emphasis.

As usual, at night we went for a stroll. Pradeep's mind was still turbulent about me. He again initiated the topic of Mitali and asked, 'Are you sure there is nothing more than a healthy friendship in your interaction? Just ask yourself; sometimes we are unable to read the signs.'

'Pradeep, I respect your concern; but trust me, there is nothing like that; and I have already told you about my love interest—it's not here; it was in Delhi; this is only a transitory phase of my life. I am neither going to settle down here nor do I have any interest in her. In fact, I respect her as a very good human being; I am happy that I could redeem my trust in myself and am able to conduct with decency. I am also exultant that my personality that I had so carefully cultivated has helped me in building such good bonding with the opposite gender. It shall be an unforgettable experience of my life. Let us not read too much into this,' I was composed and calm and he felt reassured. In my heart I admired his concern for me.

Caught Between Two Fevers

As time was running out, I utilised Sunday thoroughly. Pradeep too had to put up with me in the house as he did not have anything else to do. Poor chap! He kept on reading some magazines and even had an afternoon nap. I was deeply absorbed in my books; at times it was boring but I had no choice. I had to study per force to complete the course and succeed in my long cherished goal.

To overcome that ennui and to balm my emotions, I also wrote a letter to my mother, 'Mummy, my preparations are going on well. I am resolute and determined to achieve my goal. My preliminary exams are scheduled for 10th June, and I would be reaching Delhi on 7th morning. So, please book my return ticket for Raipur from Delhi for Monday, the 11th June.' In the post script, I wrote, 'I miss you all very much.'

At around five in the evening, Pradeep said, 'Don't you feel bored remaining in the house the whole day? Let us go out and have a cup of tea. I feel since you have been studying continuously for a full week, you should take a break. Why not watch some movie today? I am sure it's going to refresh and rejuvenate you.'

I agreed readily. He was right I felt my attention, after such strenuous hours, was wavering and I seemed to be losing focus. In no time we were headed for Indian Coffee House. We ordered some French toasts, Upma and coffee and in the meantime scanned the pages of a local newspaper.

'Why not watch *Hero* at Raj talkies? Although, I have seen the movie twice in the past it is enjoyable. What do you say?' I proposed.

'Yes, anything goes for me. And *Hero* is a nice movie with lovely songs,' Pradeep's tone was exuberant. After all he was seeking an escape from the boredom that beset him on Sundays and holidays. He was a devoted worker of the bank and didn't like sitting idle. Here, he did not have his family; hence, boredom for a singleton was obvious.

We relished the snacks and coffee over light discussions about tennis and cricket. The movie theatre was not very far, and we were there soon. Inside, everything was refreshing, unlike the heat outside. The cool air of the coolers and vibrant colours of the theatre changed the mood. The advertisements were followed by the trailers of a few upcoming movies. The movie started. Even though I had seen the movie on a couple of occasions earlier still everything appeared new. Jackie Shroff's style, his gait and mannerisms impressed me. I felt as if I was on the screen living his character. Meenakshi Sheshadari looked stunning; her lovely appearance, cute demeanour and vivacious acting were marvellous. I got totally immersed in the movie; but that song in Anuradha Paudwal's voice was riveting with Meenakshi Sheshadri dancing exquisitely:

'Nindiya se jaagi bahar,
Aisa mausam dekha pehli baar…'

All of a sudden I saw her face getting obliterated and then getting transformed into … into the face of Mitali. I could distinctly see the lively, smiling face of Mitali in all elegance and grace. Her face had the resplendence of the sun and the soothing glow of the moon; it had a lovely smile revealing her shining white teeth through her half parted lips; her black hair was glistening and flowing like a water stream; her eyes looking at me in a mystical manner with her brow arched in mischief. I remained stupefied; mesmerised by the aura and emotions it engendered in me. In the last few months it was the second time. I must say that the first time I was startled but this time I was euphoric! Her smile was sending sensations of pleasure in my mind and heart. Something had gone wrong … I felt. That feeling and the hallucination didn't end and it continued throughout the movie. It was a phantasmagoria where Meenakshi was Mitali and I felt myself in place of Jackie Shroff. Pradeep was watching the movie intently totally unaware of what I was experiencing. The song:

Tu mera jaanu hai,
Tu mera dilbar hai;
Meri prem kahani ka tu hero hai….'

with its lilting music was getting etched in my psyche, entering deep recesses of my conscience.

After the movie we had dinner. 'You are unusually quiet Rohit; what happened?' asked Pradeep.

'Nothing in particular; I am just wondering that time is fleeting, and I have to cover a lot of course,' I replied in a desperate attempt to conceal my emotional state. Pradeep was a mature man and he didn't rake the issue further. He just tried to divert our attention to other trivialities.

After reaching home also I did not feel at ease. I was going through a strange predicament. I pondered over what had happened in the cinema hall. *What interest had I in Mitali?* While in bed late at night I found Shama's sweet face reappearing, telling me, 'How can you forget me, an inseparable part of you; your soul mate; your true and only love till eternity; Mitali is only a momentary distraction … to remove your loneliness and add some transient spark in your life—your life, which in this far off place, away from your people is becoming dull, boring and empty; it is only a passing phase and you will be all right once you are transferred out of Raipur; you must not forget your goal of getting into Civil Services. Come on! try your best, and you will certainly succeed; all this is ephemeral and illusory; just to give you experiences in life so that the hesitations that you have been harbouring right since your childhood and even in your youth … of not talking to the girls are banished; after this you would be a man without any inhibitions and no distraction shall affect you.' While saying so, she stretched her hand. I took her hand in my hand with affection, caressed it and put it on my eyes and then on my lips. I could hear myself uttering, 'Yes Shama. You are my true love. How can I forget you? We had a pact. It didn't materialise in this life; but we shall be together in many incarnations … till eternity. Shama, you have taught me the meaning of love. This heart is yours. You are the presiding deity of my heart. Yes, it is all illusion; it's all evanescent. I am only a traveller, on a short sojourn to Raipur. Soon, my stint here will end, and I shall lead my life wedded to your memories.'

Shama smiled, and took her hand from my grip. Then slowly she caressed my head and my hair, and lovingly patted my cheeks, and said, 'Don't worry, we shall be together in the next incarnation. I give you my word. I could have been yours in this life too. But, you were very timid. You never sincerely tried to search for me. One just can't be a fatalist. Pursuit of love is arduous. Besides, intense love, you need efforts. You just can't attain love without exerting. I hope in our next incarnation, you won't act timid and slothful. Ha ha ha ha ha …' Shama's laughter was melodious and sharp. Then slowly she prepared to move. It seemed she was floating in the air. She waved at me very affectionately. Then she morphed into a red butterfly, my red butterfly; slowly fluttering her wings and gliding. I reciprocated her adieu. She vanished into thin air.

No sooner did Shama's apparition disappear, came another red butterfly fluttering its wings and gliding elegantly.

'Oh, Shama, you are back,' I shrieked.

But this butterfly was shining brilliantly and it was much more vibrant than the earlier one. It came nearer and then suddenly transmuted into the vivid image of a smiling Mitali, her eyes naughty and her gaze piercing.

She laughed, 'So, you will leave me Rohit. Do you think I will let you do that? You have pursued me, and now you say all this is illusory and transient. Let me see how you will forget me. You kindled this flame of love in me, and now you say it's nothing. Shama is gone. She is someone else's in this life. Is it right of you to think of and harbour feelings for someone else's wife? Is it not unrighteous? Maybe you will be with her in your next life. But I too am your soul mate. And, our lives in this life are intertwined. If you don't believe me then try. Let's see whether you leave Raipur alone.'

'But it is true that Shama is my true love. Try to understand. You are just a good friend of mine because you are a very good person ... I ...' I was arguing with Mitali.

'Shama is your past, she is history now. I am your present; I am not an illusion but reality. How can you ignore reality for something which just lives in your consciousness, which is just a memory? You are trying to deceive yourself Rohit. You love me; you have been having this desire of getting closer to me. You have been manoeuvring to reach me. You are unnecessarily trying to cling to your memory, which shall not let you move on in life.'

'But Mitali, Shama is my true love. I could understand the meaning of love because of her. She is always in my senses and my psyche,' I said.

'Ha ha ha, don't try to fool yourself Rohit. There have been two instances recently when instead of Shama you have seen me in your hallucinations. It's not for any reason. I am now ruling your psyche. You have been missing my absence in the bank. Do you think you can mask your emotions? I have watched you closely in the bank. I have seen your cheeks becoming ruddy when you have been in my vicinity. I have seen how my sight brings a twinkle to your eyes. I have seen through your planning. Why did you alone try to have full training in the bank and not Raghavan? Why have you been shifting to various desks? Was it only to learn the job? Be honest!' she asked. Haaaaa haaaa haaa. Her laughter was now resonating. I found my face losing colour. I had been caught. I became speechless and then merely blabbered, 'may be ... Perhaps ... but ... I, I, I can't decide.' I closed my ears with my palms. Mitali's laughter was now echoing ... I found my defences going down. Mitali got transfigured into that shining butterfly again and started its flight. I moved and then started running after her. 'Don't ... please don't go. I want you ...' I uttered.

I don't know when that spell melted into that unconscious state of dreams. When the next day I awoke I could vividly remember what I had seen in my dreams. I had dreams of the songs '*Tu mera jaanu hai*' and '*Nindiya se jaagi bahaar*', and in those dreams I was dressed up like Jackie Shroff and Mitali like Meenakshi Sheshadari, and we were singing the lyrics and acting to the tunes of those songs. Nature's splendour was profuse in the dream sequences and so was Mitali's beauty ... sublime, innocent and pure.

On Monday I was back at my usual desk of Savings Bank wearing my trademark blue jeans and light pink shirt. A week having been spent on a different desk, things appeared a wee bit odd. I had now returned to public dealing and the work load was a little more than cash scroll. Something appeared amiss to start with. The morning rush that continued during the normal transaction hours till three, kept me busy. Still I felt a little hollow.

In the morning, I had portrayed as if everything was normal. I just wished Mitali 'Good Morning' in my usual amiable manner laced with my natural smile. And, she too reciprocated. I didn't keep my gaze on her for long; thus giving the impression that missing her company didn't matter to me. But ever since morning I was perturbed. Time and again my eyes would try to have a glimpse of Mitali. I saw Kumar sitting beside her — both of them absorbed in their work. In fact on a couple of occasions I saw them chatting ... and I was filled with a strange sense of envy. I was reminded of the beautiful moments that I had the chance to spend with her in the absence of Kumar. I was gripped by a strange contrast of emotions of heaviness and emptiness simultaneously. Much later did I realise that I was missing her very much. Despite the crowd and colleagues around me there was a surreal melancholy. I could feel what I used to experience during the phase when Shama had left my neighbourhood.

During lunch at the Ambassador Hotel with Pradeep, I was again quiet. Pradeep, cajoled me to talk, and even raised a specific query, 'Are you all right Rohit? I hope there is nothing wrong. You look lost.'

'Oh no, I am a little worried about my exams; time is short, you know,' I replied feebly. I made a futile attempt at lying. Suddenly, I became aware of a ghazal being played in the background.

Ghazals had become a craze during that phase as Hindi film music was on the decline both as regards lyrics and even the melody. Ghazals, earlier appreciated only by the elite class, had become popular with the masses. Initially Jagjit Singh and Chitra Singh had popularised it but later Pankaj Udhas with his sweet, mellifluous voice and simple and effortless style mesmerised the masses. All of a sudden everybody was listening to Ghazals, whether in hotels, restaurants, and even in paan-cigarette shops. They became new vehicles of expression of people's sentiments. Many new singers were now cashing in on the Ghazal boom.

I could hear the sweet voice of Pankaj Udhas weaving magic:

'*Aap jinke karib hote hai, wo bade khush naseeb hote hai,*
Aap jinke karib hote hai ...'

I was immersed in those lyrics with its mesmerising tune and ... I could feel the meaning and sentiment of each of those words and the sensitivity of the rendition ... I felt an inner stirring; that ghazal was deeply affecting me, and I felt as if I was singing that ghazal for Mitali.

Pradeep was mature and experienced. With his sagacity he was reading my emotional state. He said, 'Oh come on. Something is troubling you and you are reluctant to share. Out with it! Are you not missing her company?'

Still I was adamant; I was not willing to concede. 'No. Not at all; I am just homesick,' I persisted, in a vain attempt to hide my feelings.

Rest of the time in the bank after lunch was spent in day-book writing and winding up. I just had a few glimpses of Mitali while I made two visits to the washroom. I passed by her and on both the occasions made stern promises to myself, of not betraying my state to her. That was warranted also as I didn't know whether she too missed my company or not. Later, in the evening at around 5:45, I found her seat vacant with no sign of her belongings! She had left for the day! But that one thing compounded my tribulations of the day as I felt very very lonely; I felt as if I would slump to the ground. I could feel the heaviness in my chest and a lump in my throat. I felt like going to a corner and crying. But I couldn't and my stifled feelings choked me. With a lot of effort I collected myself and when it was well past six, I left the branch with Pradeep … quiet. Quiet, yes quiet, I had really become involved though I was not willing to accept it.

Later, in the evening at home, after ablutions and all, I concentrated on my studies as those I could never ignore. A quiet dinner and then harder studies made me forget Mitali.

But late at night when I retired to bed I was left wondering: what had gone wrong? What was happening to me? I came out of the house to get some fresh air. Pradeep was fast asleep; but my mind was racing and thoughts were churning at a high pitch; one thought replacing the other, there was confusion profound. *What should I do? I was at the crossroads of my past and present, wondering which direction to take. There was Shama—my past, the anchor of my life, my sentiments and my emotions; her memories the moorings of my personality that had sustained me for more than seven years. And, there was Mitali who was so very real, and had been reciprocating my friendship; and I had now begun feeling differently about her. I didn't know what feelings she had for me; but I wanted to possess her forever …*

The next day, I thought I was in control. The previous night's resolve had made me rein in my emotions. I kept on reminding myself of my purpose, my goals and the transience of my stint at Raipur. I made myself believe that I missed Mitali's company as she was a very good individual and maybe one misses such company more. I was reminded of my childhood when I used to feel sad when my cousins would leave for their homes after spending a few days with us. I consoled myself, 'So this was also a nice association for a short while and maybe as she had behaved in a very nice and affectionate manner, she appeared to be someone like my own relative. There is nothing new in the whole episode and I should forget it. I am no longer a child. Moreover there has not been any kind of overture from her side evincing that she missed me. Why should I needlessly interpret too much into that when there is just nothing in it?'

Late in the evening, when it was time to leave the branch, I again felt dejected when I saw Mitali's empty seat. I was left wondering. But a strange event jolted me. I found Mitali's voice from the opposite side of the counter. I looked up. Apropos Tuesday she was in an orange suit; she was talking to another lady who I learnt later was her friend Seema Tiwari who worked in Punjab National Bank branch at Jaistambh Chowk. I smiled on seeing her, and then bent down feigning to be busy in my work, though my heart had started pounding on seeing her; I was rejuvenated. I wanted to see her again but controlled myself.

Then I heard, 'I haven't brought your book. I hope you won't mind if I bring it on Thursday.' Her voice appeared to be laden with honey and oxygen … yes, it was sweet like honey as ever and it also had the oxygen needed for my dipping heart.

I was startled for a moment, but recovered my poise immediately. I just replied in a feeble and nonchalant tone, 'Oh no problem at all.' But only I knew while saying so, I felt, as if I was carrying loads of weight on my tongue and my heart … yes, my heart felt an enormous ache … as if it was being pricked by thousand needles … as if someone was singeing it with a red hot iron. She stood there for a fraction of a moment longer as if reading my thoughts; but she too did not say anything further as I had not given any scope for any kind of conjecture through my forthright reply.

Whenever I sit idle, I reminisce and realise how much pain I had inflicted on myself and others by not opening up! While a little bit of hint could have saved me and others from that needless pain and feelings of uncertainty, I chose to clam up. I, in the process of projecting the image of a good boy, had sacrificed many good moments and precious times which could have been, but could not be. It is truly said, 'Excess of everything is bad.'

I returned home with Pradeep, again very quiet, lost in my own thoughts. I had a bath and as usual got engrossed in my studies. They were the most important part of my life … yes, the key to my future. The rest of the time was again spent as usual; the routine of dinner and then walk. But wherever I went, it appeared the song of Pankaj Udhas was following me, deeply affecting my thoughts and heart:

'*Aap jinke karib hotey hai …*

Wo bade khush naseeb hotey hai …'

Whether it was hotel or shops on the way; everywhere the same song was being played; in the sweet melodious voice of Pankaj Udhas, with deep emotional overtones woven in lilting tune, it had become a fad. But no one except Pradeep knew how that song was impacting me and how well it was accentuating and emoting my feelings. If all the people in Raipur knew the 'Art of reading minds', they would have easily discovered my pathetic state. But luckily or unluckily for me they were not bestowed with such faculty.

I had earlier been in love with Shama but now was feeling the absence of Mitali! What was it? I didn't know. Maybe the good words she had spoken to me and the way she had conducted herself, I had found a good friend; and, one misses the absence of a good friend. I just couldn't comprehend what was happening to me.

A day passed. It was Thursday; and on two consecutive days in a row I had not spoken to Mitali in the bank. I had seen her from a distance and just wished her. But, I felt a distance. Was it my creation? Was I afraid of the fact that what would the people around say? Was it because I was fighting some wars, as usual, within? The issue had become complex, and I had no control over it nor could I understand it. I wanted to regain that simplicity and access to her as I had earlier, but there was no way perhaps. God, however, has his own designs and he had at that moment too; and I left everything to God.

Thursday evening. I was lost in my studies as usual. All of a sudden, Hariharan dropped in. He knew that I was preparing for my exams, and unlike earlier times couldn't spend time with him or move around. Pradeep also knew that. Hariharan, however, entreated, 'Come on man, let us go out. In two days I will be going to my native place for a month. You can peacefully study then.' I was quiet. He again pleaded, 'Come on man, please.'

My first reply was, 'No.'

I do not know what possessed me. But from my tone even he could make out that I was a bit low. 'Come on pal; what happened? Is she not giving you chocolates these days?' Hariharan teased. When he saw my response was dull, he insisted, 'We must go out. We can even go out to Ballar Bhai Nagar. Let us go to her house; would you come?' I do not know what happened to me that day, at that very moment I immediately agreed ... yes, to my own surprise and more to the amusement of Pradeep. When I looked at Pradeep, he smiled and said, 'Today, you must go and see her at her house; yes, don't worry; and yes, have courage; after all she is your friend.'

Thus we embarked upon a blind but amusing quest which was impelled by some quirky feeling of my heart. It must have been seven in the evening when we commenced our expedition . We hailed a rickshaw and told him to go to Ballar Bhai Nagar. The rickshaw fellow was a bit confused and with a bewildered face asked, 'Where is this place Sir?'

Hariharan said, 'Don't you know? It is near Civil Lines.'

Much later I discovered that Hariharan too was not much familiar with the place. In fact, the indication 'Civil lines' too was at my behest as I had heard Mitali mentioning that it fell in her route. But I was sure that Ballar Bhai Nagar was in existence as when I had mentioned to Mitali that I knew where she lived, and quoted that name, she had not corrected me. But soon we learnt that we were searching for something whose existence was questionable. We moved on. Reaching Civil Lines itself took us almost twenty minutes. Now the fun started. We kept on stopping the rickshaw at various places and enquired about the name of the locality but did not meet with much success. Most of the people said they didn't know; but one person went to the extent of mentioning, 'Man, in my twenty years stay in Raipur I have never come across that name.' I was disheartened. But I really cannot fathom what force within impelled me to stay on course for that enterprise.

After meeting five persons we had to revise the search as the sixth person gave the lead, 'You see, I have not heard of Ballar Bhai Nagar but I feel it could be Vallabh Nagar.' It occurred to me that maybe Mr Singh who had entered her name and particulars on the saving bank ledger folio might have entered the words Ballabh instead of Vallabh as many people in India and more so Bengalis replace 'Vee' as 'Bee' in their speech and thus Vallabh must have been mentioned as Ballabh!

I felt like crying 'Eureka'. Instead I just said, 'Oh possibly yes. Is it nearby?'

'Yes, Vallabh Nagar is close by,' he said.

Thus in the dark alley of uncertainty, there was a glimmer of hope. *But what was propelling me?* I, who in Delhi had been so shy of speaking to girls, was perhaps under an unknown magic spell. At that hour of night, I was in pursuit of something, which in my rational senses I could never have attempted. But somehow, that day I had developed some arcane courage, and there was a saving grace: I was in the company of Hariharan who was fluent in English, had a few grey hairs; and for his age looked mature and decent; for me he had been a father figure. At around eight we finally reached Vallabh Nagar. We had to go to house No. 43.

Hariharan, an epitome of confidence till then, suddenly became conscious of what we had embarked upon. It struck him that one of his bank's customers lived in the neighbourhood. He said, 'Let me check-up; that boy lives in house No. 38; he would guide us whether we are looking for the right house; otherwise at such an hour in the night it would be a major faux pas.'

The Chase Begins

Knock at the door of house No. 38 brought us face to face with an amiable young man in his late twenties. He was surprised and exuberant to see Hariharan and wondered what had brought us there at such an hour. 'Oh it was just a routine walk,' said Hariharan with his characteristic nonchalance. 'We had come to meet somebody in house No. 43 and thought of meeting you also.'

'Oh! You actually came to see Mr Majumdar,' Rajesh, the young man, exclaimed.

'Do you know them?' I asked, with inner hope, but I kept my voice casual and my emotions in check.

I should not sound too enthusiastic and the glimmer of hope should not reflect a gleam in my eyes, I thought.

'I just know of them; I am not closely acquainted with them. But what brought you here?' he asked with restrained curiosity.

'Oh, nothing in particular; I happen to work with their youngest daughter in the State Bank, and thought I would just see them as I had come thus far to Civil Lines,' I replied in a casual offhand tone. The guy apparently believed me; and perhaps Hariharan's demeanour and his elderly looks must have convinced him that there was nothing ulterior.

'Are you working with the younger daughter? But I thought only their elder daughter was working in the State Bank,' it appeared a revelation to him. 'I actually thought they have two daughters and a son; in fact, almost half an hour ago, I had seen their eldest daughter going out on the scooter with their son.' While saying so, there was a twinkle in his eyes. *Grown up girls in any family are always a matter of interest to the young men around.* It seemed he too must have been cherishing a desire of becoming friendly with the family if he had an opportunity!

We spent ten minutes with the boy out of politeness and decency, and then making an excuse that going to Mr Majumdar's house too late would be odd, we took leave.

The real drama was yet to unfold. In two minutes we were at the gate of Mitali's house. The ambience around appeared very melancholic and silent as there was hardly any sign of street light or any activity around. The house was like a kothi in Delhi. The inner courtyard was very large, and there was a long distance between the main entrance and the outer gate. There was no sign of any bell. Some feeble sounds of television were emanating from deep within. It was eight thirty; it seemed *Chitrahaar*–the programme of selected songs from new and old Hindi movies was about to end. I could distinctly hear the last few lines of a song:

'Kaali ghori dwar khadi'

from the movie *Chashmebadoor* together with bouts of laughter from the inmates. We clanked the gate by hitting its clamp to the body. But there was no response. There were mixed feelings in my mind. I knew it was odd, and I was wondering how I would face the family members and what explanation I would tender for my visit at such an odd hour; there was no specific business to be transacted nor was there any message from any senior officers of the Bank that required my presence at their house. But the decent and elderly company of Hariharan and some pressing desire in my heart goaded me to somehow accomplish the mission which I had undertaken, and which to me too appeared to be shrouded in mystery.

When a few more knocks didn't elicit any response, we decided to enter the gate invoking the almighty to bestow us courage. We reached the main entrance through a pathway that was lined on both the sides with well-trimmed potted plants of various varieties; the entrance was enclosed by a grill door through which we could see the foyer leading to the entry for the drawing room. A small name plate in the dim light read, 'H.D. Majumdar, Project Director, Dandakaranya Rehabilitation Project'. There, besides the name plate, was a switch for the bell which I pressed with bated breath. There was some whispering inside the house and in no time an innocent looking boy of hardly fifteen appeared and started unlatching the grill door.

'Hullo! I am Rohit; I work with your sister Mitali in the State Bank of India, Kutchery branch.' Before I could finish my sentence, he smiled and ushered us to the drawing room. I was not prepared for such an easy entry, and quickly did some introspection. *Maybe I too was an innocent looking boyish young man of twenty-three who appeared to be around eighteen to twenty in blue denim jeans and white T shirt with prominent but thin black lines. I definitely didn't look like someone with a creepy demeanour and Hariharan too had gentle looks with thick spectacles and almost half of his hair grey.* We sat with an uneasy calm, uncertain about what was in the offing.

After about five minutes a pleasing young lady entered the drawing room accompanied by Mitali's father and we learnt that she was her elder sister, Shefali. She was very friendly and even garrulous. She had typical Bengali features, short but impressive stature, her complexion neither very fair nor dark. Her dark shapely eyes with arched brows evinced enough resemblance to Mitali.

I introduced Hariharan and myself and explained, 'We had just come to see Hariharan's friend in House No. 38, and thought we would drop in, having come thus far.'

She immediately made us feel comfortable in total contrast to the apprehension we had harboured on our entry. She talked to us on a number of topics, and in fact Mr Majumdar spoke for lesser time; but whatever he spoke about had substance and erudition. 'So, you are a Probationary Officer in the SBI. How do you like the bank? I don't think it's bad. Nowadays there is so much of political pressure on the Civil Servants,' he observed.

'But, I am still trying for Civil Services. It is my last chance,' I replied.

'Oh, you must try seriously. Civil Service is still the best. You get lot of power and prestige. There is so much of variety in the job,' his tone was encouraging.

Shefali intervened with a lot of enthusiasm, 'Are you staying in a lodge or house? Where do you have food?'

I was surprised by the lack of any inquisitiveness from their side about the purpose of our visit. Neither any uncomfortable questions were posed nor was any resentment expressed at our unannounced visit, at such an odd hour.

The treatment encouraged me to enquire about Mitali. *I was wondering at my audacity; in an unknown house and amongst unknown people, I had the temerity to specifically ask for her.* Mitali came. She was dressed in a normal night dress. She looked a bit slim but her eyes looked puzzled, it had to be; she must not have envisioned my presence in her house and that too so late!

Her sister now retreated from the scene and Mitali was there as a silent spectator to the conversation that her father was not ready to terminate. We too, like adept and good listeners, listened to something that was highly mature and full of wisdom. He was sharing his experiences of life as a Civil Servant and the kind of political interference he had to face; and how he had countered that without sacrificing his honesty and integrity. To me that was highly appealing as during those days my youthful energy and zeal would get fillip by the talks of honest Civil Servants standing up for a just cause. Hariharan's and my interjections made Mr Majumdar to carry the conversation further. I deliberately ignored her presence by not looking at her. Mr Majumdar was now smoking, and Mitali who throughout had silently been watching and hearing the exchange; intervened twice giving a mild rebuke in *Bangla* to her father for he had spilled the embers of cigarette on the table cloth. Mr Majumdar heard once but he appeared to have forgotten the reprimand for he was too engrossed. Mitali felt embarrassed; but she had to coax him, and gave a slightly stern refrain which jolted him; yet he gave a mild answer and continued. I just looked at her and smiled. In fact I used her interjections as the perfect excuse to look at her. Actually, my mind was there in the conversation while my heart was desperate to just behold her. *After all, I had come all the way to see her only. But I did not indicate that; I just posed as if it was purely a natural visit.* Mitali was perplexed, but it appeared that she was happy too as her demeanour didn't reveal any signs of annoyance.

It was getting late, and we took leave of them. Mitali and her father came to the gate to see us off. Since the things had become quite comfortable, I just joked, 'We had been standing at the gate full five minutes but didn't hear any reaction from your house; why don't you keep a dog? It appears a little unsafe.'

'Oh! We have been staying here for the past six years, and luckily never faced any difficulty. Our house is strange: we kept a dog but it never barked; we had a cock, but it never crowed; there is something wrong here, so we have stopped thinking on those lines,' Mitali spoke in a lighter vein. We burst into laughter. Wishing them good night we returned after a very successful jaunt. It gave me memories to cherish.

We reached Hotel Girnar for dinner and now the depression that had afflicted me before the onset of the journey was replaced by euphoria. I was grateful to Hariharan for his assistance and company and told him, 'Today's dinner is a treat from my side; you can order whatever you want.' Dinner was followed by ice-cream. 'But Hari, please don't read too much into this. It was merely a friendly visit to a good friend, albeit of the opposite gender. There is nothing serious; it was just because I was feeling lonely. My family and my goal are foremost to me; this is just an experience and a memory that would boost my confidence and help me in becoming a good individual.'

Hariharan laughed it off, 'Oh, I know man.'

On returning home late at almost ten forty-five, I found Pradeep waiting. 'I waited for you guys till eight thirty and then proceeded to Hotel Ambassador. There too I ate slowly but on finding no sign of both of you, I had no choice but to finish up. By the way, how was your trip? Were you joking or did you really venture to go to her house?'

I was anxious to brief him and in no time fed him with all the details and also qualified the whole story with my stand on the whole episode that I had shared with Hariharan.

Pradeep smiled, 'Anyway, are you happy now? When you left you seemed restless and your voice had a tinge of sadness.'

'Oh, yes, I am perfectly all right; it has given my personality a different dimension that is worth cherishing, but there is nothing serious about the whole affair; I just wanted to visit a good friend who is also a very good person.'

The dreams of that visit wafted through my sleep on that night. Time and again the scene was getting replayed in my dreams; when I woke up the next day, it was a feeling of freshness, verve and bliss!

Friendship Blossoms

I felt highly confident and at ease when I met her in the bank the next day. Perhaps, I had broken further ice; was it ice or the iceberg that I had demolished through my courageous foray into her house and met her father, sister and brother? I felt more at ease now as the wall of mystique had crumbled and my apprehensions had died with it too. I saw her: she was dressed in a sky blue dress — kameez, churidar and white lace chunni; with her two braids, and a bindi of matching hue.

After finishing my desk work at around two in the afternoon, when the crowd had thinned, I stole a few moments and sat in front of her. I had taken that step for the first time since we became friendly. 'I hope you didn't mind that I came to your house? You know, it was just a casual visit as I happened to be in your area, and just felt like visiting your place,' I clarified while looking at her bright shining eyes, which were dazzling like the reflections of the moon in a lake on a serene moonlit night.

'Oh not at all, why should I mind? By the way what brought you there? I understand you stay very far away.'

'Oh, it was because of Hariharan; you know I keep on moving around with him. He had to meet his friend Rajesh who stays in house no. 38 in your vicinity. I just asked Rajesh about your house, and there itself I thought of visiting your place.'

I wove the reply that appeared credible.

There was a startled look on her face. I, perhaps, had become a good actor now, and posed as if everything was normal and nothing was amiss.

Now, my interactions with her became very normal and my hesitation had vanished. I would come in the morning and while going past her would wish her; she would smile. Off and on, whenever I found time and opportunity, I would pull up a stool or a chair; sit in front of her, discussing just anything that would be of interest. Then I made a request, 'I am running short of time. Will you please return that GK book? And, one more thing; can you get me the lyrics of that ghazal, by Talat Aziz?'

Mr Mathur's son had sung that ghazal in Bhubaneswar.

A day later, she brought the book and also informed that it contained lyrics of the ghazal too. I was too curious to see her handwriting, and somewhere in my heart there was a craving to see something different. *Why that craving was there? I didn't have the answer to my inner rumbling*. I reached home and told Pradeep, 'I got my book back.'

'Have you got a letter stashed in the book too,' he chuckled. I enjoyed his remark in good humour, 'No, no letter, but she has given me the lyrics of the ghazal I desired. I am so happy to develop such a fine and healthy interaction.'

Pradeep smiled and later on at night during our after dinner stroll we discussed the ghazal. Pradeep was good in Hindi and Urdu and he helped me in understanding the true purport and depth of the lyrics. I thoroughly enjoyed that fine piece. I wondered if Mitali too knew the same or she had just perfunctorily jotted them down for me!

My preparations were in full swing and the disturbance and the turbulence that I had in my mind had subsided. Almost a week later, when it was last week of May, I got a surprise from her. While we were chatting, she surprised me with an unexpected proposal. 'If you are free on Saturday, you can come over to our house for dinner, say around 7:30,' she told me calmly but with a twinkle in her eyes.

I was wonderstruck. 'Well, I don't have any problem; I think I can come,' I replied coolly.

'Do you have any food preferences,' she went on.

'Oh no, none at all,' I said, 'anything goes for me; I feel home-cooked food is definitely better than what we get in the hotels; thanks a lot for the invitation.' I was jubilant and broke the news to Pradeep while returning.

'Oh something strange is brewing,' he mused, 'I hope it is not a marriage proposal like the song:

'*Shayad meri shaadi ka khayal dil me aaya hai,*
Issi liye mummy ne meri tumhe chai pe bulaya hai.'

Pradeep quoted.

'Oh, what are you saying?' I protested, 'It is just a plain and simple invitation; you are reading too much into something innocuous.'

'Just joking dear.'

I was ruminating how in a short span Pradeep had become so close to me that I could discuss everything with him. His company gave me a comfort zone similar to my family. I passed those few days with a lot of excitement, and on Friday I deliberately went to her and got the confirmation. And, then on the D day …

I spent the whole of Saturday wrapped in studies as the countdown had already begun. It generally happens that as the time approaches, butterflies start fluttering in one's stomach as the will to do well and succeed also gives rise to fears of uncertainty. Similar apprehensions were also ruling my heart and mind when in the evening I was getting ready to go to their house. I got ready at six lest I may get delayed. I decided to be near their house by seven and calculated a rough commute time of forty-five minutes. I thought I would hang about in that locality for a while and shall present myself sharp at 7:30. While calculating thus I must have combed my hair at least ten times and might have appraised myself and my attire an equal number of times in the dressing table mirror. In my heart I also thanked my landlord Mr Bakshi for providing me that luxury of a dressing table which gave me enough confidence.

Dressed in my light pink shirt with light brown lines and matching light brown trousers and with brown half boots, I boarded the rickshaw for Vallabh Nagar. Suddenly the sky became overcast, announcing the possibility of pre-monsoon showers; a dusty wind started blowing, and on the way it started drizzling. I didn't want to spoil my dress and found the rickshaw puller too not very keen to move on. So we took a break at Jaistambh Chowk. We took refuge under the awning of a tea stall beside the road. I was constantly worried about my hair and the wavy puff that I soulfully cherished. I didn't want to get delayed too and prayed to the heavens, which had opened up, to rein in the rain, and leave the benevolence of the clouds for some other time. Luckily my prayers were answered and the drizzle stopped.

My journey recommenced and to my delight I was at Vallabh Nagar by seven. Butterflies in my stomach now started a ballet and in no time it was transformed to salsa and tango as my breathing quickened. Anxiety of facing the uncertain had increased as I didn't know how the encounter with all the family members would turn out to be. I kept looking at my watch and somehow killed fifteen minutes roaming about in the colony; each minute was like an hour. Then at 7:15, I started the march to her house and calibrated my speed with the time and the distance; finally, sharp at 7:30, I found myself entering their house through the main gate, and in no time my finger pressed her doorbell. I waited with bated breath. In a minute I heard footsteps approaching.

I discovered through the grill that it was Mitali in a blue sleeveless kameez and salwar of the same hue; her untied black glistening hair was flowing like a fountain down to her knees; she had a white diaphanous dupatta unsuccessfully covering her upper torso and arms; her eyes had kohl; a medium sized blue bindi adorned her brow, it accentuated the glimmer of her face. I was disconcerted by her presence. With a faint mysterious smile she welcomed me, and in no time ushered me to the drawing room. I just followed her as if under a spell. She made me comfortable, and her confidence was tremendous. I was feeling a bit awkward but I tried to put up a brave face.

'How did you manage? Did you have any problem because of the sudden drizzle?' she initiated the conversation.

'Oh, it was fine; the drizzle luckily stopped in time, so no problem,' I replied. *Life and times make you gain self-control and poise when it is required the most*.

She talked about my preparations. I asked, 'Where is everybody else?'

'They are inside, will join us shortly' she said. 'Wait, let me call them.'

After a gap of almost five minutes, came her sister Shefali, followed by her father. She was talkative like in the previous visit; I liked her promptness and straightforward nature. She was very childlike and affectionate as I learnt during the course of our conversation.

'How are your parents? How many brothers and sisters do you have? Where do they stay?' she asked many questions and put me at ease.

'I have one sister only. We are from Delhi. My father is currently posted at Ludhiana. He comes to Delhi during weekends,' I answered.

'Do you eat in a hotel or do you cook at home?' her question and her manner touched me.

'I am here for only six months and there is no provision for cooking; besides, there is paucity of time too; so I have to resort to hotels only.'

'How old is your sister? Don't you miss your family?' was her next question. It touched another emotional chord in me and I felt so much at home while talking to her. Mitali's father too joined the conversation and enriched the same with anecdotes of his experiences as a career bureaucrat. I too, with my youthful energy, idealism and feelings of bringing about a change in the society enjoyed such discussions; Raghavan's taunts had changed me to a different person; from the raw youth who had landed up at Raipur. I just couldn't keep track of how fast time progressed that evening.

'Can I meet your sister who is studying for the IAS? I am keen to see how other aspirants look like,' I interjected during the discussions. 'I will call her,' saying thus Mitali disappeared; she had been a silent observer and had been keenly appraising my conduct. I had been looking at her throughout from the corner of my eyes, but had been posing as if she did not exist. In five minutes entered another beautiful young lady with large eyes, fair-complexion and smiling face. But she was a bit reticent compared to Shefali; she was Dipali. I found all the sisters to be very elegant. I had already met their brother. So the only person remaining was her mother.

And, to my amazement she appeared, very gracefully attired in a typical Bengali cotton saree–white with a red border. She was wearing spectacles and her slightly grey hair imparted her a very dignified appearance. And, I was immediately reminded of my mother. I was totally mesmerised by her personality; I bent and touched her feet. She too was overwhelmed by the gesture. 'Do you take proper care of yourself? Your mother must be really worried about you; how many members are there in your family?' she showered all the questions in one go.

'I am the only son and I have one sister; she is younger to me and presently studying in 12th standard,' I replied. I don't know why I felt totally at ease in Mitali's house; besides, the conduct and affection of her family members was so much like my own family.

I just didn't realise how time flew past till Mitali announced, 'Dinner is ready. Let's go to the dining room.' Other members of the family barring her father and myself remained in the drawing room. While he was guiding me to the dining room, I expressed a desire to use their washroom. He said, 'Oh I will show you the way.' Then only did I learn that they had a small washroom attached to the drawing room with a very small door that hardly indicated whether such provision existed there. Inside I marvelled at myself how life had changed for me … from being a total stranger to Mitali and her family, I had been conferred the honour of dining in her house and now I had become so informal with her father as to seek direction to the loo. When I came out, I found her father waiting for me patiently. He immediately escorted me to the dining room and there, I must say, I was treated like a prince.

Her mother and Shefali going overboard in extending all hospitality, and enquiring, 'What dishes would you prefer? Do you have any favourite? We don't know whether you would like our Bengali preparations.' I was overwhelmed by the affection, even more than the delicacies that were being served.

Her father also intervened, 'We people are basically non-vegetarians. So the probability of the vegetarian items not being good is very high; but still they have tried their best.' I was touched by his highlighting this fact.

I reassured them, 'Oh no, everything is delicious; I am thoroughly enjoying the food. And, even more than the food, I am enjoying the affection and love you people have mixed in it; it is very special for me.' My voice became a bit choked conveying my emotions. I saw Mitali giving me appreciative looks with her gleaming eyes.

Dinner over, as it was late, I took leave of them, thanking them profusely for the trouble and efforts they had undertaken. Mitali and her father came up to the gate to see me off. I hailed a rickshaw, and on the way kept on thinking about an extraordinary evening that I had never foreseen …

On my return I shared my experience with Pradeep who heard my account with suppressed amusement. While I was recounting he was constantly appraising my visage and my mannerisms, trying to read something. My ebullience couldn't remain concealed from his piercing gaze. Slumber at night had many dreams and trains of thought.

A Mother's Doubts and Fears

The day next, while on our way to the bank, I asked, 'Now that I have become so friendly with Mitali, even to the extent of having been invited to her house for dinner; should I not buy her something she enjoys?'

'Why not? Of course you must,' Pradeep responded.

'I can buy some chocolates; She is quite fond of them,' I said, and we proceeded to a confectionary shop. I bought a 'Cadbury Five Star chocolate'. Now I had ammunition to strengthen our friendship…

Once inside the branch, I kept looking for an opportunity to meet her and got one when the workload was less and customers few. I deliberately planned a visit to the water cooler area, and on the way found her sitting idle looking towards the table of the Accountant and the Head Clerk. I just stopped on the way and using the concealment of the pillar next to her, bent near her table drawer, and whispered, 'How are you? Here is a small gift.' I spread my hand, half concealing the thing from the public view.

She was astonished, 'Oh, for me!'

I just smiled and proceeded to the water cooler. On my return after five minutes, I came and sat in front of her.

'I hope you liked the dinner yesterday,' she asked while her eyebrows danced and her eyes beamed.

'Very much! And, you people had laced it with your love. When I go to Delhi, I will tell my people about such a nice family in Raipur,' I replied innocently. I could see the glint in her eyes gaining in intensity. That day I felt some stirring inside me. During lunch, in the restaurant, a song was being played in the deep and mellifluous voices of Jagjit Singh and Chitra Singh from the movie *Saath Saath*:

'*Tumko dekha, to ye khayal aaya;*
zindgee dhoop, tum ghanaa saayaa.

Tum chale jaayoge to sochenge,
tum chale jaayoge to sochenge;

Humne kyaa khoya, humne kyaa paaya;
Zindgee dhoop, tum ghana saaya.

Aaj phir dilne, ik tamana kee,
Aaj phir dilne, ik tamna kee,
Aaj phir dilko, humne samjhaya
Zindgee dhoop, tum ghana sayaa
Tumko dekha to yeh khayal aaya ...'

What that song meant for me or for my life, I did not know but there was some magic in the song: in its lyrics, in its music and its rendition which captivated me, which enchanted me. There was something mystic in it which I could not fathom at that moment. But the song became an inseparable part of my psyche, constantly resonating in my mind and ears.

When I returned to the branch, I carried the fond lyrics and tune of the song in my heart and mind—without any conscious effort. The day passed and with that also passed the time. It became my routine to give chocolates to Mitali and chat with her, whenever I got the opportunity. I even mentioned this aspect in my letters to my family, '*I have a nice friend who gave me chocolates; now I too am reciprocating. I was once invited to their house for dinner.*' While writing thus I didn't have even an iota of hesitation; it was with all the innocence of a child. I even got a reply, '*We are happy to learn about your friend. But be careful that you should not get distracted or get entrapped into something.*'

A week before my departure for Delhi for my exams, Pradeep left for Ujjain, his native place as he also wanted to avail of joining time. I was left alone and maybe for the better as I could fully concentrate on my studies, and my confidence started soaring with every passing day. So, there was no tension on that count. In the branch, I was able to relieve my boredom and also kill my loneliness by talking to Mitali off and on besides my regular conversations with other colleagues.

The day of my departure had arrived and on 6th June I went to the branch only for half day as I had to catch the train at 2:30 pm. I planned to leave the branch by 1:15. At around 12:30 while I was sitting at the Savings Bank counter, I heard a little rustle behind me and then to my astonishment, I found Mitali opening my drawer and whispering, 'This is a sacred flower from God's temple; please carry it with you when you go for your exams.' With those words she vanished in a moment leaving me stupefied. I just became blank. *She is so much worried about me and my career! Why?'* I was befuddled. I looked into the drawer and saw a rose flower packed in a small polythene packet along with some prasad. Had I not been in the bank surrounded by staff and customers, I would have wept; I felt an immense sense of gratitude.

While leaving the branch, I just passed by her, waving at her with a smile. In the train I looked at that flower on a number of occasions while rummaging through my handbag. I ate the prasad, and deep in my heart I wished Mitali all the love and peace in the world. My heart was enthused. Her simple gesture had kicked up many storms in my heart. I hadn't imagined such reciprocation. *What was it? Was it her love or was it the concern of a good friend for another?* The latter appeared a bit odd as people say *that persons of opposite gender seldom become good friends; friendship undergoes transformation sooner or later*!

A simple thing had become a conundrum which only time would settle. I too consigned the matter to the backburner since my immediate concern was to address the seriousness of my exams. I picked up my books and magazines and tried to read whatever I could in the train, though my concentration was constantly disturbed by the intermittent arrival of the hawkers, the stoppage of train at various points; and the regular movement, influx and exit of passengers. The train would chug, drag and screech; and there were potent mixtures of cacophony of all shades, frequencies and pitch. The theoretical aspects of India's economy, politics, geography and the historical perspectives were getting alloyed with the realities of crowd and accentuated by the motley collection of personalities, voices and their tantrums. The only constants were the coordinates of my existence at that moment. The tumultuous affair was getting calming balm of the serene memories of Mitali and her present: '*God's flower*'.

And, after twenty seven hours, next evening I reached Delhi.

As usual, the arrival at Delhi brought back nostalgia, along with the craving of just remaining in Delhi, ruing my decision of having left it for greener pastures. The auto-ride from the station to home, traversing the familiar paths, streets, buildings and markets, returned the fond memories of all that I had experienced and enjoyed in Delhi. My arrival at home was as usual greeted and celebrated with the same fanfare, love and affection: hugging, wet eyes, fondness and attestation of eternal familial bond. But this time there was curiosity and anxiety too. After all, I had created a slight flutter by mentioning Mitali's name and our friendship! When the topic was broached during lunch time conversation, I warded it off politely branding it as a good and healthy friendship. I had to as I still didn't know the true import of all that had happened. I managed to set my mood for my studies; the exam was two days away.

But, I did not know that with the advent of Raj Mamaji and Mamiji, the matter would acquire a different twist. It was 6:30 in the evening. I had covered a great portion of my planned target. I was confident and obviously my systematic studies, past experience and the lighter magnitude of the Prelims had lessened the tension to a great extent. At that moment Raj Mamaji and Mamiji came to our house as they had information of my pre-announced programme. They enquired about my welfare and my preparation for the exam.

'I don't foresee any difficulty in your clearing this exam; it is only the Prelims and you have got experience of two years; we are very hopeful and confident; yes, much more than you are,' Mamaji said with fervour. 'We are very proud of you; in our family you are the only one who has taken up the challenge of Competitive Exams and have been successful in some of the prestigious ones,' his eyes brightened while saying so. Mamiji nodded in the affirmative. I could understand his sentiments. He was the one who had motivated and guided me when I was in a dilemma, suffering depression. His inspiring words had extricated me from the morass of diffidence and instilled self-belief in me. I acknowledged their gracious outpourings.

When the mood was light and conversation progressed, mummy ignited the issue which I least expected of her. 'He has made friends with a Bengali lady–his colleague in the bank; she gives him chocolates; and he has been to their house also for dinner,' mummy said enthusiastically with a twinkle in her eyes. Nalini gave a mischievous smile.

'Oh! That's great. How old is she?' was their immediate query.

I said with a little hesitation, 'She is around my age; may be an year or so younger.'

'Is she also an officer?'

'No; she is in the clerical cadre; she had also joined the bank in December.'

'How many members are there in her family? What does her father do? How are they? Do they have their own house? How come they have settled down in Raipur?'

They let loose a volley of questions.

'They are also refugees like us; from East Bengal. Her father was the Project Development Officer for the Dandakaranya project for rehabilitation of refugees from East Bengal after the Partition. He retired almost six years back; nowadays he is working with a private company, making their project reports. Her eldest sister too works in SBI in Raipur; the other sister elder to her is doing Masters in Music; and her brother, who is the youngest, is studying in 10th,' I gave her family's bio-data in one go as if I had done research. 'She used to give me chocolates and I also started exchanging the same. Then she invited me to their house for dinner; it's nothing, it is just a healthy friendship.' I concluded on finding Mamaji and Mamiji giving me amused and suspicious looks.

'Yes, yes, I can make out. But there is no harm if this healthy friendship is transformed into a permanent lifelong affair,' his eyes twinkled.

'Oh sure, why not; if you had become a doctor, you would have preferred a doctor wife and aptly so; and, now when you are a banker, there is nothing wrong in choosing a banker wife,' Mamiji supplemented despite mummy's whimpered protests.

'But they are Bengalis who eat non-veg and are not Brahmins either,' mummy emphasised.

'What are you talking about? These are modern times when the old social mores are undergoing change; after getting enough education if we still talk in this manner, we would be no less orthodox than others who are not ready to accept modern currents; I feel we should go by our hearts; if he likes her and she likes him, I don't think we should be stumbling blocks in their alliance; you should leave everything to destiny. I know he is mature enough to distinguish between right and wrong,' Mamaji retorted.

Mamiji too joined him with equal vehemence.

Mummy was a bit indignant at their stance, but she didn't express it in too many words or overtures. Her mild disagreement was however expressed by her little interjections and resentful shaking of her head. I was both startled and amused by such support coming from unexpected quarters.

But, then Mamaji concluded his sermonising with the strange statement, 'I was just joking. Don't take it seriously. Everything should be left to God; life is on a predestined course, and we never know what is in store for us in future; the future is uncertain and has an element of surprise; that is its beauty, and we should not unnecessarily waste our time and energy in thinking what is going to happen. My intention was to inculcate that our minds should remain open to all possibilities and we should be ready to accept what God has designed for us. And, let me tell you what He ordains cannot be stopped by anyone. Let your path be illumined by His grace. We have full faith in your simplicity, rationality and maturity.'

I was speechless; but I smiled, and then gave a muted laugh. I had never foreseen that a small disclosure about my friendship with Mitali would become the topic of such detailed debate; that I would get such hints from Mamaji; that he besides being a guide for my competitive career would also become a beacon for deciding my life partner!

They left on a very happy note, but left a lot of rumblings in Mummy's mind.

'Don't take their conversation too seriously. It is easier to preach to others; but you see for their son—who is settled in America—they have been looking for an Indian wife. It is easier to profess dual standards in one's own life and tell others to become modern,' Mummy insinuated, expressing her reservations unequivocally.

My spirits which had touched the seventh heaven now dashed to the ground. But it was not the time to indulge in any arguments. I had to focus on my exams.

I got ready for the Prelims. Luckily this time the examination centre was very close to my house; just walking distance. And this time apart from the regular puja by my mother, and applying of that auspicious tilak on my forehead, I had a 'special flower' with good wishes from one other well-wisher … Mitali. I had kept the flower with a lot of care and concern in my pencil box.

During the exam, I did not face any difficulty. My systematic studies and experience of two years made me sail through the arduous exam. In any case it was Prelims and the Main exam was still far away. Yet this too was an achievement as many a good candidate would fail or falter at the first stage itself either due to complacency or getting overawed by the occasion. Throughout the exam, I was caressing that 'precious flower'. That 'precious flower' imbued with God's blessings gave me the necessary support and alacrity to my faculties of remembrance and recall.

In the evening, I returned home with a victorious smile and a sweet-sour pain in my heart. Something had gone seriously amiss!

Late in the evening we went to the nearby market at Kamla Nagar whose acronym 'KNAGS' is highly popular amongst students at the North Campus in the Delhi University.

Mummy purchased two T shirts for me from a known vendor. One was round necked, collarless; its sleeves being very short, just two inches from the shoulders; it was white coloured with prominent thin wire stripes; just two buttons. When I tried it in front of the mirror, I felt a bit awkward although it looked awesome … my wheatish complexion and innocent face with my bouffant hair added a distinct vivacity to my personality. Another one was of bright sky blue shade with normal collar and half sleeves. It was dazzling. I protested as I didn't want to look flamboyant. But mummy and Nalini liked them and said, 'This is the latest fad and you should not lag behind.' Even the vendor said candidly, 'For your age they look good; you must sport such clothes. If not now, when? When you are old?'

Mummy also said with a naughty smile, 'They are nice and I am sure *she* will be mesmerised on seeing you in these clothes.' Nalini's eyes too twinkled with mischief.

I didn't know what was happening around me. It all appeared to be a dream. And, throughout I maintained that 'she' was my friend.

Late in the evening I did go to meet my cousins also as I had not seen them since I had landed up in Delhi. It was a sweet meeting. We had tea and snacks. In fact, it was my second visit to Delhi since I had joined the bank. I told them, 'I couldn't come to meet you all as I had my exam and was running short of time. I promise, in my next visit in the month of July, after completion of my first branch training, I will spend enough time with you people.' Neelima had joined Life Insurance Corporation as an Assistant Administrative Officer after leaving her job as a clerk in the State Bank. But she was not very happy in the same and was trying for a Probationary Officer's position in various banks. I wished her all success. Even though she had been close to me, I didn't tell her what I had been undergoing throughout. Om Mamaji and Mamiji showered their affection as usual.

I had to catch the train in the early morning for Raipur and had to hurry up. I had to share many things with Neelima; but they had to be postponed for some other moment.

That very evening the movie *Saath Saath* was telecast on television; and there was my favourite song in the voices of Jagjit Singh and Chitra Singh:

'Tumko dekha to ye khayal aaya,
Zindagi dhoop tum ghana saaya …'

While passing by various homes I overheard that song. But we had missed that movie. Maybe I would see that some other day.

In the sweet company of Mummy and Nalini I spent that night talking about our future with the hope that someday all of us: Mummy, Papa, Nalini and I, would be together again!

Is it Love?

The next day, early in the morning, I had to catch the train. Needless to say, my mother had woken up early for preparing breakfast and lunch for my long journey.

Sharp at seven I reached Nizamuddin railway station and boarded the train. Setting foot inside the compartment again filled me with that nostalgia: the day I had boarded the train for Raipur the first time on that fateful day of December for joining the State Bank. The whole scene played before my eyes: my mother, sister and Raj Mamaji waving at me while the train was chugging out of the station. My eyes became moist; I felt a choking in my throat and heaviness in the chest. It appeared as if something was getting lost; the receding platform, the bookstalls and tea stalls; the wetness in my eyes became intense, taking the shape of droplets trickling down my cheeks when the train reached Tughlakabad. '*Why? Why? Oh My God, Why does it happen?*'I wondered, '*Why does one have to leave near and dear ones for pastures that appear greener, for a future that appears bright; but in the bargain one's past, one's proximity is lost and what remains is only the treasure of memories which one has to savour in the lonely times; in the hope that the time of reunion would arrive soon.*'

On the way when I gained composure, I could make friends with a nice, innocent looking boy of almost twenty who hailed from Bhilai. He somehow developed a liking for me and we clicked well. With the passage of time we became so intimate that he even revealed, 'I am in love with one girl for almost five years; and our love is so intense that even if I get a chance to have a film heroine in my life, I would never like to part with my beloved. It has now become a life-long bond, and only death can separate us.'

I was bowled over by his emotions and found reflections of my own thought process and emotions. I too had tasted love, after all; yes the true, pristine love of Shama, and I also had the privilege of divine friendship of Mitali. It was marvellous. I told him, 'I too had fallen in love when I was sixteen; that love is unforgettable.' It was really nice to share such feelings with someone who was like-minded. I encouraged him to move on with his love and maintain the same intensity. 'You are lucky my friend; only the privileged and blessed few are destined to have true love; preserve it, cherish it and savour it as nothing in the world is comparable to such wealth; yes the wealth of love and the ornamentation of the heart,' I said in one go, and was wondering since when I had acquired the credentials of advocating the philosophy of true love. I could see a sparkle in his eyes. I wished him all success and the best of his life with his companion.

He shook my hands and said, 'I find you too are made for love marriage only; I have hardly come across somebody who talks like you and is appreciative and understanding of the flame of love.' I simply blushed. But that was true that I had experienced the flame of love, my Shama (the flame), who had been my soul mate for more than seven years. *But what was happening to me of late?* I didn't know whether that qualified as love. Time just passed on, and I realised the increasing darkness of the night from the window, and with that the lights of the compartment getting switched off. I tried to read some magazine under the night lamp, but to no avail. I was not able to concentrate as life had brought me to a strange crossroad! *I didn't know what was in store for me.*

The train journey was long. And, even after waking up and having finished breakfast, Raipur was still at least two hours away. In the early morning too, that boy narrated more details about his love; he appeared to be totally intoxicated with the elixir of love. *Love is really a strange feeling. Only those who fall in love or who have fallen in love can understand its true import.* He got down at Bhilai leaving my mind in turmoil.

At around 10:30 I got down at Raipur and straightway headed for my house at Tatyapara. Monsoon had arrived. The weather was pleasant. I readied myself quickly. I chose that newly purchased collarless T shirt with short half sleeves along with my blue denim jeans. While looking in the mirror, I myself fell in love with my looks. It had given me a 'personality switchover'. I rushed to Indian Coffee House and had dosa and idli. When I entered the bank, I felt everyone was eyeing me in a queer manner; I greeted them with my usual pleasant smile. I was given some light charge in the Savings Bank counter, and got busy with it.

In between everybody was just enquiring about my performance in the exam. Two hours passed. I stole a few glances at Mitali whenever I got the opportunity. I felt restless and had a strong urge to meet her and have some conversation. Ultimately while returning from the washroom, I smiled at her, and in a swish pulled a stool, and sat before her. She was not perturbed; perhaps she had been expecting it.

'How was your exam?' She asked with a glimmer in her eyes.

'It had to be excellent; after all your good wishes and that pious flower were with me,' I surprised myself saying that. *How did I get so much of confidence, so suddenly?* I wondered.

'How is everybody at home? Did you have a nice time?' she asked.

'Oh it was fantastic. I met them after two months. You know, I learnt there that I have been allotted 'Delhi and Andamans & Nicobar Islands Civil Service' on the basis of my first attempt. I need to seek your father's guidance about its prospects *vis-a-vis* the bank.'

'Did you see the movie *Saath Saath* on TV on Sunday? I remembered you when the song "*Tum ko dekha to ye khayal aaya*" was played,' there was a question and an expression in her words.

'No, I couldn't see it as I had been to the market and to see my relatives; but I certainly missed the song; I like it very much.'

We talked about a few more things, but time was running out, and people's prying eyes were on us. I had to get up although I wished time would stand still. She was magnetic. I just didn't know why it was happening. 'Okay, see you,' I said and got up. Later, I got immersed in my work and also in conversation with other colleagues. Much later when I realised that it was time to go, I thought of stealing a glance, but to my chagrin she had vanished for the day.

I felt totally lost; as if I would sink to the ground. I felt as if my knees were unable to bear my frame of 5 feet and 10 inches with 70 kgs. My heart became heavy and vision dimmed. *What had happened to me? I didn't know*. I stood still beside the counter for a few moments which appeared like aeons.

'Hey man, are we not going home? It's already past six,' I heard Pradeep Kulkarni's voice.

'Yes, yes let's go,' I mumbled.

When we came out of the branch, a mild drizzle started. We waited for ten minutes and then boarded a rickshaw. 'Why not take a round of Shankar Nagar, the weather is so good? I am not very keen on going home so early. After all I have just gone through the ordeal of that exam; I wish to hang around for some time,' I proposed. Pradeep couldn't refuse. We boarded the rickshaw for Shankar Nagar and aimlessly moved around, and reached 'Civil Lines'. The scene was beautiful. I had never realised earlier that Raipur too had pockets worth seeing. There were lush green trees laden with flowers. Sun rays were passing through their interstices in lovely iridescent beams. In the soothing rays of the receding sun, the water droplets on the trees and leaves were shining like pearls. Fragrance of flowers was wafting in the cool breeze; the ambience was enough to stir and evoke the poetic hearts; and one could imagine what it could do to the love besotted hearts.

We gave up the rickshaw, and started moving around on foot. We met a bank colleague who wondered why we were in that area. We just gave a plausible explanation, leaving him to construe and comprehend. After chatting for about five minutes the colleague left. When our purposeless pursuit killed almost half an hour, Pradeep said, 'Do you have anything special in your mind or can we wind up and go home.'

'No, nothing in particular; let's go home.'

The moment Pradeep turned around to hail a rickshaw; something hit me.

'Pradeep, I feel like going to her house. Why don't you just come along; I don't think it is far from here.' I was insistent like a child. Had Hariharan been there he would have readily agreed. But Pradeep was a bit reluctant and hesitant.

'You can go alone man. I hardly know them and I also feel a bit awkward. You go if you feel like. I can push off from here, don't worry, you may even have dinner if they offer; I will take care of mine,' he chuckled.

I agreed. And the moment he boarded the rickshaw, I thought of going to her house on foot. I had been to that place twice, but every time the path looked new. I felt a bit hesitant; but I don't know what kept pulling me towards that home.

In almost ten minutes, I was at the gate. The sun had now receded into the horizon leaving its dimming redness all over; the weather was pleasant with the after breeze of the drizzle that had ceased. I could see the lovely flowers, green grass and the nicely lined up ornate flower pots, many shrubs and small trees in the courtyard. Those idyllic surroundings and some mysterious magnetism were tugging me. I slowly opened the gate as the last two visits had increased my confidence; moreover, I remembered that any sound of the gate was not enough to alert them, and continuous cranking of the gate would be annoying. So, I felt it would be decent to ring the bell after crossing the veranda. I gently rang the bell, and after almost two minutes Mitali appeared near the grilled foyer. I smiled at her; she too smiled inquisitively. She was wearing a long peach coloured skirt and a matching shirt with her hair bound into two long ponytails. She opened the door half surprised and half expectant.

'I just felt like meeting your father. Is he there?' I said. She motioned me to sit in the drawing room without saying a word, and vanished into the house. After some time, as usual, her sister Shefali entered the room. She too was a bit surprised, but maintained her composure.

'You had been to Delhi, I understand?'

'Yes. I returned just today.'

'How is everyone at home? You must have had a nice time there. How were your exams?'

'Everybody is fine. It was a nice change. I did well in my exams; let us see what happens. Incidentally from my first attempt I have been assigned 'Delhi and Andaman & Nicobar Islands Civil Service', a Group B service. I thought I could just discuss the matter with Uncle. I hope he is at home.'

'Sorry, today Mummy and Papa have gone to meet some relatives; they may return after two or three hours.'

I felt that my ruse of coming there was over and I may have to leave. After all other than that there was no reason for my being there.

'No problem if he is not there, you can sit and talk to her; after all you have come from so far off. What would you have: tea, coffee or some cold drinks?'

My thought process was broken by her words, and I felt those words very soothing. I gave up my hesitation. It was always better to talk to her in her house than in the bank where one had to face the uncomfortable prying eyes of other colleagues.

'I won't mind some tea if possible. The weather allows that liberty,' I replied with confidence.

'Okay,' Shefali smiled, and moved out of the drawing room.

I sat there appraising the interiors. I liked the all-white ambience, nicely lined cushions on the steel and wooden furniture, which was simple and elegant. There were books, with white covers, stacked in glass closets. Dried flowers and long leaves of palm and some other plants were painted in golden and silver colour, and were beautifully set in glass bottles and flower vases placed on small Japanese tables and stools. Still there were enough vacant spaces in the room to add elegance and grace. Far in the distance were a *tabla*, *harmonium*, *tanpura* and *sitar* on a Kashmiri carpet, arranged in style, enhancing the sophistication of the room.

My focus was disturbed by a little whoosh of the curtain and rustle of clothes. I saw the elegant figure of Mitali with her lovely face with lunar luminescence; her dark twinkling eyes finely lined with kohl and a small round bindi adorning her forehead; *enough to bowl anyone over*. She entered with a small tray containing a tea cup and small plates with biscuits and rasogollas. I was awestruck and stood in deference. 'Oh why have you stood up? Please be seated,' saying so she kept the tray on the table, and sat right in from of me. I was no doubt a bit stunned by her presence and her deportment.

'Have something,' she broke my reverie. 'I lifted the tea cup and somehow managed to prevent my hands from trembling. I held the cup firmly and tried my best to contain my nervousness. I took two sips and looked blankly. I didn't know what to say to make the conversation going.

'Where is your sister?'

I broke the silence while having another sip.

'She is busy with her preparation for the music class.'

It was a jolt for me. In the absence of her father and the garrulous Shefali I didn't know how to keep the conversation going.

'Have some sweets, you are only taking tea,' Mitali tried to break the silence, 'By the way, how was your journey?'

'It was good, but the distance is too much; and twenty-seven hours is a long time; besides, in the train the food also was not very good; I had to somehow kill time. But since I had good company, the journey otherwise went on well.'

'I hate travel; it upsets your daily routine,' she interposed, 'I remember when I was away in a hostel and I had to travel to meet my parents, it was an uphill task for me; I used to wonder when it would be over.'

The conversation progressed.

'You were referring to that movie *Saath Saath*. I didn't see it. How was it?'

'It is a beautiful and sensitive movie with Deepti Naval and Farookh Sheikh in the lead; it has melodious songs by Jagjit Singh and Chitra Singh.'

'I haven't seen the movie nor am I aware of the story; but that one song I heard, it is beautiful,' I said.

'I understand you sing well; why don't you sing that?' I cajoled her, 'You had told me that you sing duets with your brother.'

'No, I don't sing so well. Why don't you sing, I know you sing very well,' she said casually just to ward off the request.

But, I was just looking for that opportunity.

'Me, I don't think I sing well; but I like this song; if you want I'll sing; I hope you won't mind that,' I replied.

'Why should I mind; in our house singing is a very normal thing,' she said with insouciance.

I needed no more goading. I immediately coughed and cleared my throat, and then just to brag a bit, I said, 'I don't know how it will be as my throat is not very good due to the food I had in the train.'

'Don't worry,' she encouraged me.

I began coughing again to show some attitude. I remained silent for a few seconds to set the mood, and then started:

'Tumko dekha, to ye khayal aaya;

Zindgee dhoop, tum ghanaa saayaa.'

I sang the song with all emotion and pathos; while singing I was looking either into space or keeping my eyes closed. In between I opened my eyes and looked at her as naturally as possible. Her eyes were fixed on the floor. I attempted to capture her image in my eyes in all detail. I felt an urge of possessing her forever. But that was a craving, just like those wordings of the song:

'Aaj phir dilne ik tamana kee,

Aaj phir dil ko humne samjhaya....'

I felt a deep pain in my heart when I finished the song. She appreciated it, but her approbation was not hearty; it was restrained; perhaps it was because she was in her house. We sat quietly for some time and then I said, 'I must leave now.'

All of a sudden, I heard a giggle from behind the curtain. It was Shefali with her childlike face, but there was something lurking in her eyes, a strange naughtiness. I found that very odd.

'I had gone out for cycling,' saying thus she mysteriously vanished. I felt a bit uncomfortable, and then expressed my desire to leave. Mitali nodded. I found that I had spent almost two hours in their house!

On my way, I kept marvelling at my luck, my strange gumption and my expressions through that song. On top of that I was concerned about the manner of her sister's appearance on the scene: her stealth, her mischievous smile and her mysterious giggle, and her equally queer disappearance. Everything happened in a cinematic manner or like the script of a mystery novel.

While returning, I didn't take a rickshaw. Even after the gruelling train journey, I don't know why I walked back, for full forty-five minutes. And, at the hotel I felt hungry ... yes, very hungry. While having those tandoori rotis with dal fry and alu matar, I don't recollect how many times that scene of my singing that song, and her listening to it with rapt attention, got re-enacted in my mindscape. I was in a trance, which would be broken only by the regular intrusion of the waiter, enquiring about the requirement of more rotis, vegetable or dal. Now those means of nourishment appeared too dull in comparison to the nourishment I was getting for my heart.

Pradeep was reading a sports magazine when I entered the house. 'Hey man how was your evening? I kept on waiting for you till eight, and then thought we would be meeting in the hotel. There too, no trace of you. I hope everything is fine,' Pradeep expressed his concern. I narrated everything with all interest and relish. He listened to the whole story with amusement but it appeared that deliberately he didn't want to comment on anything. After all he was a mature guy!

Sleep that night was sweet and heavenly. I got disturbed on a number of occasions when the events of the day replayed in my dreams. Yet I woke up all fresh and enthusiastic. I felt as if my mind and body had been injected with a morale boosting tonic. The spring in my step had increased and my gait had acquired more style. The nervousness of earlier times had gone and there was confidence galore.

I got ready in my cream coloured shirt and brown corduroy jeans and was on to my daily routine with Pradeep. I felt my hair had acquired a few more waves; my half boots had improved my gait, I felt like an army man and also like Jackie Shroff of the movie *Hero*.

In the bank now my eyes were centred only on Mitali; it appeared as if nothing else existed for me. I had to just go through the motions of my work: attend to the public without looking at them; take their cheques; post them in those thick heavy ledgers; post the entries in the passbook; wait for the messengers to take the ledgers to the officers, and if they were not to be found, lift the ledgers and pile them over on the officer's table. In between, I would constantly try to have a glimpse of Mitali as and when I was presented an opportunity by the circumstances; whether by default or by design. I would use my forays to the toilet side or the water cooler as the stopping point to meet Mitali; now I had given up the hesitation of looking at her furtively. Somehow I felt emboldened and was now unfazed by the possible prying eyes of the other staff. I knew she liked chocolates and would buy them regularly; in the process I too had become a voracious eater of chocolates. She would also talk to me without hesitation; but I felt that she was a bit lost, and my sixth sense told me that she wanted to tell me something. Three days passed like that.

In the meantime, I wrote a letter to my mother informing about my safe arrival in Raipur and about my visit to Mitali's house. This time from Delhi, I had also brought photographs of my mother, sister and father. In two photographs she was in a kirtan in a temple, dressed up as

Lord Krishna and dancing with a flute with another lady who was dressed up as Radha. My mother, besides being good looking, also looked much younger than her age. Many people couldn't believe that she had such grown up children.

On Thursday, I took those photographs with me to the bank, and on finding an opportunity showed them to her. 'Guess who could be my mom amongst these ladies,' I quizzed. And when she couldn't, I pointed to the most beautiful and youthful person in the photo.

'Oh really,' She was surprised. I showed my sister's and father's photos too. She was happy to see them.

Then I asked her, 'I have a feeling that you are perhaps hiding something from me. It appears that you want to tell me something but are reluctant to do so. I hope my visit that day didn't cause any problems in your house.'

'There is nothing as such, but I certainly wanted to talk to you about something. I am not sure whether I would be able to express that in the office. I don't know where I can tell you.' Her reply stirred in me many of the things that Raj Mamaji and Mamiji had spoken about. I wondered whether something interesting was in the offing; a female offering to speak something, and not being comfortable about telling that in the office! I didn't know what to construe. I was totally flummoxed. Anxiety and curiosity made me mull over.

I said, 'I too cannot think of another place.'

Then I hit upon an idea, 'Can't we go to your friend's bank … that Punjab National Bank at Jaistambh Chowk?'

'No, I won't be comfortable there.'

'Then I need to think it over,' I replied.

On my return and even during dinner time, I discussed the issue with Pradeep, 'What does she want to say? I am curious to know; but the problem is certainly of the place; she is neither comfortable in our bank nor in her friend's bank; what to do? I just don't understand.'

Pradeep was casual and cool, 'Simple, man; why don't you invite her to some restaurant; oh I remember even the Indian Coffee House has a family room. You can call her there. I feel it is high time that you know what she wants to reveal. And, be a man, have courage to move with her. If you are able to talk to her in the bank and even go to her house, you must not hesitate to be seen with her in the cosy family room of Indian Coffee House. You can propose to her to come over there on this Saturday after the bank and see if she accepts.' The topic remained hot on our agenda throughout our post dinner walk.

'What has she to tell me that she is calling me outside? I hope her parents were not upset because of my visit,' I blurted.

'I don't know what repercussions your visit had that day, but I am sure that you committed one mistake. How could you sing in her house when her parents and sister were not present? That appears to be a bit inappropriate. Why did you become so overenthusiastic? Restraint, man, restraint should have been there. Anyway now since you have taken the plunge, you must proceed. You must gauge her feelings and find out what she wants to tell you ... without meeting her it's not possible,' Pradeep sounded concerned.

I agreed to propose a visit to the Indian Coffee House on Saturday. 'But how should I make the plans, and how to proceed?' I was very anxious.

'Why do you worry? On Saturdays the bank is for half day. Both of us can come out at the normal time and proceed to the Coffee House. After reaching there we can wait at the main entrance. You can tell her to come out of the bank five or ten minutes after we go out. We will certainly be able to see her from a distance. The moment we see her, I will proceed to the normal hall, and you can escort her to the family room.' Pradeep sounded very confident, and I felt lucky to have him beside me during those tense moments.

The night was spent in planning for the next day. My heart was agog with what would be in store. How would I proceed? How would I talk and conduct myself?

But the next day went off well. Pradeep had instilled enough confidence in me. I carried two bars of Five Star chocolate, delivered them to her at an appropriate moment, and then in a whisper that appeared to be normal, and when no one was within hearing distance, I laid bare the plan in English that Pradeep had so painstakingly devised for us. To my amazement she heard me out patiently and after absorbing the details, nodded in affirmation.

Her eyes twinkled but there was a deep sadness in them which left me wondering, 'What was that she wanted to convey; was it positive or negative?'Anyway one can only conjecture; only time knows what it carries in its layers that it manifests at the appropriate moment. Things become clear only when the truth unfolds and reality dawns like the rising of the sun, the twinkling of the stars and the serenity of the moon. My moon had to take a little more time to reveal and there was nothing I could do except to be patient and wait … yes wait for that moment to arrive.

The D day arrived, and I got dressed in a sky blue shirt and blue denim jeans. My hair was well shampooed and fluffy; with very little oil, just to impart them a little shine and to hold them in the vantage positions. As usual, I appraised the fairness of my face, after applying the thin layer of *Fair & Lovely* cream. My eyes gleamed at the immaculate aura I saw of myself in the mirror. *Whatever may be one's complexion, contours or angles, everyone loves oneself and one's image. And, we don't lose any opportunity to appraise our images anywhere: be it in a mirror or any polished surface with mirror finish. Everyone is afflicted by narcissism—the difference is only of degree. I too was not untouched by that feeling, and wanted to present myself in the best possible manner. And a satisfying image in the mirror gives us the added boost.*

In the bank, I kept on counting the hours and minutes, waiting for the time; in between to ensure certainty, I even stole an opportunity to meet Mitali and asked, 'I hope the programme stands and there is no change from your side.'

'Why any change? If, I fix a programme, I stick to it. I am not fickle,' she was emphatic.

Her reply made me nervous; though I made full attempt to pretend that I was okay. And, then came the moment to leave. Being Saturday, the banking hours for the public were over by 12:30. The Day-Books for the day were finished by 1:30; we could go out at two. I passed by her seat after having been to the water cooler and conveyed through my eyes that it was time and I was going out with Pradeep. She nodded.

Pradeep and I went on foot and as decided remained at the entrance of the Indian Coffee House. We waited for almost ten minutes; but then my patience ran out. I started praying that she should not change her plans; that she must come, as I had that constant anxiety of listening to what she was so eager to tell me. When the thirteenth minute passed, Pradeep said, 'She is coming.' Initially, I couldn't see her; then I saw her at a distance; in her pink saree, in her two braids and accompanied by one lady of the bank. For a moment I was befuddled, 'My God! Is she coming with that lady? How would I talk to her in the presence of that lady?'All my calculations came crashing down for a moment; but to my relief, I found that the other lady had left her and was passing across the Coffee House on the road as I hid myself near the book stall in the foyer pretending that I was browsing through some book. When she stepped inside from the entrance, I immediately guided her to the 'Family room' whose entrance was from the foyer. It was curtained. We entered the room, and saw there were almost eight tables with four chairs for each table. We chose the one that was far away from the entrance; at that moment only one family was seated in the family room, that too near the entrance. I kept on wondering that the bearers of the Coffee House who had so far seen me either with my male friends or alone, would be surprised at my being in the company of a beautiful lady. But, I had to face them as thinking too much about them would have made me nervous. *Love teaches you many things and it also gives you confidence and assurance to act in the new situations that emerge when you are on the journey of love*.

We sat down. It was little awkward for both of us to meet in a place that was different from the bank and her house. 'What will you have?' I asked.

'I generally don't like South Indian food,' she said.

'But, today you don't have much choice as we have to present a legitimate reason to be here,' I said. With a lot of reluctance she ordered two idlis, while I being hungry settled for masala dosa and idlis.

Now the service time and the privacy so accorded had to be utilised to the fullest effect. I only started the conversation as I didn't want to miss the opportunity: 'So, tell me what you wanted to convey. It is high time that I should know.'

She took time to assemble her thoughts and then proceeded, 'In our house we are all very frank. And the first time you came to my house, I couldn't make out the reason. But, there was no problem as people keep coming to our house just like that, and we entertain them too. When I became friendly with you, I liked your conduct and felt comfortable to invite you on my own. In fact my family members readily consented as such things are normal in our home. But the last time when you came, your visit caused some consternation, and the reason was my sister Shefali.'

I immediately recollected Shefali's mysterious exit and then entry into the room that day; the way she had giggled and then vanished with a sly smile.

'What was it that annoyed your people? What did she say?' I was excited and anxious. And what she revealed later set the chain for many more interesting things.

'You see, I have been very candid in my interactions with people as I don't harbour any complexes. But sometimes I land into problems. I try to remain simple but my parents don't trust me. The reason relates to what happened a few years back when I was a student … doing research after my Masters in Organic Chemistry; there was a boy … an year senior to me. He was a genius and very smart. He was like a hero for the college. All the girls were after him. But I don't know why he was always ready to help me; and would take special care of me. He would fetch chemicals and other necessary materials and apparatus for me; I didn't have any kind of feeling for him.'

The waiter brought idlis and sambar, and I requested her, 'Please start.'

'You first,' she said. We somehow broke one piece each and then finished an idli each. Silence prevailed. I found her gathering her emotions, and I myself was puzzled by this new turn of events. I was thinking that what came out was totally contrary to my imagination.

On regaining her composure, she continued, 'But when he went to Delhi, he wrote a letter which as such didn't contain anything objectionable. However, my sister Shefali's friend who was his class fellow told her something about us. My sister believed her friend more than me, and presented a convoluted picture before my parents. Since that day, my mother never reposed faith in me. Whenever I would get late, all sorts of uncomfortable questions would be posed. Same thing continues till now. That day your visit to my house led to controversy and even my father scolded me. I think you should not come to my house as it is likely to create problems for me.'

While saying so she looked so innocent and more beautiful, but that beauty was more of her heart than the physical one. I didn't know what to say, but in the process I gulped one glass of water. I had different plans of saying something to her that to a large extent was because of my inner churning and also for what had been fuelled by Raj Mamaji and Mamiji. I felt as if my small world that I had created in a few months and especially in last few days came crumbling down. I debated whether I should leave it and say goodbye to her forever, follow her advice, and give up the idea of ever going to her place. But somehow, my inner voice was not agreeing to that stance.

'Would you like to say something,' she asked when she found me quiet and serious, 'I hope I haven't hurt you?'

'No, I am all right; but yes I want to say something as I don't think I would get this chance again. You see, I came to this branch more than six months back. I am basically a shy person. I don't know how coincidentally you were the first person I met in the bank. I generally don't talk to girls or ladies much. And here too, I hardly ever tried to come near you or tried to talk to you on some pretext or other. In fact, things would have remained the same; and I would have gone away from this branch on completion of my training in July. But that stint of seven days beside you, when that clerk Kumar, went on leave, changed everything. I found you a very good person, and then our conversation made us good friends. Before this in my life I hardly had such long conversations with any girl. I didn't feel much during that period; but when, on your colleague's return, I was asked to go back and work at the 'Recurring Deposit counter', I felt a strange emptiness. When you are in the branch, I hardly look at you. But that day and even later, whenever, you would leave the branch, I felt very very alone; as if everything would come crashing. I don't know the reason. That day when I was separated and I felt very alone, I can't explain what made me search for your house and reach there, even though it eventually turned out that your address in the ledger was incomplete!'

While saying so, my throat choked, and I felt that familiar lump in my throat. My voice became heavy and I found it difficult to say the last few words. Actually in completing the last sentence, my voice gave way, my tone vacillated and fluctuated and two tears made desperate attempt to get away from the confines of my eyes; howsoever, hard I attempted to contain them, I was failed by my emotions. And, ultimately, they trickled down. I desperately pulled out my handkerchief and wiped them and immediately controlled any further flow. I saw that her eyes too had become moist. She took out a handkerchief from her purse and rubbed the corners of her eyes. The scene was straight out of some movie, and I felt very elated that my emotional nature had found true expression, and it generated equal reciprocation.

She said, 'You know, I too was in the Punjab National Bank earlier, and I joined just a week before you joined here. In late May there was an offer of my going to Chief Regional Manager's office at Shankar Nagar and it was for you that I didn't go there!'

It was strange; I was important in her life and indirectly perhaps she liked me! While listening to her I gulped my glass of water. Then overwhelmed by emotions and without any premeditation, I picked up her half-finished glass of water, and put it on my lips. She protested, 'Please don't; I have drunk from it,' But I continued and finished the same.

My act was guided by my past experience in the college. Once along with three friends of mine, I was having snacks in the college canteen. After finishing we had to push off for some function. My friend Navneet wanted to have water and when he found that the waiter was taking time to fetch that, he picked up my half-finished glass of water and drank from it. When I protested, he simply smiled and didn't answer. When I had raked up the issue casually with my mother, she had laughed that when you drink water or eat whatever has been touched by another one, your love and affection for that person increases.

That day while sitting in front of Mitali and after learning that she had been reprimanded because of me and that she had not gone to CRM office because of me, I felt a powerful surge of affection for her, and almost without any contemplation, I drank the left-over water from her glass. It appeared that she too had been deeply moved by that gesture of mine.

Our conversation veered to a few general things while being intruded by the waiter. In between I had also ordered a couple of masala dosas even while she prevented me. Having finished the same and somehow managing to buy some more time, we continued our exchange. 'You know, I had mentioned about you to my elder mamaji and mamiji too. My mamaji has been my friend, philosopher and guide during my period of trials and tribulations. I don't hide anything from him,' I said. But deliberately didn't divulge what all had actually transpired in that context at Delhi. She was perplexed by such a revelation.

I glanced at my watch. We had been there for an hour. It was time to leave. She gave me four Five Star chocolate bars.

'My God, so many. Please, I won't take all.'

'No, you will have to take them all,' she insisted, and said, 'You are a good person; I like your nature. You should remain like this only.'

'You should not bother about anything; everything happens for the best. I assure you that I will pay heed to your request; I will not visit your house and will not create any problems for you,' I responded.

I felt that any dreams that I had harboured for future may have to be nipped; and I may have to remember it as a very good friendship for the rest of my life.

On my return, I narrated the whole episode to Pradeep in all detail and gave my own conclusion, 'Perhaps, this is the end of the whole story, and now she would be a good friend of mine. Nothing further should be interpreted in the matter.'

Pradeep smiled in a sly manner, and said, 'It is too early to write the end of your story; let us see what happens in future; but I am proud of the manner in which you conducted yourself, and I am equally proud of having a person of your nature as a friend. Don't worry; we can't say anything now; let us leave it to God and destiny.'

I couldn't comprehend what he meant; but from my side this story didn't have any serious ramifications and like the 'Shama chapter' of my life it had to become part of my sweet memories.

Yes, It Is Love!

On Sunday, the weather was very pleasant. While having breakfast at the Indian Coffee House and perusing the newspaper, Pradeep proposed, 'I hope you won't mind watching *Sohani Mahiwal* at Jaistambh theatre; it is an India-Uzbekistan collaboration. It has Sunny Deol, film star Dharmendra's son and the heroine is Pooam Dhillon, that innocent one of *Noorie* fame.'

'Oh, yes; it is really difficult to spend Sunday in the confines of our small house,' I agreed.

The newspaper preview highlighted that their story was one of the seven popular tragic romances from Sindh compiled by the famous Sindhi scholar, mystic and poet *Shah Abdul Latif Bhittai* in his opus *Shah Jo Risalo*. The other six such tales are *Umar Marui*, *Sassui Punhun*, *Lilan Chanesar*, *Noori Jam Tamachi*, *Sorath Rai Diyach and Momal Rano*. They are commonly known as 'Seven heroines'. The story runs thus.

Mahiwal, a rich trader from Bukhara, during his business trip to Punjab comes across Sohani's house and requests for water to quench his thirst. Sohani, the daughter of one of the potter families, serves him water from her pitcher. He is instantly besotted by her. He gets employed as a cowherd in her house. Sohani too is mesmerised by Mahiwal. On learning about their love, fellow potters of that area conspire to have Sohani married to a cantankerous fellow of potter clan. Sohani is left with no choice when the baraat comes to their house unannounced. Mahiwal instead of returning to his land, stays back, and starts living as a cowherd in that area across the river Chenab. Sohani learns about this. Driven by his love, she goes across the river on an inverted earthen pot and meets him. Their love is rejuvenated, and she starts meeting him every day by adopting the same mode. One day her sister-in-law finds out her secret forays and parleys. She deliberately removes her earthen pot from the place it used to be stashed, and instead, replaces it with a half-baked earthen pot of the same appearance and dimensions. The unsuspecting and innocent Sohani is drowned in the river when her earthen pot melts in the water. Rattled by the sight, Mahiwal jumps into the river; and they are united in death.

An eternal classic was immortalised in an equally captivating way on the screen. Poonam Dhillon was beautiful, charming and innocent. Sunny Deol with his half smile, macho looks and dreamy eyes, twinkling with the pathetic yearning of a diehard lover, was superb. It was a treat to watch; and the icing was the lilting music with some heart-warming songs especially this one:

'Bol Do Meethe Bol Soniye,
Bhed Dilon Ke Khol Soniye;
Sone Ka Hai Mol Soniya,
Mitti Hai Anmol Soniya ...'

I was transposed to another world, and on many occasions in the movie, felt that I was Mahiwal and Mitali was Sohani; the love, the intensity and the longings that poured out of their hearts on the screen appeared to be ours.

Much later, when the movie was over, and we came out ecstatic, the thoughts of my rendezvous with Mitali on Saturday, and all those moments when I could open my heart to her, the emotional overtones that were expressed in the restrained tears from our eyes ... all lingered vividly in my mind. I realised that those moments are precious in the world. Those moments could have been with Shama too but destiny didn't permit it, and maybe then the time was not ripe; perhaps I was required to attain more maturity and also to accomplish something in my life to be prepared for the moment. When Shama had entered my thoughts, I was just a student and a raw youth of sixteen; now I was a Probationary Officer, earning a decent salary, and as the whispers went about—an eligible bachelor. Raj Mamaji's wordings reverberated in my ears. But, that was not to be, I thought, as she would only be a good friend, and maybe after my training at the branch, I may not be able to meet her.

On Monday, I reached the bank as usual with Pradeep. And, in a routine manner I wished her, and then proceeded to the Savings Bank counter; and became busy. In between I saw that she was in a lovely sea green saree, her hair nicely tied in a braid, and a light coloured bindi was on her brow. She looked absolutely stunning. It seemed that Saturday's meeting didn't have any negative impact on her outfit or face. She looked fresh and revitalised. She had taken pains to dress up to the minutest detail as everything was looking nice about her. I was astounded. And, on top of that, the poor Accountant came with a new directive, 'Today, you may have to manage Cash Scroll as Kumar has not come.'

I grimaced, 'Why am I being shunted from one place to another?'

'Oh, what can we do man? You have handled that counter earlier, and moreover you are quick and efficient.'

I expressed some reluctance though my heart leapt with joy, and the butterflies danced in my stomach. 'God is really a great playwright,' I thought while proceeding to that desk with slightly heavy feet to feign my disinterestedness.

'I have been asked to come here again,' I said, 'I don't know why your colleague chooses to go on leave so often, and why do they find me the best replacement?'

'Why don't you refuse straightaway if you find this an ordeal and so heavy a punishment?' she whispered. 'They will post someone else, and you would be happy. Won't you? Then you may not have to bear this.'

I saw there was a naughty smile on her face. She could make out what my heart desired and that all my tantrums were farcical. In a feeble voice I said, 'No, it is not a big deal. If the bank is paying me salary, I have to work where they want me to,' while saying so I looked at her, and both of us burst into laughter though it was a little restrained as we did not want to attract undue attention to ourselves.

It is amazing that when man does not even plan, God showers his bounty when it is least expected. Her presence instilled a sense of completeness and banished all those thoughts of emptiness that haunted me occasionally. We had conversations on various issues; I would narrate many funny instances of my past and also plans about my future. 'I wish to become an Indian Police Service officer and bring about changes in the society that I had long cherished,' I said.

'Oh, I like it,' she chuckled.

I talked about my mom and sister. She also informed me about her father's postings to the remote tribal areas of Bastar District. 'My father was so much imbued by the sense of compassion and duty to his fellow refugees from East Bengal that he gave up a cosy posting, and joined as a Project Officer in the Dandakaranya Project for their rehabilitation.' Anecdotes of her father's travails and fight against all odds in those interior areas inspired me, and my idealism got reinforced. I asked about her interests, and learnt that she enjoyed art and craft. In between I also pestered her with the question, 'What exactly did your sister say that day?'

But somehow she dodged that question.

Two days passed thus. On the third evening when she picked up her purse and was about to leave at 5:15, I just asked innocently, 'Are you leaving?' She nodded.

'So early!'

'I have finished my work, and why should I wait here now? Should I remain here for sweeping and dusting the branch?' she posed a counter question.

'No, I thought you could carry me also in your bag,' I joked but she saw my sad face and my eyes which were cajoling her to stay back. I could understand that she could recollect my wordings of that day.

She said, 'Okay I will wait for some more time till you finish your Day-Book.' After almost five minutes, while I was writing the Day-Book she asked, 'When is your training going to be over for this branch? And what would you do when you leave this branch? That day you were saying that when I leave, you feel very lonely. How would you survive then? And you know,' she continued, 'I am going to be sent for Hindi training to Indore from 2nd July to 14th July; what would you do then? There is also a possibility that I may be transferred to the Chief Regional Manager's office in the next week. How long can you tell me to remain in the bank for you?'

I just looked at her and was about to say something when Pradeep came, and asked, 'Have you finished your Day-Book? When do you plan to leave?'

'In another five minutes,' I replied. While saying so I found that Mitali had picked up her bag and was leaving, looking at me from the corner of her eyes. I could feel heaviness in my heart; but, where was the choice? Both of us were required to move to our respective destinations, without any convergence. Only our hearts and minds had converged but our physical and material existence was separate from each other — demarcated by society.

Before I left the branch that day, I got a letter from Mummy. It was in response to my letter in which I had informed her about my visit to Mitali's house. Mummy's letter was instructive and replete with apprehensions. She was perturbed by my frequent and uninvited visits to Mitali's house. *She exhorted, 'Uninvited visits lead to loss of prestige. You are a good boy; you should refrain from all this. You haven't turned 24 yet; your focus should be on your aim of becoming an IAS officer; only five months are remaining for your Mains exam; you should avoid such distractions. Don't take that conversation with Raj Mamaji and Mamiji seriously. You know any indiscretion at this stage shall bring opprobrium to you and our family; the welfare of the family should be foremost on your agenda. You jolly well know that our economic condition isn't very good; Nalini is still studying. You should think of her future and her marriage first.'*

Mother's letter jolted me. In the evening, I discussed the issue with Pradeep. I told him about Mom's letter and also about Mitali's impending transfer and her training at Indore. I wanted to say something but was hesitant.

Pradeep understood my predicament, and said, 'Whatever is happening, let it happen. Do not stop the flow of the river. Please see things through and listen to your heart.'

'What are you saying Pradeep? I don't understand,' I said with a bit of discomfort.

'Don't deceive yourself, my dear,' he said, 'You may be a bit confused, but others are not, I especially am not; we can see what equation you have with her, and what your feelings are, and what she feels about you. Rohit, my pal, it is difficult to get true love in life, and if you have got it, you must value it and take it to its logical course.'

He sounded philosophical but earnest, 'Your eyes, your mannerisms, and your voice all indicate that you have fallen in love, well and truly, and above all she too loves you very much; in fact she adores you. You don't know that I too had fallen in love; to be specific we were in deep love; I will not tell you the name, but I have experienced it; it is a different story that our parents did not agree, and we had to give it up.'

While saying so his voice faltered and choked and his eyes became moist, 'If in your house there is no problem about inter-caste or inter-regional marriages, then you should go ahead; such moments in life do not come again.'

Our late night conversations after dinner continued and Pradeep came up every time with stronger arguments.

'Suppose, my parents agree, what is the certainty of her people agreeing to the whole affair?' I countered. 'And moreover, I have not yet checked up whether she likes me or not, and if she is ready for such lifelong association.'

'See, she has thrown a subtle hint, girls do not express everything so explicitly; boys only have to take the lead. She has given you enough feelers and what are you doing? What else do you want?' His voice was authoritative.

In that one instant, everything became clear to me. The mist that had enveloped my eyes and my mind had receded and I could hear the craving of my heart; Mitali's rejoinders, her actions and her questions were being replayed before me like a movie. Now I could hear and understand what answers and replies she wanted from me.

Pradeep suggested, 'First of all you must tell her very clearly that she should get her transfer to CRM's office cancelled as you are going to be here till 14th July and you don't want her to go before that; secondly, tell her to postpone her Hindi training for the time being; such trainings occur at regular frequencies and she can join that later, I think the next one is going to be in September. You can, instead, suggest her to get it rescheduled for September, and tell her that as you will be in Dewas during that period for your second branch training you may be in a position to meet her there; Dewas is hardly twenty-five kilometres from Indore. And, thirdly you should now persuade your mother to come to Raipur. I know she loves you very much, and will not decline. To dispel her apprehensions you may make it amply clear that all you want is for her to come and approve of Mitali; once she accepts Mitali, the marriage could be considered only after four to five years. After all, Mitali too has two elder sisters and their marriages are likely to take that much time. In the meanwhile your sister's proposals might come, and her marriage might materialise. This shall remove your mother's misconceptions. It would also give you enough time to improve the economic situation of your house as the bank pays you so well.'

I was again wonderstruck at the meticulous plan that Pradeep had conceived, and was filled with admiration and gratitude. I was really fortunate to have been bestowed such care and concern by someone whom I hardly knew a month and a half back! *God certainly has his own designs; not only that, he carves out special mediators for you if your love is genuine so that it may flourish*.

Although the outcome was uncertain, there was enough effort and support for me. And, quite significantly Pradeep had rendered this advice just two days before he was to leave for Ujjain!

Time was short for me too as I would be leaving Raipur forever on 14th July.

It was Thursday and I was itching to put Pradeep's plan and advice into action. During the course of the day while talking over routine issues, I asked Mitali, 'Why don't you have your transfer postponed to CRM's office till 14th July?'

'Why? What is the significance of 14th July?' she asked nonchalantly.

'14th July is going to be my last day in this branch. That day I would be relieved for Dewas, my next branch for training. And, I want you to be here till then.' My eyes and voice conveyed entreaty. She looked at me for a moment, studying my expression, and then said, 'Okay, Mr PO.'

'I have one more request,' I said in a deep voice, 'You told me that you are going on training to Indore from 2nd July to 14th July. Please don't go. I would feel very lonely and you know that. Why don't you defer it for some time? I have learnt that the next training could be in September. You can go to Indore during that period. And if you have no problem, I can come to meet you from Dewas, as it is hardly twenty-five kms from Indore. Now, you know me well and I leave it to you.'

She heard me, thought over for a moment and said, 'All right, I will try both these, but it is not in my hands; still I will try my best.'

Her words were music to my ears and balm to my heart. Pradeep's plan was working to some extent and it also proved beyond doubt her feelings for me. Later, in the evening I asked, 'Why do you wish to go to CRM's office? Earlier you didn't want it.'

'Everything and each corner of this branch shall remind me of you, and it will become very unbearable. Your presence here now matters to me, and when you won't be here it would be difficult for me,' she was now becoming emotional, and I could see the mist of tears in her eyes, 'Would it not have mattered to you if you were in my place?'

I grew nervous with her reply and her emotional state and didn't want those tears to escape her eyes. There was a strong possibility of the same if my reciprocation was equally sentimental. To make the moment lighter, and to distract her I said, 'No, why should it matter to me? It doesn't matter to me.'

My apparently innocuous reply upset her. Her facial expressions changed to one of hurt, and she became stern, 'If it doesn't matter to you then why bother about all this?'

I tried to calm her down but she said, 'What is the point if my feelings don't matter to you?'At that very moment, an officer came to me for some clarification. After some time, I saw her picking up her belongings and going out of the bank. My heart was broken and I was repentant. There were no means of reaching out to her. *There was no mobile phone for me to call or SMS her during those days unlike today's instant world of gadgets to assuage one's feelings and clarify things*. She was gone for the day!

I had to inform Pradeep in the evening.

'You have committed a major blunder; everything was going as per plan. How could you come up with such an outlandish idea? So churlish! So boorish! I appreciate you didn't want her to break down publicly, but it could have been handled more delicately; with more sensitivity. You made it a disparaging joke; her annoyance is right. Now, since you know her feelings, you must learn to appreciate and respect them. You are a good person. How could you commit such a crime? Anyway, if your heart is pure and true, things will get rectified. You need to apologise to her immediately in full earnestness.'

The next day, I tried to talk to her, but she was reticent. Her replies to my queries were very succinct and curt. I kept on sulking throughout. During lunch time, Pradeep had some work and he moved out quickly, and I had to take lunch all alone at Hotel Ambassador. I ordered only vegetable biryani and curd as I was in no mood to have rotis. While having food I evaluated my behaviour; and was full of remorse and pain. I felt very dejected. All of a sudden I became aware of one Pankaj Udhas ghazal being played in the background, its lyrics by poet Nasir Kazmi epitomising the pain and anguish of a separated lover. Its music with equally sombre tone, replete with notes of *sarangi* overtook my senses. I found resonance of my own mental and emotional state in the ghazal:

'Dil, Dhadakne ka, sabab yaad aaya
Woh teri yaad thee, ab yaad aayaa;
Aaj mushkil thaa sambhalana ai dost,
Aaj mushkil thaa sambhalana ai dost,
Tu museebat me bahut yaad aaya;'

My condition was pathetic. Had it been a private place, I would have broken down. I was feeling very morose and forlorn, and that sad tune of *sarangi* had aggravated my condition. I collected myself and somehow finished the last remnants of the vegetable biryani. I again evaluated my chances. Still there was time to mend fences.

I came out of the hotel, and bought five bars of Five Star chocolates, two Dairy Milk and three regulars; and paced towards the branch with a new resolution of seeking apology at any cost. I had hurt her; so I had to be contrite, leaving aside my bloated ego.

Once in the branch, I calmly moved to my seat and saw her seated in a glum mood. She had finished her meals, and was taking rest, bent on the desk with her arms crossed.

'One should not sleep in the bank in such a manner; this is inappropriate,' I said in a commanding voice.

'What should one do when the work is finished for the time being? Should I stare at people's faces?' she said in a curt manner while lifting her head from the desk.

'You can talk to the people who bother about you; for whom you are important; who miss your presence in the bank,' I said with authority but in a whisper, 'and please, forgive me; I have committed a grave blunder. I have hurt your feelings; but you know my feelings for you.' I continued, 'And, I don't know whether you believe me or not; but I deliberately uttered those words as I discovered that you were on the verge of tears. If those tears had rolled down, I too would not have been able to hold back my tears. And, that would have been embarrassing, for both of us. I did not want that. Please forgive my insensitivity. I had unintentionally hurt you … please please,' saying so, I handed over that pack of chocolates taking precaution to ensure that no one was watching.

She accepted them and smiled with effort; but then the heaviness of the pack made her exclaim, 'So many!'

'Yes, still they cannot compensate for the amount of hurt and pain I caused.'

'When are you coming to my house?' her question surprised me.

'Why should I come? To increase your discomfort? I may not come.'

'You will have to, someday,' she confounded me further.

Pradeep was exultant on hearing the news, 'Now you are maturing on this path of love. You have surmounted one hurdle; it is crystal clear that she likes you; in fact she loves you. Now you have to persuade your mom.'

Persuasion

On June, 21st I wrote the first of my persuasive and pleading letters to Mom. To some extent it was part of Pradeep's plan but the language that was scripted on those A4 sheets was imbued with my true yearnings for Mitali; they reflected my deep concern for her and though I tried to portray that my mom had to just come and see her once, and that her decision to continue this relationship would be final; the tone and tenor was that my mother had to come and approve.

I wrote in the first letter:

Dear Mummy,

... I can't forget the way you came running with that towel and tears when I was leaving for Raipur. 'O Mama' only I know how much I miss you. I showed your photographs to my 'chocolate friend,' and she remarked that Mama is very sweet; that Nalini doesn't resemble me; and that I resemble Dad.

I think things are becoming serious now; Raj Mamaji's words are coming true; she has indirectly conveyed what you all wanted to know, and there were tears in her eyes while saying so. She told me that when I would leave this place she would be missing me. She was about to be transferred to CRM's office and also she had to leave for training to Indore during July, 2nd to 14th, but at my instance she has agreed to stay back till I get relieved.

Mama, when she gets up in the evening to go home, I feel very lonely and insecure. I want you to come here on July, 8th, and stay here for one week till my relief; then we can return to Delhi together. Before coming, you can send me a telegram. I would come to receive you at the station. Mama, you know me well and I will not take any decision till you approve of her.

On 26th June I wrote:

I have learnt from my seniors and outsiders that I should quit the bank and join that Delhi and Andaman's & Nicobar Islands Civil Service as it has better prospects despite being a Group B service. I would be staying at Delhi and it would save us expenses of two establishments. It would provide more power and prestige as I would be given the initial posting as a Sub-Divisional

Magistrate or a Sales Tax Officer with a red beacon vehicle, and most probably a house in Delhi. Then I will be under your control and you won't be having any worries about my going astray or not following your command.

I got a response on 29th June, which was not favourable and my mother had again questioned my commitment for the Civil Service exam and also towards the family.

When I found that Mummy was not relenting, I shot off two more letters on 29th June itself saying:

I don't know how many times I have to repeat that without your approval nothing will move. For me you and your decision are supreme. I am writing to you as only you understand me well. I just want you to come and see her. My main aim is to become an IAS, and nothing can distract me from that goal. If you approve of her, we can wait for three or four years till I settle down; in the meantime our problems and economic condition shall also improve. I have checked up with her; they too are middle class people like us; they are not very rich. She is a nice and innocent person. If you don't like her I would give up the idea. I just want that you should at least see her so that I don't suffer from this feeling that I had not shown her to you; that I left such a person in lurch without letting her meet my mom. Have faith in me, I will not let you down.

Please do come … … Mama, please do come … …

Thus I wrote on all sides of the letter: '*Please do come … … Mama, do come … O Mama, I am waiting for you … … Mama, I am feeling very lonely …*'

I remained very tense during those few days and especially on Saturdays and Sundays. Pradeep had left for Ujjain on 23rd June and Hariharan had not come back. It had been raining and I was sulking all alone. In the branch I had been shifted away from her. Pradeep returned on Sunday evening, and I told him about my travails.

'Don't worry, leave everything to God and be positive; things would move now according to God's will and at the right time; you have done your best. Come on, I am famished. Let us feast today at Girnar. Let's hope Monday brings something positive.'

We had a sumptuous dinner comprising Malai Kofta and Navratan Korma, followed by ice cream. The delicious dinner lifted my spirits too, and I felt that God would do the best for me, though there was a lurking fear of Mummy remaining adamant.

I reached bank on Monday with mixed feelings: 'Would there be something positive or another acerbic letter from my mom?' Nothing appeared till 1:00 pm, and I got absorbed in my work. Time and again I would look towards Mitali and feel pity for her and my situation. Her feelings of love for me had now manifested in full intensity.

Would it be another failure for lovers like us as history had not been too kind to true lovers? Only in Hindi movies they were shown as lucky.

I felt immense love for her as I knew that our plight was similar.

Then at 1:05 pm came the bombshell in the form of a telegram. I slowly opened it when delivered by the postman:

'MUMMY REACHING RAIPUR BY CHHATTISGARH EXPRESS ON 8TH JULY; COACH NO. S-10 … PAPA'

I folded the telegram and pressed it tightly against my chest and deep inside me I chanted, '*Jai Mata Di*.'

During lunch time, I broke the news to Pradeep. He was ecstatic, 'Your parents really love you very much and God is on your side. Great; your mom has agreed to come. Now let us think about the future course of action,' he said seriously, 'How would you introduce Mitali to your mother? Where shall they meet? And, will you take your mother to their house?'

Now my mind also started working fast. God gave me an idea. 'Pradeep, I don't want that people should come to know that my mother has come to see her. But it is also true that I cannot take them out straightaway. They need to be introduced first. I feel the ideal course would be to have some suspense. I think, my mother can come over to the bank as a customer. She can come a little late say by 1:30 in the afternoon during rush hours when there are many customers. At that time she can easily be inconspicuous in the crowd. I would show her the branch in the evening, and from Tatyapara, it would not be difficult to reach here as the path is straight and easy. We would be at the front counters. She would come and stand before my counter, and in a very casual manner she would ask me something. And, I would tell her to go behind and meet her as she is the only good looking and young girl. My mother is very smart and she will not find any problem in figuring her out. Besides, Mitali has seen Mom's photograph and with a prior intimation she too will not find it odd. They can then have conversation in the ladies common room for some time,' I said in one go and marvelled at my idea.

Pradeep applauded me, 'Wonderful! Now you are moving in the right direction.'

'It is the impact of your company and maturity,' I acknowledged. He was pleased at my compliment.

'But, thereafter?'

'Don't worry; just before we come out of the branch Mitali may help Mom in boarding the rickshaw at around three for the Indian Coffee House. And, we shall join Mom there for lunch. I think Mom, as you say is smart; will not find any difficulty in tracing out all these places. After all it is a prominent one, and we shall join her there for lunch. Rest of the action will depend on what opinion your mother forms about her. I am sure she is certainly going to approve her. The only issue is whether you will be visiting her home or not,' Pradeep was confident about all the happenings as if he was the Director of the show that would unfold in the days to come. The plan was complete.

I wondered how in a short span of twenty days since my return from Delhi things had taken such a course. It is rightly said: *Where there is a will, there is a way*.

On the same day Hariharan too returned from Chennai. He had never thought that my 'chocolate episode' and that 'Ballarbhai mission' would come to such a pass. He had his reservations on the issue, 'I understand, as things have opened up now that you have fallen in love, and that she too has reciprocated. Your mother has also relented to come on your persuasion. But this is not the end of the matter. Even if your mother agrees and you keep it on hold for say four years; things won't end there. It is going to be a major issue of inter-regional marriage, and I am doubtful that her parents would agree. Bengalis are in any case wary of Punjabis; in fact all regions are in awe of Punjabis, and there are so many cultural differences. It's going to be very difficult as the lifestyles, language and eating habits vary a lot. The couples may say that they may adjust; but it is not merely the adjustment of the couple. Marriages in India also bind the families and there are many social functions where the cultural differences get pronounced leading to too many problems. It is very easy to say that we can adjust as you are in love; but to lead a whole life in an alien culture is very very difficult for a girl.'

'Don't be so pessimistic Hari,' Pradeep interjected sensing that he was being highly dissuasive, and also understanding my emotional state which had brought things so far, 'You may be right but our history is replete with many such matrimonial alliances e.g. Jagjit-Chitra, Sunil Dutt-Nargis, Nawab Pataudi-Sharmila Tagore, Sunil Gavaskar-Marshallein, Raj Babbar-Smita Patil, Shashi Kapoor-Jennifer Kendall, etc.'

Hariharan conceded a bit but added, 'All of them are celebrities and celebrities are above social norms.'

'But you hardly know any successful couples who are not celebrities; without a proper survey we cannot say that your theory is entirely correct. These are modern times, and we, educated people, we alone can help break such myths.'

I acknowledged mother's telegram the same day through a return telegram and a letter appreciating her gesture:

'Mummy,

I know I am causing you much distress. Just for me you have accepted this ordeal of coming to Raipur all alone. Mummy, for me, you are the most important person in the world. As you only understand me truly, it is befitting that you are coming for this moment ...'

Pradeep had a thermos and he proposed, 'We can bring tea from that stall nearby. We can buy some snacks and biscuits. And, as we have enough time in the morning, we can fetch breakfast like puris or parathas or even other items from the market, and have breakfast with Mom at home. For lunch we would return from the bank a bit early in the afternoon, and instead of moving on foot, we would take a rickshaw, come home and take mother out for lunch. Thereafter she will reach home on her own and we would go to the branch. And, we shall have dinner together anywhere.'

Hariharan, despite his reservations was now enthusiastic, and said, 'Okay, I too am going on Sunday to the station to fetch Mother.'

My interaction with Mitali in the bank increased as she too realised that there was not much time remaining for my relief. On Thursday, I said I wanted to tell her something and for the same it would be appropriate that we meet somewhere outside. 'We can meet at the same place in that family room of Indian Coffee House,' I proposed.

'No, I don't like that place as there is every possibility of known people coming over there.'

'Then where? Suggest something better.'

'We can meet in JK.'

'Where is it?'

'It is near Shankar Nagar and at a little height; when you move towards Shankar Nagar, it is almost at the beginning of the elevation.'

'Okay,' I agreed. 'By the way you didn't reveal what your sister had said on that day,' I posed the same old question which she didn't want to reply. I talked about many other things to continue the conversation but was interrupted by the presence of a customer at my counter. Time had stood still as it appeared that nothing else in the branch mattered to me. I was just going through the motions of life. I was physically at some place and my heart … my heart was now tagged to hers.

Friday just passed like that.

Saturday, being half day, I finished my work and enquired about the certainty of the plan.

'Yes, I will be reaching there by 1:15, you also try to be there by that time,' she said. I saw her when she was leaving at one, and so as not to raise any suspicion, I came out after five minutes. I moved on foot thinking that the place was nearby only. But it took me little longer. By the time I reached there it was already 1:20. When I entered the dimly lit dining hall, I found it difficult to focus my eyes. After a few seconds, I saw lush black hair of one lady, sitting alone beside a table, with her back towards the entrance. Far away at a distance there was one couple. I could recognise her by her dress, a sky blue chiffon saree with light floral prints. I went near her. She looked stunning in that dark background, her eyes shining and her long well-trimmed eyebrows, and kohl-lined corners of her eyes bowled me over. I was hypnotised for a moment.

'Always late,' her remark unsettled me.

I somehow gained my composure and said, 'I was not familiar with the location and miscalculated. I came on foot. Had I known, I would have come by rickshaw.'

'Leave it; come on place the order; I have to go back; you know my parents and how inquisitive they are about me,' there was both command and request in her voice.

'Why don't you order as you are familiar with the hotel; you might know which dishes are good here.'

'Paneer butter masala, one mixed vegetable, a plate of rice, one raita and some soft rotis,' she ordered in an instant. I was surprised at the alacrity of the order and the clarity of thought. While she was ordering I was enthralled by her face and mannerism. She looked very elegant and graceful. 'So, are you leaving on the 14th?' her voice broke my trance.

'Yes.'

'You must be very happy leaving this place.'

'Do you think so?'

'You appear to be very enthusiastic.'

'I used to be earlier; but those seven days in your proximity caused by the absence of your colleague have changed everything. I may not like Raipur, but now I feel, I would not have minded my extended stay here if the bank permitted. We have to follow the training schedule, and it is not in our hands. I hope your transfer to CRM's office has been stalled for the time being. What about your Hindi training?'

'Yes my transfer has been deferred. I have checked up; the training for the next batch is going to be in the second week of September. When I would be there, would you come to meet me? I don't know why I started liking you,' there was depth and pain in her voice and she spoke the last lines with deep sigh.

'It is all ordained by God. You don't know how much I have felt in those few days. I was deeply pained when I unintentionally hurt you.

In the process, I also learnt about the intensity of your feelings and my feelings too. It was good in one regard that all confusion in my mind was over.' I said. 'And, I would like to mention that I wrote to Mom about you, about everything that has happened in the last few days; that what I think about you and you about me. And, after my repeated requests, Mom has agreed to visit Raipur.'

'What? Mummy, she is coming to Raipur!' she said.

'Yes, she is reaching here tomorrow. I wanted her to meet you. She is going to visit the branch as a customer; you have seen her photograph; hope you may be able to recognise her. She will meet you; you can talk to her in the Ladies' common room. I hope you won't mind meeting her.'

'Day after tomorrow! And, in the bank!' she was flabbergasted at my disclosure.

'Yes. I have conceived this plan. Any problems?'

'No, it is okay. In fact, it's like a movie.'

'What to do? Hindi films have too much of influence on me. And, you asked about my meeting you in Indore. Obviously, when you are coming to Indore only for me and at my request, I have to come, I will come. There is no doubt about that.'

I couldn't discuss with her about our future as it was too premature. Everything was uncertain: approval of my mother, approval of her parents and then the time of her elder sisters' marriage. Only one thing was certain: our love for each other; yes the love which for me had been so beautifully reciprocated; God had really been very kind to me.

We parted on a happy note. She tried to snatch the bill from me; but I held it firm. She was insistent and showed some resentment. I told her, 'There would be many more moments in future; let it be my privilege as just two days back I received fifty-eight rupees as "dearness allowance arrears". Bill payment need not be an issue between us.'

She left; and, I kept looking at her trail with a heavy heart. 'After one week all this would become only a memory,' I felt, 'I will be craving to see her; I will be far removed from her!'

Course of True Love Never Runs Smooth

Chhattisgarh express was just ten minutes late than its normal arrival time of 10:30. Pradeep, Hariharan and I had reached the station almost half an hour earlier. There was so much of anxiety in my mind: about my mother's welfare and what she will be telling me.

'*Whether there will be reprimands?*' was the lurking thought as I knew my mom and her domineering nature. She could be firm in certain issues if she wanted. She loved me and also dominated my psyche. I used to be afraid of my father up to some stage till he was physically more powerful than me. Much later I found that compared to my mom he was more pliable and understanding. So ultimately it had to be mom whose opinion was going to be of concern. Papa, I was sure, would always give in. This stature I had acquired by my sheer dint of hard work, and he was very much appreciative of the support I had started giving to the house. My bargaining position with him had become strong after my selection in the Civil Services and on my joining as Probationary Officer in the bank. *For mothers, perhaps these things don't matter; for them you remain the same small child whom they have given birth and reared. In any case sons are more attached to their mothers*.

My train of thoughts was broken by the announcement of the arrival of the train. We all moved fast to be near coach S-10. The moment the train stopped, we entered and started looking into each cabin. My heart leapt every time I couldn't locate her. And, then after eighteen seats, I could see my mom, and shouted, 'Mummy.'

'Rohit,' Mummy responded with enthusiasm; her face happy and radiant. I embraced her, and we all immediately picked up her luggage. The moment we landed on the platform and my mother again embraced me, I was shaken by uncontrollable tears. Pradeep, Hariharan and my mother were all stunned. Such a grown up man of twenty-three was crying so openly on the platform. It was the manifestation of the pain and feelings of melancholy that I had been experiencing for the last few days.

'What are you doing *beta*,' she said, 'what will people say, such a grown up man crying?'

But I was inconsolable.

We all returned to our house in two rickshaws. My mother had brought only two bags.

My landlord Mr Bakshi and his family were also surprised at the sudden turn of events, and they were equally amazed to discover that Mummy was so young. Mr Bakshi had two grown up daughters and two sons; all of them were in the age group of eighteen to twenty four. But I used to be so shy that when crossing the passage to the main gate from my room, I would only wish Mr Bakshi and his wife and at the most smile at his sons; but I had made it a point of not looking at his daughters at all. They all knew my nature. Mr Bakshi specially sent his son to inform that we could take lunch with them that day. He also sent tea and some snacks for us.

Mom found the home quite small. But somehow we had to manage there. After she got ready, we had lunch at Mr Bakshi's house. Once earlier too, I had lunch with them; almost one and a half months back. I marvelled at their hospitality. That day for the first time, I had seen them properly and they talked and laughed with us.

'We had nicknamed him "Ravi Shastri,"' Mr Bakshi's wife and daughters told Mummy. Many people had told me that I resembled Ravi Shastri, the famous cricketer; with the passage of time such comments and comparisons had increased. My face, hairstyle and movements did resemble his.

And, as is the common tendency of people I too would bask in the reflected glory of my doppelganger. Mere mentioning of such comments from people would fill me with elation. I remembered one instance when Hariharan had taken me to an old gentleman's house. On seeing his face I recollected that I had seen him in Kutchery branch on a few occasions. He would come and stand quietly behind the counter and I used to offer him help, be it telling the account balance, updating his passbook or posting his cheques. I asked him, 'Uncle, do you have a pension account in State Bank?'

'Yes, I do,' he replied.

'I have seen you in Kutchery branch many times,' I said. Hariharan introduced me, 'He is Rohit, working as officer in the State Bank.'

'No, he can't be Rohit. He is Ravi Shastri,' the old man quipped. I laughed. The gentlemen advised me in a lighter vein, 'You resemble him so much. You should start posing as Ravi Shastri only and give autographs to people.'

My mom told Mr Bakshi's family, 'In Delhi too he was considered Ravi Shastri only.'

In the evening we went to Hotel Girnar. I wanted to treat Mom well and dispel her concerns about the kind of food I was taking. She enjoyed it and also felt proud that I now had the competence to entertain the family in good restaurants. *I had climbed up the social ladder*.

We took a walk around, and came up to Kutchery branch. I showed her the front-lit board of SBI with its blue logo against the white background signifying:

'*Come, Let us move together*'

For me it was apt; when I had come to Raipur for the first time, I had seen that logo with interest. At that time, I had not foreseen that by the time I would be leaving the branch I would get tied in a pious knot with someone with the promise, aspiration and vision of moving together for the rest of my life. My mind had been made up and there was no going back. I had found the chosen one of my heart … my heart–throb.

I explained to Mom how the next day she had to take a rickshaw and reach here, and how we would be meeting subsequent to her meeting with Mitali.

Mom was smart, and she had soaked the plan.

The next day went as per plan.

We reached the bank as usual without anyone getting a whiff of what was about to happen. At around twelve, I met Mitali and informed, 'As planned, Mom would be coming.'

She was dressed in an elegant pink saree, her luxuriant and lustrous black hair was nicely combed in a simple ponytail with a dark pink band; a light pink bindi adorned her forehead; her lunar face was radiant; her eyes had been well lined with kohl. She looked like a married lady. She was exultant; her eyes had a magnetic twinkle, her face a magical smile.

I thought, 'In a few days I would be missing all this!'

'I am nervous; I don't know what Mummy would think about me? It is an awkward situation,' she murmured. Her voice was barely audible.

'Everything will be all right,' I whispered, though I was equally apprehensive. 'Hope for the best for both of us.' Mummy's consent was most important to me. It was the first step in the long and arduous path of winning Mitali.

I moved back to my counter and resumed my work. But, my mind was constantly haunted by the apprehension of the impending arrival of Mom. I waited with bated breath. It is one thing to conceive a plan, but one remains nervous about the successful execution of the same, and prays that there are no hiccups. I kept on praying that Mom may quickly get a rickshaw and reach the branch; let there be no problem in locating the branch. She had seen the place during night time, but generally the day changes the complexion of a place. Time went past and my watch showed 1:20. Now my main focus remained my mother. Any work on the counter, the customers and the calls from other officers were not relevant at all as I didn't want Mom to miss me at the counter. Then she would be forced to enquire about me; and the whole plan that I had so meticulously prepared with Pradeep, could go awry.

Those ten minutes appeared like ten years and then sharp at 1:30, Mummy entered the branch. I could figure her out from a distance: wearing a dark pink saree and sporting brown sunglasses. She was looking very smart and elegant. The sunglasses had added mystique to her personality. It was so conspicuous. Slowly she came near my counter, and then asked about Mitali in a whisper. I surreptitiously pointed towards my back and whispered, 'She is at the back, and the entry is from there.' While saying so I acted as if I was guiding a customer. Mom moved away, and my worries got over. But now I was having butterflies in my stomach, 'Whether Mummy would approve of her?' How time fleeted I couldn't realise till I found it was 2:15.

I went to Pradeep, 'Let us get ready; we have to move fast so as to reach there in time.' At around 2:25, I found Mom going out with Mitali.

I moved out at three, and didn't allow anyone a hint of what was going on. I posed as if it was just like any other day. I told Raghavan, 'I am going out for lunch early as I have to come back early.' Raghavan didn't know that I too was going to Indian Coffee House. And, Pradeep stayed back as he planned to go with Raghavan.

I reached the family room of Indian Coffee House in ten minutes and found Mummy and Mitali absorbed in amiable conversation. On seeing me they smiled: Mummy's face and eyes evincing wholesome appreciation and affection for her son and Mitali's expressions embodying love for the beloved. I was at the pinnacle of happiness. I had never imagined earlier that so soon I would see Mummy, who encompassed the whole world of my affection, face to face with the one whom I had loved wholeheartedly in the prime of my youth, whom I wanted to be my life partner!

I moved with all alacrity and sat next to Mummy. I didn't want to show any indiscretion by sitting beside Mitali. We had not become as modern as to negate the presence of our elders. 'You order what you think is the best,' Mom said. Mitali was not much interested in South Indian food but there was no choice. We persuaded her to take whatever she felt comfortable with. After all, the family room of Indian Coffee House was the safest place if we didn't want the people known to us to be around or have any inkling of our real motive. We discussed about general things. We just talked about ourselves. Mom had brought a few more photographs which she showed with a lot of enthusiasm, and I just intervened to guide Mitali in getting an idea about the faces in the photos and our relationships with them. Mitali told a bit about her family, her father, her mother, her sisters and her brother and about her father's postings. She elaborated on the interests and dispositions of her people.

In between the topic of inter-caste marriages also arose to which Mitali's reply was very positive; though she did say, 'Yes, Bengalis are a little wary of Punjabis.' Throughout Mitali's eyes were fixed on me with a look of adoration, which made me nervous. I never knew that a time will come in my life when I would be loved so much by a girl! I was on the seventh heaven of delight with my love having been reciprocated with equal vigour.

In the midst of all this, the waiter kept serving the delicacies that we had ordered. He was the same one who had served both of us on that eventful

Saturday! While last time he was full of curiosity, there was appreciation in his eyes now. He came beaming from ear to ear whenever we summoned him. His movements were swift and his mood upbeat.

Almost after an hour Mitali sought our permission to leave. I too had to hurry up. We dispersed on a positive note and smiles. She left first, and after five minutes Mom and I came out after settling the bill. I hailed a rickshaw and after briefing the rickshaw puller about the destination, helped Mom in boarding it. Seeing her off, I moved towards the branch. My heart was jumping with joy; it appeared as if a part of the battle had been won. On seeing me, Pradeep smiled and queried, 'Was everything fine?'

I smiled broadly conveying that things went on as planned. We got engrossed in our work and at 5:00 pm called it a day. I deliberately didn't disturb Mitali.

But, I could feel something in the attitude of some of the officers and staff of the branch. One of them being Sunil Banerjee–a clerk; he was standing next to me in the morning when Mom had approached me before I guided her to Mitali. He was looking at me with distrustful eyes. He was always suspicious. He was a perfect shirker and would act like a union leader. He didn't have any positive trait in him. I remember once he had commented, 'Mr. Rohit, don't work so hard and show too much of enthusiasm. You would be saddled with more work.'

I had replied, 'Howsoever, I may try, I can't change my nature; I just can't be lethargic in movements if there are customers standing before my counter. I always empathise; fully appreciating that everyone wishes their work to be done expeditiously.'

Banerjee had remarked with sarcasm, 'You are saying so now. A day will come when overwork will lead to fatigue and all your stamina and enthusiasm shall wane.'

I had replied with a bit of irritation but a lot of confidence and conviction, 'Mr. Banerjee, I guarantee you that unless I am afflicted by illness, you will find the same zest and enthusiasm even after twenty years.'

My reply had unnerved him. I felt that in his heart he never liked my free conversation and interaction with Mitali. He was also a Bengali but Mitali had never given him any importance. Banerjee, however, felt that being a Bengali, he had the first and natural right to talk to her. Mitali disliked his negative and intrusive personality and his trade unionist attitude.

For a moment I felt whether he could make out that my mother had come to the branch, and if so had he spread canards about me. But I consoled myself that calling my mother to Raipur and arranging her meeting with Mitali in the branch was a positive thing which would have dispelled any notions that people might have had about my seriousness in the matter; *that I was not a flirt or a philanderer*. But something had leaked out I felt. My doubts were confirmed in the evening when Pradeep on the way told me an amusing thing.

'Do you know the first thing that Raghavan asked me in the afternoon?' Pradeep asked with a hearty laughter.

'What?' I said.

'Approved by mother?' Pradeep stated jocularly.

'What!?'

I was aghast. I had never foreseen such quick leakage of our meticulous plan. Perhaps Mom and I needed more training in acting. Or, perhaps it was my resemblance to Mom that had exposed our secret!

Pradeep looked at me and laughed again, 'Why do you worry man? You have not committed any wrong. Calling your mother and showing a girl in whom you are interested is perfectly all right. You have come of age, and are an eligible bachelor. So your mother has every right to see the girl. Why should there be any guilt? You should be happy that one part of the mission has been successful. Prospective mother-in-law and daughter-in-law have met in the most salubrious surroundings, and the meeting too has gone off well. You should celebrate. Your next course of action should actually be to find out the reaction of your mother, and work out further plans,' he continued in the same vein. His views and guidance reassured me.

We went home carrying some fruits and snacks. Mummy was lying on the bed, listening to songs on Pradeep's transistor. Our knock made her take notice of our presence. 'Would you like to have tea?' I asked. Her nod made us move to the nearby stall with a thermos flask.

Late at night, when I was alone with Mummy after dinner, Mummy broached Mitali's topic.

'I didn't like the girl very much,' her first sentence sent my dreams crashing down, 'she is okay, but I found her quite ordinary looking.'

'But Mummy, I too am not all that good looking,' I protested.

'I know, but all mothers want beautiful brides for their sons even if their sons are short on looks. I too have a right to that,' she continued, 'and, besides they are Bengalis; it will be very difficult for her to mingle in our family; different cultures, food habits, different value systems; I don't think even her parents are going to agree to this match.' Her wordings were like burning scimitars, piercing my heart; they caused me enough anguish as I was under the cosy impression that she had good vibes with Mitali. What an anti-climax!

'But Mummy, both of us like each other,' I implored.

'So what my dear boy, life is long and you will come across many more girls to choose from; it isn't necessary that you have to marry the very first one you like. In our social set-up we have to see many more things than merely liking of the individuals. You are reciting her name so much; do you know if her parents are going to approve of your relationship and let it materialise? It is a difficult proposition. I have come here just because I felt that you might be missing us and would be emotionally low. Don't take us for granted. We won't approve of this.'

Her words spoilt my euphoria. I didn't know what I would tell Pradeep. He was at a distance not privy to our conversation. '*Would it be the end of my story?*' I wondered. But I couldn't have conveyed the whole thing to Pradeep. I thought I must wait for a day or two.

Next day in the branch, I met Mitali as usual. She didn't ask any question about Mummy's reaction. It appeared she had felt that Mom had liked her; I didn't want to change her notion. I wanted Mom to visit their house. Maybe, she may change her viewpoint after meeting Mitali's parents and after seeing their house. Now the question was whether it would be proper for us to visit them. After what Mitali had narrated about the repercussions of my last visit, I was a bit wary; but I had to take a chance; else all efforts would go waste. Raipur was so very distant from Delhi, and one couldn't afford to visit it often.

If at all there was a time, it was now. But Mitali had to give me the green signal.

Mitali herself raised that topic, and said, 'I want to invite both of you to my house.'

'Won't it cause problems?' I asked.

'Why should it?' her voice had more of optimism than realism; 'Anyway, I will talk to my people and let you know tomorrow.'

On Tuesday, I took Mummy to the residence of one Mr Nagarajan, a senior officer of the SBI Main Branch whom I had visited earlier with Hariharan. They were a good couple. His wife especially was very affable and we used to discuss many general things about life. Their hospitality was tremendous. Once at the instance of his wife I had sung my favourite Jagjit Singh song from the movie *Arth*.

Hariharan only had insisted that we visit them. It was a nice evening although we didn't have dinner despite their repeated insistence. As we had not given them advance intimation, it would have been too much to expect the lady to cook. Just some light snacks and coffee; but all were served with so much of love and affection.

Wednesday morning Mitali told me, 'You people can come tomorrow.'

'Is everything fine? Have they given their wholehearted consent to the invitation?' I asked with concern when I felt discomfiture in her demeanour.

'No, no problem at all. You people can come for tea say around 7:30,' she said calmly. But I don't know why I felt that she was concealing something. It was not the time to probe further or change the plans. I needed to take Mummy there as it was the last opportunity for me.

I took Pradeep's views, and he concurred with my decision. He also remarked, 'See, her true love for you is guiding her to take such a bold step. There is a possibility that there might be some problem in her house. But everything is fair in love and war; make the most of all the chances that come your way. You must proceed with all confidence. Pray for the best.'

'We are going to Mitali's house tomorrow. She has invited us,' I declared on my return on Wednesday before we started for Mr Shukla's house. As I had informed Mr Shukla also about Mom's visit, he had extended an invitation for Wednesday.

'Have her parents agreed to meet me? What would they think of the visit? You have become really shameless, taking me to a girl's house without confirming if they would welcome us,' mother was sceptical and concerned.

'Why do you worry? I would just tell them that I had told my people about them, and my mummy just wanted to meet the people in Raipur with whom I had been interacting. We can always meet people in such a manner. Don't you remember that in Bhubaneswar too we used to visit many houses just like that? Why the fuss? I think we should just meet them casually and things would be okay. You have also not made up your mind. Why have any preconceived notions?' I said.

Hurdles and Obstacles Galore

A significant day or should I say evening of my life had arrived. We got ready and boarded the rickshaw. My mother wore a nice light pink saree, and I must concede that she was looking very beautiful. It was God's gift that my mother looked very young. Mummy was hardly twenty when I was born. In olden times people used to be married off at an early age, especially girls. This, coupled with her special efforts to take care of her physical attributes, had kept her young even though she was forty-four when she came to Raipur. People around would not believe that she had such grown up children, and one of them was a Probationary Officer in the Bank! Mummy's youthful appearance and her equally youthful thinking had always made me comfortable in my interactions with her; and it was also perhaps the reason that I had been so confident that Mummy would agree to my lifetime association with Mitali.

We reached their house on the dot at 7:30 pm. Mitali came out to receive us when I pressed the bell. It appeared that she had been waiting for us, unlike earlier occasions, when I used to wait for a while for someone to open the door. She was in a pearl white salwar kameez and a white lace dupatta. Her hair was in a ponytail, and her broad forehead had a perfect sized red bindi. She was looking awesome and for a moment I felt my heart missing its beat. She sat and chatted with us for some time and then brought some tea and snacks. *Eerie silence pervaded the house*.

Her father and mother came after almost twenty minutes which was quite unusual and alarming. They came and just talked in monosyllables. Her mother's opening remark for my mother was, 'Your mother looks very young.' Otherwise, it appeared that we were not very much welcome. I enquired about Shefali and expressed whether we could meet her. Her mother uttered a noncommittal, 'Yes.' I talked to her father too for some time but the conversation was stilted and his manner cold. He too vanished after a while. Her mother went inside to call Shefali and returned. I kept waiting but Shefali didn't appear on the scene. I was now seething with anger. I felt insulted. Her mother kept on persuading us to take some snacks but we didn't, and had tea after a lot of effort and that too without any enthusiasm.

I found that Mitali was throughout in the room sitting next to my mummy. She was asking her to put on her spectacles, which really suited Mom. I found their conversation and interaction most amicable and natural. She too was feeling that we had not been treated well. Her mother disappeared from the scene and we waited for a long time for Shefali to appear, but to no avail. It was very shocking for me as in the past Shefali was the most interactive and natural amongst all. Her role now was becoming suspicious and dubious. I was left wondering, 'Why did she hide behind the curtain that day, laugh mischievously, and then disappear? And now why was she not coming out to meet my mother?' We waited there for a pretty long time and when she didn't turn up we decided to leave. Her mother came into the room and wished us goodbye. In a shallow manner she told us to come again. We also said that they should visit us when they come to Delhi.

Only Mitali came up to the main gate to see us off. She said, 'I am sorry; but there are certain problems which I can't explain to you now. I wish to meet you again before you people leave. Can I meet you tomorrow at the Coffee House?'

Before I could react, Mummy said, 'Okay.'

I must say that though I was very much annoyed by the attitude of her people, my love for Mitali had increased. But I had also foreseen the end of the story through her people's conduct.

My head was spinning with whatever had happened. On the one hand my mother had shown reluctance and now her parents' conduct had fortified the argument of my mother that they would not agree, and this match should not be pursued any further. On the way mother reiterated her stand, 'There is no scope in the match.'

I was thinking, 'Then, why has mother accepted Mitali's proposal for meeting at the Coffee House?' I didn't feel like raking up the issue any further.

It had grown late. So, instead of going home we thought it better to have dinner. To get the taste of the forgettable out of our mouths and minds, I thought I must treat Mummy to a good dinner at Girnar. As usual the favourite items were navratan korma and paneer butter masala with nans and rotis.

I was still upset at what had happened and what Mom had been iterating. Around ten minutes later, the waiter served the food after setting napkins and our plates. While having food I don't know what had smitten me. The sweet innocent face of Mitali fiddling with my mom's spectacles and indulging in innocuous conversation with her, flashed before my eyes. I tried my level best to focus on my food but to no avail. I was overpowered by a sensation of gloom and depression and felt as if everything had been lost. And, without my conscious knowledge, tears started rolling down my cheeks. I used the napkin to hide them. But I started losing control. I kept the plate aside and stopped eating. Mummy was initially unaware of my plight due to the dim lighting that the restaurant people deliberately maintained. But when she realised that I had stopped eating and was constantly wiping my tears, she became concerned.

She asked, 'What happened? Why are you not eating? Are you all right?'When she didn't get a proper response, she too was upset. 'Are you crying? What for? Why??'

I couldn't give any reply as my throat was choked, and I knew that if I attempted to answer, my voice would crack; I may even break out into sobs.

Mummy held my hand tenderly and asked again, 'What's the matter? Are you upset at her parent's reaction? Are you upset because of her? Are you upset because I have rejected her?'

I couldn't reply. But deep inside me I felt a profound loss. It appeared that the dreams that I had woven for Mitali and myself were torn asunder.

She repeated, 'Why such a plight? Is it Mitali?' I didn't reply. She found me inconsolable. She said, 'What will all these people around think when they find a grown up man crying? You are embarrassing both me and yourself.'

I was the life and soul of my mother; she couldn't tolerate my distress. She cajoled me further, 'Have your food and let me see what I can do.' Her soothing words tinged with a hint of conciliation were enough to assuage my feelings; I managed to control myself and somehow finished the food. We returned home without much of discussion.

At night I couldn't sleep for a long time; *future's uncertainties nibbled at the colours and contours of my dreams that were still embryonic; those dreams that were craving to flourish but there was no certainty if they would survive the onslaught of inclement events*. I didn't know whether this love too would die before it could bloom ... like my first love for Shama. But I resolved that even if it happened, then like my first love this too would find a cherished place in my heart forever. *Mitali's love had further made me evolve in life. I thought that I would take the resultant pain too in my stride and enjoy it throughout. It is not imperative that everyone may succeed in matters of love. I thought* that as usual I should leave everything to God as he would do what was best for me. I fell asleep with such arguments and counterarguments raging in my mind. In the morning only did I realise that I had had a strange dream wherein Mitali was looking at me with her large and shapely eyes and a very loving smile, and saying with intense conviction, '*You can't escape from me; wherever you go, I will follow you like a ghost*.'

It was effectively my last day in the branch, I was going to be relieved for joining at Dewas. In the morning I reminded Mummy about meeting Mitali during lunch hour, 'If you confirm, I shall come to fetch you by 2:30 and we can go together.'

'Okay,' she said.

The moment Mitali entered the branch I looked for an opportunity to meet her, and I got one after about fifteen minutes. Her sharp and straight gaze rattled me. Her eyes showed a cold resolve, and I was instantly reminded of the previous night's dream.

'Are you coming for lunch? If so, I will go home early and fetch Mummy,' I asked her cautiously.

'Why such doubts or confusion? I had told you clearly yesterday. I am *certainly* coming.' Her reply was emphatic. Her looks were possessive as if she was ready to announce to the world that I was hers and that she had complete control over me.

'Okay, then I will bring Mom. By the way, I may not find much time now to talk to you. When will you come to Indore? And how do we communicate? Should I write to you at SBI address or that PNB address where your friend works?'

'That Indore training is likely to be in the month of September, and I would like to meet you there. And, you can write to me at the PNB address in the name of 'Ms. Seema Tiwari' as it will be risky in the SBI,' she elaborated, and then asked, 'What time are you going to go and get Mom?'

'Since I have not been assigned much work, I may be leaving by two,' I replied.

'And, how would you go?' she just asked casually.

'I will first go to Indian Coffee House on foot from the back entrance, and then I'll take a rickshaw. I don't think I should take a rickshaw from here itself.'

It was the last day and I was not assigned any work. Same was the case with Raghavan. We closed our accounts; got Demand Drafts made, and completed the necessary formalities of leaving the branch with a clean chit. Throughout I cast furtive glances at Mitali, and found that she too was noticing me with a lot of concern. I felt as if her eyes were imploring me to stay. I too wanted to remain there for ever … forever, *but … had to obey the bank's diktat.* Earlier I was jubilant when I received my Training schedule, and was a bit enthusiastic about the prospect of seeing different places. But now, I wanted my life to swing on the fulcrum of Raipur, and I wanted to lose myself for ever in the deep lake of Mitali's eyes; I desired to ever remain a beholder of that luminescent face; I wanted to hide my face under the cascade of her glistening black hair.

At around two, I left the branch; and adopted a short route from its backyard towards Indian Coffee House. As such, I used to walk fast. When I reached halfway, I could see ahead of me the lissom figure of Mitali draped in a purple saree going in the same direction where I was going. I was awestruck. I wondered where she was going as I had told her that I would be coming to the Coffee House with Mummy only by three. I thought of changing the track for a moment; but then decided that I must move. Since my speed was good and it was difficult for me to reduce it, I could catch up with her in no time. On reaching near her I just quipped to banish my nervousness, 'Where are you going at this time? Are you not coming as planned?'

'You ask too many questions. I had told you that I will be coming and even confirmed in the morning. I think you should have more faith in me,' she replied while we walked along. 'Here is a pen for you which my father had given me. I know you like fountain pens,' saying so she handed me one silver colour fountain pen of a foreign make. I was startled. *So it was a ploy to meet me outside the office and hand over that gift*! I was deeply touched and marvelled at my fortune of having been blessed with the love of such a beautiful person. Mitali appeared divine to me. I didn't remain there for much time.

'Thanks a lot and see you soon,' I increased my speed and moved ahead of her. I didn't want anyone to notice our meeting. I didn't want that she may have to hear anything because of me once I left the branch for good.

I boarded the rickshaw. On reaching home, I found Mom was ready. We were at the Indian Coffee House five minutes before three. Mitali appeared five minutes later. Everything was as planned. But what was not planned was our destiny, and that hardly could be. On the way, Mom told me that there wasn't any point in wasting time as Mitali's parents won't agree. Like a typical mother in a Hindi movie she said, 'I feel today, you must consider this as your last meeting and then forget about the whole episode as a dream that could never become reality. Our culture, our system, our language and our standards of living are totally different. Moreover, you have seen their attitude. I, despite being the boy's mother, came all the way from Delhi, and see what treatment they gave us! Even if one doesn't agree to a proposal, one should behave properly. There are ways of telling people, and besides, for an intelligent person a mere sign, an indication is enough. We too have our self-esteem. We shouldn't kowtow to anyone's diktat.'

I heard the whole thing through without protest but found the same totally incongruent to my relationship with Mitali. Whatever treatment we had got from her parents was of no relevance to me as I knew how much Mitali loved me, and I wanted the whole thing to be decided by destiny. I wanted the whole affair to be left to the probabilities of life and be given a fair chance; maybe it could succeed, though the odds against were more than the odds in its favour.

When Mitali arrived, Mom was also amazed by her grace and appearance. After the usual placement of order and service by the same waiter with his benign smile, the proceedings started. I looked at her so as to capture and freeze her image in my memory in all details as I didn't know when I would be able to meet her and see her again. It seemed that she too perhaps had the same intention and leanings as she was not much perturbed by Mom's presence. *True love is not awed by the conditions and presence of others*. While having dosas with coconut chutney and sambar, Mummy initiated the topic and repeated the same words to her what she had told me on the way.

'What can you do? Your people are not going to agree to this proposal and we have seen the reality. You can forget the whole thing and treat him as a very good friend,' Mom emphasised her point.

Mitali picked up her glass of water, took a sip and said in a very calm voice, 'I am a stubborn girl with strong determination.'

She didn't elaborate it further. But her tone, tenor and her twinkling eyes evincing steely resolve, said it all.

At least I was convinced that my love was not dead and it was too early to write its obituary. There was so much to happen in future. Mom was not much convinced as to what an apparently timid girl could do, and moreover we wanted everything with her parent's consent; and at that juncture the fructification of the whole proposal was distinctly 'impossible'. We chatted about many other things, and with the clock showing four, we had to wind up the conversation. She got up to move, and all of a sudden touched Mom's feet. Mom was moved by the gesture; she patted Mitali's head and embraced her. Mitali moved out and I kept looking at the empty space which a few moments back was occupied by Mitali!

After about five minutes we also came out. Mom boarded the rickshaw and I marched on foot to the branch.

After reaching the branch, I went to Mitali. I took out my Chinese pen of *Wingsung* make which I always adored, and gave it to her.

'This is my gift. Whenever, you will write with this you will remember me. I am sorry for whatever I have done, for whatever hurt

I have caused to you. But I promise that I will never forget you. You are so very precious to me,' I whispered lest anyone else might listen to our conversation. I could see her eyes had become moist. She didn't say much. And the moment I left her desk I could see that she had rushed towards the ladies common room. I knew what might have been her plight. *True love knows the other; their hearts and minds feel and think at the same wavelength and frequency. They can understand each other's anguish and pain.* My condition was the same except that I managed not to break down. I had to meet other people in the branch ... yes one last time before I left that branch.

That day I returned with a very heavy heart. I felt as if a part of my existence had been lost; as if I was incomplete and my heart had been torn.

Pradeep asked me on the way, 'How is everything?'

I told him the whole story and added, 'I don't find much scope in the whole affair. All seems totally lost. She had met mother today in the restaurant but it doesn't seem that Mom has changed her stand all that much. Basically her attitude, to a large extent, has been shaped by the rigid stand that Mitali's parents have adopted. So it appears that Mom is taking for granted that they are never going to budge. But Mitali appears to be defiant and I don't know the basis of her resolve. I don't feel that it would be possible for her to convince her parents. Although for me her love is supreme and I would always cherish it till I hear the final "No" from her parents.'

Pradeep was a bit reflective and then he spoke with a deep voice, 'See, you have done your best. Now leave the rest to the almighty. Of course, I find it will be easier for you to convince your people and I find there is ample scope for that. But, it is a question of time. I am only worried about Mitali. You know, in the branch, people are now talking about your affair. It seems the whole branch is aware of this. I heard them saying that now Rohit's mother has come to approve the girl and they are going to be married. Things have become serious. And it is very important for girls, you know. As far as you are concerned, you will be going to a different place; in fact to different places. But, she has to stay here forever. And, she may have to hear from the branch people; people enjoy spreading rumours. They may say that she had an affair with a

Probationary Officer of 1983 batch. I don't know how you feel about it. But if you see from a girl's perspective, it is a highly sensitive issue.'

I heard him and felt pain and empathy for Mitali!

Mummy had planned to go to Bhilai to meet one of our distant relatives. Pradeep had already left for the Branch. We were getting ready. I wore brown corduroy trousers and a light peach colour shirt. While combing my hair in front of the mirror, I felt I had been made for Mitali only. But whether we would unite was uncertain. My movements were unenthusiastic and my limbs were heavy. What Pradeep had told me yesterday was weighing heavily on my mind.

'Is everything all right? I hope my visit has remained low key and your colleagues didn't have a whiff of the real purpose behind that?' Mummy asked.

'In spite of all our efforts and planning, things have not remained hidden,' I said, 'the office people are discussing that you came here to approve of her; and as you have already approved her, we shall be getting married.'

'What nonsense? How can people indulge in such loose talks? It is a serious issue now. That poor girl; I can understand her position. How is she going to bear such embarrassment when people talk regularly like that? You will be leaving this place and she has to put up here only. I can well appreciate how the girls have to endure all the taunts and slurs. I wish I could talk to her. Is there any way of reaching out to her today?' I could sense the same concern and anxiety, as Pradeep had expressed, in Mummy's voice.

Suddenly it struck me that we could meet her in the Punjab National Bank where Seema Tiwari, her friend was posted! I told Mom about that. And then without wasting much time we boarded the rickshaw for the Jaistambh Chowk branch of PNB. Being Saturday, there wasn't much time available as public dealing would close by 12:30. I had never been to that PNB branch. The advantage of public dealing in the bank is that you can enter the branch as a customer and the guards don't stop you unless you look suspicious.

After entering the branch, I told Mom to wait on an empty sofa kept for customers. Luckily, I didn't face much difficulty in finding Seema

Tiwari. She was on the first counter, posting some vouchers in the accounts ledger.

My interaction with Seema in the past was bitter and sweet. I had been introduced to her once when she had visited SBI to meet Mitali. On a later date Mitali told me, 'Seema has alleged that you had laughed at her while she was going in a rickshaw near Raj Talkies.'

I was surprised and upset at such an allegation. I tried to clarify with some bitterness when Seema came to SBI a few days later. Seema, on sensing my resentment and caustic tone, had immediately conceded, 'I am sorry. It must have been some misunderstanding.'

And, there I was standing before her with confidence!

The moment she lifted her head she was startled.

'Hullo, Madam. Could you recognise me?' She nodded in affirmative but was puzzled.

Before she could say anything, I assuaged her apprehensions. 'My mom has come along with me; we wanted to meet Mitali. Would it be possible for you to phone her up and call her here? You know it is a little awkward for us to go to SBI now as I have already been relieved. I don't want people there to know this,' I whispered and was surprised at my own candour.

She was taken aback for a moment. She regained her composure and said, 'Yeah, I remember, Mitali had told me some time back that your mother would be coming to Raipur.'

She came out from behind the row of counters and met Mummy with warmth, and expressed, 'Today, public dealing time is short. I will tell Mitali to come fast. I hope she has come to the bank.' In almost five minutes she reappeared; elated. 'Mitali will be here soon. I'll finish my work meanwhile. Why don't you people have some tea or coffee?'

We readily agreed for tea while she vanished behind the counters. I wondered how life is full of infinite possibilities. I never knew that one day Seema would be playing an important role in our lives! That she would be the recipient and conveyer of my future letters addressed to Mitali! That PNB was going to be the safe haven of my love letters but it would also be the place of my last meeting with Mitali!

We waited there, observing the hustle and bustle. Due to limited hours for public dealing, there was a lot of activity. Some employees of the bank were a bit curious as they had not seen us earlier and were wondering at the purpose of our visit. After fifteen minutes, I saw Mitali entering the bank, elegantly dressed in a coca cola saree and a matching blouse. Her hair tied in a ponytail and a dark brown bindi on her brow. Her walk was graceful. Her eyes were looking for us. A lovely smile flashed on her face the moment she found us and her eyes sparkled. I didn't talk much except to inform her that we would be leaving for Bhilai to meet our relatives.

Mummy spoke to her, 'I am very much distressed and concerned to know about the loose talk amongst your colleagues in the branch. You are like my daughter. I don't want your name to get spoiled.' Perhaps she dropped a hint or it was interpreted that Mitali was acceptable to her if her parents agreed. From my mother's eyes now I could read that she had grown more appreciative of Mitali. The battle was half won!

'What time are you people leaving on Sunday?' Seema asked.

'By Chhattisgarh Express which leaves at 2:30 pm,' I replied.

'By the way, where are you staying?' Seema asked.

'I have been staying at A 46 Tatyapara; the house is owned by Mr AK Bakshi of SBI Main Branch.'

'I have been to Tatyapara earlier. Is it on the main road?'

'No, it's in the second lane from the main road,' I replied casually. We talked about general things and then Mitali prepared to leave. Her eyes were constantly on me. I too couldn't take my eyes off her. God had been kind to me to give one more glimpse of Mitali which I had not envisaged when I had left the branch on Friday.

I kept looking at her trail and then into vacant space, and then we thanked Seema and came out of the branch.

We boarded the rickshaw for the bus stand and took the bus bound for Bhilai. It was an hour's journey. And, when on our reaching there we boarded a rickshaw for Sector 6, it started raining. It took us almost half an hour to locate the house. Our relatives welcomed us and we had a nice time. It was a nice evening when we munched the tasty pakoras with hot tea. We were chatting but I don't know why I, in between, was having hallucinations of Mitali in all her moods and dispositions: her arched and twinkling eyes were beckoning me from all nooks and corners. On a few occasions that aunt of mine remarked, 'He seems a bit distracted.' I denied but my mom replied, 'He is like that only.'

They insisted that we have dinner too. Later, my uncle dropped us on his scooter to the railway station from where we could board a train for Raipur.

It turned out to be an eventful day which I hadn't dreamt of earlier. So, the next day was going to be our last day which I thought would be spent in just packing and the like. Pradeep told me that Hariharan had come to meet me in the evening and that he would be coming the next day for seeing us off at the station. We packed most of our items in the night and waited for an otherwise uneventful Sunday.

Mr Bakshi had told us that we would be having lunch with them the next day by 12:30 pm so that we could leave for the station in time.

Hope Springs Eternal ...

It was like any other morning except that we would be leaving Raipur for good. We got ready early. Pradeep and I brought puris and alu sabji from Bhagtan di Hatti near Sharda talkies. That would be a good breakfast on a Sunday and that was also the delicacy of Raipur which I wanted Mom to enjoy on our last day there.

After having breakfast Mom was giving finishing touches to our packing. After the slight drizzle the day before, the weather had become pleasant. I was as usual in my jeans and banyan while Pradeep was in his lungi and shirt. We were casually chatting in the front balcony of our portion when all of a sudden my eyes caught some movement at the main gate that opened into the main courtyard. I just couldn't believe my eyes. Was it a hallucination? I rubbed my eyes again. Mitali and Seema were entering from the main gate.

I shrieked, 'Pradeep, she has come with her friend.'

Pradeep too was caught unawares. I picked up my T shirt while he his trousers and we rushed to the bathroom gasping and telling Mom in the process, 'Mitali has come with her friend Seema; we are going to the bathroom to change. You please handle the matter till we come.'

I was absolutely befuddled by the turn of events. Mitali, in our house, was unbelievable! And, I also wondered what Mr Bakshi and his family must have been thinking. Now the whole story would be out why Mom came to Raipur. Yet it was a pleasant surprise too, and it also manifested the intensity of Mitali's love. We could hear the expressions of surprise that my mother emitted on their arrival in the room. We too came out in five minutes somehow managing to keep our appearance unruffled. My beaming smile matched Mitali's. And, Seema sported a naughty look. Pradeep wished them and went out while I stayed put. We only had a double bed which was used for seating too. Only problem was that it had four aluminium pipes meant for fixing the mosquito net that would come out of their sockets the moment someone pressed one's foot against the same. The bed rest was high on one side and with little margin on the other side. Now we four were sitting on the four corners of the bed and had to manage either remaining seated or reclining or squatting on the same.

'To what do we owe this honour of a visit?' I chuckled.

'Maybe we wanted to surprise you and see your reaction,' Seema said with a mischievous twinkle.

Mitali smiled. She looked so innocent. She was in a brick red polyester saree with black border which I always liked because I felt that it enhanced her looks. Her shining red bindi, her kohl lined eyes, her arched eyebrows and her lovely face were before me. I felt so lucky that I was loved by such a simple and beautiful person. And, now she had thrown caution to the winds, knowing well that a couple of officers and staff of the bank stayed in this colony. It was my privilege to meet her on the last day of my stay at Raipur in the benign and blissful company of my mom whose approval was the most important to me. Seema and Mom talked about other things and in between Mitali's restless feet would dislodge the aluminium pipes creating distractions. And, I would be dutifully fixing them each time while she would be begging sorry for the act. Exuberance of our meeting was too much for her to bear, and her feet kept on dislodging the pipes while I patiently fixed and re-fixed them. At every chiding by Seema she would giggle; that accentuated the luminosity of her face and made it lovelier. 'How privileged I was!' I wondered.

After ten minutes Mom told me, 'Why don't you fetch tea from the nearby tea stall?' I promptly went out with our thermos flask. Pradeep who was just loitering outside to give us space saw me and joined me. He said, 'Now there isn't even an iota of doubt about what Mitali feels for you. And, I feel after this, your mother too has been won over. Thus sixty per cent of the battle is already won. Both of you can now meet in Indore when she comes for her training and then bide your time till there is a green signal from her parents. I personally feel that this may take three to four years. And, in any case you should wait for that much time. It will help you in settling down, in completing your ambitions, and all else. And, my dear friend I must concede that you are lucky to have been blessed with the love of such a beautiful person.'

We came back. It seemed Mitali had been waiting for me only. We had tea. Suddenly Seema asked, 'You don't have any photograph of yourself?'

I thought for just ten seconds and recollected that I had one spare copy of a lovely photo that had been clicked two years back. In that I resembled Ravi Shastri even more than I did now. In those times mostly black and white photos were taken. I took that out from my personal file and handed it over to Seema. She showed it to Mitali too. Seema held on to it and said, 'Now it will not be returned.' I feebly protested but secretly I was glad. Then I gave in. In any case I too wanted Mitali to have it. Now there was no looking back on this journey of love. And I got that love in abundance. I had loved Shama but that was unrequited. But here I experienced true expressions of love: mutual and reciprocal!

A few moments later they prepared to leave. They couldn't say anything directly as to a large extent things had been conveyed. Seema had the last punch line, all encapsulating and emphatic, 'You should not marry for three years.' Those words kept ringing in my ears for a long time. Mom immediately responded, 'He definitely is not going to marry for three to four years at least. He has to fulfil his dream of becoming an IAS.'

While leaving Mitali's eyes were moist. She touched my mom's feet and Mom embraced them one by one. She said, 'You are like my daughters.' I repeated my request to Seema, 'Can I write to her at your bank address?'

'Oh sure; we have already discussed that,' Seema winked.

They left. I kept looking at Mitali with yearning eyes till she closed the outer gate. I felt highly energised with God's elixir. True love is an elixir, bestowed only on a chosen few.

Time was running out. Mr Bakshi sent us the message that lunch was ready. We had a sumptuous lunch with Mom suo moto explaining, 'Those girls who just came to our house are our long time acquaintances from Delhi. We had visited them here and they paid us a return visit.' I don't know whether they were convinced. Anyway, nothing mattered now as I knew my moorings and my resolve.

We were full of gratitude for all the hospitality that Mr Bakshi's family had extended. God had been very kind to me, I felt. He had given me good friends like Hariharan and Pradeep in Raipur. When I came there seven months back I was so sceptical. The city gave me my love to cherish and the affection of so many people that I would never have imagined.

Then it was time to move. We hailed two rickshaws, loaded our luggage and proceeded to the station, and after settling down in the train had full ten minutes for casual chit chat with Hariharan and Pradeep. I expressed my gratitude to both of them for their nice company and the help they had rendered. I embraced them. Pradeep touched Mom's feet and we discovered that tears were rolling down his eyes.

God has given everyone emotions. Some people express them, others try to hide. Tears reflect the person's true feelings; their purity and intensity. They fall when one reaches the pinnacle of one's emotions. They purge you of all misgivings and chicanery.

Mom blessed both of them and then the train whistled signalling it was ready to depart. They got down and from our windows we kept on waving till they could no longer be seen. Thus ended my Raipur saga of those seven months; transforming me into a different individual submerged in deep and pure love of my Mitali.

But there was a big question mark. Will her family agree to our marriage? Or like the Shama chapter will this too remain an unfulfilled dream ... only a memory!

A little later the train entered open space, with greenery and foliage on both sides. And I spotted a red butterfly, my red butterfly with black and white dots and striations, flitting and gliding in all exuberance ... and then it transmuted into Mitali in her brick red saree with black border ... waving at me and smiling at me. My Red butterfly!

Far away a marriage function was going on, and my favourite song from the movie *Hero* was emanating from powerful speakers:

'Tu mera jaanu hai, tu mera dilbar hai,
Meri prem kahani ka, tu hero hai,
Par prem granth ke pannon par,
Apni taqdeer to zero hai ... ...'